The Language of Adult Immigrants

D1590052

MIX
Paper from
responsible sources
FSC
www.fsc.org   FSC® C014540

NEW PERSPECTIVES ON LANGUAGE AND EDUCATION

Series Editor: Professor Viv Edwards, *University of Reading, Reading, Great Britain*

Two decades of research and development in language and literacy education have yielded a broad, multidisciplinary focus. Yet education systems face constant economic and technological change, with attendant issues of identity and power, community and culture. This series will feature critical and interpretive, disciplinary and multidisciplinary perspectives on teaching and learning, language and literacy in new times.

Full details of all the books in this series and of all our other publications can be found on http://www.multilingual-matters.com, or by writing to Multilingual Matters, St Nicholas House, 31–34 High Street, Bristol BS1 2AW, UK.

NEW PERSPECTIVES ON LANGUAGE AND EDUCATION: 39

The Language of Adult Immigrants

Agency in the Making

Elizabeth R. Miller

MULTILINGUAL MATTERS
Bristol • Buffalo • Toronto

Library of Congress Cataloging in Publication Data
Miller, Elizabeth R.
The Language of Adult Immigrants: Agency in the Making/Elizabeth R. Miller.
New Perspectives on Language and Education: 39
Includes bibliographical references and index.
1. English language–Study and teaching—Foreign speakers. 2. English language–Business
English–Study and teaching–Foreign speakers. 3. Immigrants–Education. 4. Adult educa-
tion. 5. Literacy programs. I. Title.
PE1128.A2M5523 2014
428.0086'9120973–dc23 2014001719

British Library Cataloguing in Publication Data
A catalogue entry for this book is available from the British Library.

ISBN-13: 978-1-78309-204-8 (hbk)
ISBN-13: 978-1-78309-203-1 (pbk)

Multilingual Matters
UK: St Nicholas House, 31–34 High Street, Bristol BS1 2AW, UK.
USA: UTP, 2250 Military Road, Tonawanda, NY 14150, USA.
Canada: UTP, 5201 Dufferin Street, North York, Ontario M3H 5T8, Canada.

Website: www.multilingual-matters.com
Twitter: Multi_Ling_Mat
Facebook: https://www.facebook.com/multilingualmatters
Blog: www.channelviewpublications.wordpress.com

The policy of Multilingual Matters/Channel View Publications is to use papers that are
natural, renewable and recyclable products, made from wood grown in sustainable for-
ests. In the manufacturing process of our books, and to further support our policy, preference is given to printers that have FSC and PEFC Chain of Custody certification. The FSC
and/or PEFC logos will appear on those books where full certification has been granted
to the printer concerned.

Typeset by Techset Composition India(P) Ltd., Bangalore and Chennai, India.
Printed and bound in Great Britain by Short Run Press Ltd.

Contents

Acknowledgments   vii

1   Agency in Second Language Research   1
       Introduction   1
       Agency and Second Language Learning   3
       Organization of the Book   9

2   Theories of Agency and Language Learning   11
       Agency as Socially Mediated   11
       Vygotsky and Semiotic Mediation   14
       Bakhtin and Interactional Mediation   18
       Agency of Spaces and Ideological Mediation   20
       Performativity and Constituting the Agentive
          Individual   23
       Conclusion   27

3   Analyzing Agency Constructs in Interview
    Discourse   29
       Undertaking an Interview Study   29
       Interview Talk as Discourse   33
       Mobilizing Language   36
       Analyzing Selected Linguistic Constructs   38
       Conclusion   40

4   Agency and Responsibility: Positioning Self in
    Subject-Predicate Constructs   42
       Agency and Grammar   42
       Subject-Predicate Constructs and Agent-oriented
          Modality in Discourse   44
       Discursive Agency: An Overview of the Interview Corpus   47

Subject-Predicate Constructs in Discursive Practice:
  A Micro-Analysis   52
Conclusion   70

5 Stance and Subjectivity: Evaluating Agentive Capacity   73
   Agency and Stancetaking in Discourse   73
   Dialogic Construction of Evaluative Stance   75
   Analyzing Stance: An Overview of Patterned Constructs   76
   Stance in Discursive Practice: A Micro-Analysis   82
   Conclusion   92

6 Performing Agency and Responsibility in Reported Speech   94
   Agency and Reported Speech   94
   Researching Reported Speech   95
   Producing Reported Speech as Evidence   98
   Analyzing Reported Speech: An Overview of
     Patterned Usages   100
   Reported Speech in Discursive Practice: A Micro-Analysis   103
   Conclusion   117

7 Local Production of Ideology and Discursive Agency   119
   Constituting Reality   119
   What is Ideology?   120
   Ideologies and Discursive Practice   122
   Ideologies of Language Learning for Immigrants to
     the United States   125
   Ideologies of Agency and Responsibilization   130
   Conclusion   133

8 Conclusion   135
   A Researcher's Account   135
   Overview of Linguistic Constructs Produced by
     Interviewees   135
   Implications of Treating Agency as Socially Mediated   142

   Appendix   146
   References   148
   Author Index   162
   Subject Index   166

Acknowledgments

I am forever grateful to the 18 people who allowed me to ask them questions about their experiences learning and using English. In addition to making this book possible, their conversations with me gave me entrance into dynamic multilingual spaces that I otherwise might never have known about, even though some of them are only a few miles from where I live and work. I also want to thank my colleagues (in alphabetical order) who helped put me into contact with some of my participants: Pilar Blitvich, KimMarie Cole, Boyd Davis and Paula Eckard. I am thankful to Sherrie Smith for her careful, tireless work in transcribing the audio-recorded interviews. A Faculty Research Grant, sponsored by the University of North Carolina at Charlotte, provided financial support for this project. And, finally, I want to thank my husband and best friend, Steve Hageman, who supported me throughout the writing of this book and understood why so many of my weekends and holiday breaks were spent working at my computer.

1 Agency in Second Language Research

Introduction

As I finish writing this chapter, members of the Congress of the United States are debating whether and how to implement immigration reform as federal policy. The issues involve increasing the numbers of work visas granted to 'high-skill' and 'low-skill workers', the perennial call for increased border security and, among many other contentious issues, the need to create 'a path to citizenship' for the millions of undocumented immigrants living in the United States. At this point, it is difficult to determine whether any lasting change will emerge from such debates. The current iteration of this decades-long debate, as in the past, casts the benefactors of the proposed policy changes as an undifferentiated population of '11,000,000 illegal aliens', a monolithic 'problem' to be solved, rather than as highly diverse individuals with unique aspirations.

Feldman (2005: 214) argues that such 'banal' legal and political discourses performatively constitute the nation and individual subjectivity simultaneously. He notes, 'that which the nation-state identifies as an objective, external intrusion into its territorial/cultural space, performativity sees as a discursively-produced encounter that generates the effects of pre-given and mutually exclusive "sovereign nations" and "immigrants"' (Feldman, 2005: 214). He adds that these identities of nation and immigrant are only intelligible in relation to the other, a 'mutual constitution' (Feldman, 2005: 216), and further, that the identification of perceived threats to the nation owing to the arrival of culturally, linguistically and legally defined Others, in fact, has the 'positive' effect of legitimating and consolidating the identity of the nation and those who 'naturally' belong to that nation (Feldman, 2005: 221).

In adopting a performativity perspective, Feldman argues that identities, whether national or individual, become meaningful and recognizable as they emerge from or develop in discursive practices – sometimes as binary opposi-tions such as *citizen* vs. *illegal alien*, rather than arising out of their fundamen-tal essence. It is, he claims, the 'proverbial [discursive] equation of individual, culture, territory, and state' that enables the construction of a cultural Other and, as such, a 'minority problem' (Feldman, 2005: 237).

This notion of performativity, i.e. the constitutive effects of discursive practice, is developed in this book in relation to conceptions of language learner agency among adult immigrants to the United States. Researchers such as myself, who do qualitative research, have the luxury of interacting one-on-one with individuals who can be identified as 'immigrants', rather than needing to conceptualize research subjects in terms of large-scale popu-lations. In conducting an interview study with a small number of adult immigrants (all documented or legal) to the United States, I co-produced discourses on immigrant language learning and use that are much more situ-ated and nuanced than policy-level discourses, talk that was mobilized as interviewees generated stories about their individual experiences. In such contexts, interviewees are 'addressed' or 'constituted' (Butler, 1997) as 'indi-viduals', and often, as agentive and morally responsible. As such, these local, face-to-face discursive practices are performative too, in much the same way as the public political discourse on immigration reform (i.e. Feldman, 2005); they are simply small-scale 'socio-political production[s]', as Hantzis (1995: 204) reminds us. In referring to these moments as performative practices, I mean that we *constitute* what come to be regarded as the real and relevant social realities and social identities as we reiterate, enact and/or transform discursive practices.

Anthropologist Alessandro Duranti (2001) notes that the term *agency* was first introduced to the social sciences by influential social theorists such as Giddens (1979) and Bourdieu (1977a, 1990) who wanted to create a theory of social action that would avoid the deterministic vision of human action outlined in structuralist and Marxist visions of the social world. Another anthropologist, Laura Ahearn (2001), offers an explanation for the notable increase in agency scholarship across a wide range of disciplines. She con-tends that social movements in recent decades, such as the civil rights activ-ism of the 1960s and 1970s, and the social and political upheavals in central and eastern Europe lasting through the early 1990s, have demonstrated the effects of human agency in transforming social structures. The 2011 activism in Middle Eastern countries provides more recent evidence of individuals' and groups' capacity to change long-standing political and power relation-ships, even though the emerging political arrangements remain highly problematic. Ahearn adds that shifting theoretical frameworks across the social sciences, primarily the adoption of constructivist, practice-based, post-structural and other postfoundational approaches have created an interpretive framework for understanding the dynamism of social constructs, thus advancing views that reject a determinist understanding of social structures constraining human actions. This increased focus on the role of agency across the social sciences has also been taken up, somewhat belatedly, in language learning scholarship.

Agency and Second Language Learning

Second language researchers, especially those who engage in qualitative research, recognize that the identities of their research participants are far more interesting and complex than merely as 'non-native speakers' (see Firth & Wagner, 1997, 2007). They recognize, for example, that the language learning aspects of any one person's lived experiences, while often highly consequential, never define that individual fully. At the same time, second language researchers *do* tend to focus on language learning to the exclusion of other important aspects of their research participants' lives. This exclusion is necessary to some extent, I would argue, for the research to proceed. Researchers will likely never account for everything that contributes to language learning and use in an individual's experience, let alone for all of the sociopolitical influences that comprise such an individual's experiences beyond language learning. For this reason, it is important for researchers who adopt sociocultural and/or poststructural approaches in researching language learning to acknowledge the limits to what they can know (Miller, 2011a) and to be cautious in how they attribute causality for particular agentive actions given that language, learner identities and learner agency are, I argue, fundamentally social and thus deeply complex constructions.

As you will find in the following pages and chapters, I too have chosen to focus on a very limited facet of the complex totality of individuals' lived experiences: the notion of agency as a socially mediated phenomenon in relation to learning and using an additional language. I analyze adult immigrants' interview accounts on language learning and use as part of that exploration process. The concepts of performativity and the relational or social ontology (Gergen, 2009) of individual agency are developed more fully in the remaining chapters, with particular attention to their theoretical basis provided in Chapter 2. The remainder of this chapter focuses primarily on how issues of identity and agency have been construed by second language researchers.

Research from the past two decades, which has adopted a sociocultural approach to language learning and/or which has focused on issues of identity, often from a poststructural perspective, has increasingly treated learner agency as an essential consideration. Van Lier (2008: 179) in fact argued that agency ought to be regarded as a 'central construct' in language learning research. The shift in focus from 'linguistic inputs and mental information processing to the things that learners do and say while engaged in meaningful activity' (van Lier, 2007: 46) has contributed to the enhanced attention given to learner agency. Even so, in an essay on identity in applied linguistics, Block (2009: 219) commented on the 'lack of clarity' in second language identity research that includes agency as one of its conceptual components. He is particularly critical of the ambiguity in identity research informed by poststructural perspectives. Such research views identity as socially constructed, but often treats individual research subjects as agents, by default, without further interrogation. Block attributes the prevalent lack of consideration for how agency itself is constituted and constrained as partly owing to the fact that much identity research in applied linguistics uses case study methods in which only a few individuals are studied intensely as they interact in their varied social milieus. The problem, he suggests, is that such intense scrutiny of *individuals* in action often engenders interactional analyses in which research participants are positioned as 'active shapers of their realities while leaving behind more explicit mention of how social constraints are at work at every juncture in their activity' (Block, 2009: 223).

While I agree with Block that agency is often treated simplistically and remains under-theorized in applied linguistics research, and in identity work more generally, I am less inclined to see this issue as primarily an effect of the research methodologies adopted by many scholars. It seems to me that the problem lies in the fact that agency remains under-theorized no matter which research methodologies are adopted. Our research methods certainly do shape how we 'see' research participants, but the selection of 'individuals' for research can just as well be understood to emerge from our understandings of agency as a phenomenon that *belongs*, more or less straightforwardly, to individual persons. Though I too explore interview data co-produced with a relatively small number of individuals in this book, I hope to advance an understanding of agency as a fundamentally social phenomenon for second language research. In taking such a view, I orient to 'the social' as structured and structuring (e.g. Giddens, 1979), but also as reconstituted and transformed in discursive practice. That said, my understanding of agency in language learning is indebted to the transformative perspectives advanced in early second language research that has incorporated agency into its theoretical and analytic frameworks.

One of the formative pieces that incorporated agency into its approach to second language learning is McKay and Wong's (1996) ethnographic study of Chinese immigrant students in a secondary California school. They traced the social and learning trajectories of four of them for two years and found that by accounting for the kinds of identities available to these students in the varied aspects of their lives, one could better understand their sometimes limited and even decreasing investment in learning some aspects of English. For example, 'Michael' invested in improving his listening and speaking capacities in English as he socialized with English-speaking students who shared his interest in sports. But he did not invest in learning how to write in English or in a student identity. The authors explain his lack of investment as a strategy of resistance to his powerless positioning as an English-as-a-second-language student. Over the two years of the study, he frequently misbehaved in class and often openly resisted his teachers' efforts to have him do assigned school work. As McKay and Wong (1996: 594) note, Michael's lack of investment in developing his ability to write in English was ultimately 'self-destructive' given that it prevented him from advancing to mainstream classes, but it was also 'quite understandable'. That is, they observed that Michael gained enough agency and positive social recognition when positioning himself as an athlete and popular student and when positioned by others as such that he saw little need to develop his academic capacities as a student, an identity that he seemed to regard as bringing him little desirable social recognition.

McKay and Wong (1996) further note that it is only by understanding the complex and often contradictory social discourses in and through which individuals live their lives that scholars can begin to address the often perplexing situation in which some learners exercise agency by taking advantage of every opportunity to advance in a language while others seem to act against their best interests and make little headway. They add that in recognizing language and identity as 'sites of contestation', one comes to understand language learners as 'subjects with agency and a need to exercise it ... while positioned in power relations and subject to the influences of discourses, [who] also resist positioning, attempt repositioning, and deploy discourses and counterdiscourses' (McKay & Wong, 1996: 603). They thus contend that among the secondary students in their study, immediate 'agency-enhancement and identity-enhancement' (McKay & Wong, 1996: 603) were often far more important than was a commitment to their future Selves as strong(er) users of English.

Not only did McKay and Wong (1996) highlight the important role learner agency plays in the language learning process, they also emphasized its inseparable affiliation with identity and its socially and discursively shaped nature. Much of the burgeoning research on language and identity in the years since McKay and Wong's study has incorporated agency as a component of language learning. For example, Norton and Toohey (2001) analyze the language learning successes of two of their research participants (from the authors' earlier separate studies), one a young child in an English preschool program and the other an adult immigrant female. The authors describe the agentive actions taken by these two learners as they drew on available resources in order to gain access to desirable social networks, efforts that enhanced their learning of English. Norton and Toohey comment on the need for researchers to consider how these individuals' actions developed in relation to how 'others in their social context determined the worth of their contributions' (2001: 317). They further note that 'the proficiencies of the good language learners in our studies were bound up not only in what they did individually but also in the possibilities their various communities offered them' (Norton & Toohey, 2001: 318). In this way, Norton and Toohey propose a view of learner agency that is exercised *in relation to* the social world.

Relatedly, DaSilva Iddings and Katz (2007), who investigated young Hispanic students who were learners of English in a primary school in the United States, found that these students' home identities were often devalued, and indeed the voices of parents or other non-school adults in these young students' lives were often silenced or delegitimated in school discourses. The authors advocate for the need to integrate home identities for such students into school contexts, and among many recommendations for making this happen, they argue that teachers need to work to position these students (and their families) as having 'identities of competence in the classroom' (DaSilva Iddings & Katz, 2007: 312). Such a positioning, DaSilva Iddings and Katz (2007: 312) argue, 'may increase possibilities for students and their families to exercise agency'. Essentially, they criticize the many subtle ways in which school practices legitimate a very limited range of possible ways of using language, which then severely limit students who are not as expert in the dominant school language to 'exert will and autonomy and to affirm themselves as active social agents' (DaSilva Iddings & Katz, 2007: 312).

Morita (2004) too found that institutional practices frequently limited how much older students, international graduate students at a Canadian university in this case, could participate in their new learning environments. Among the six focal participants in her study, she noted that one student actively resisted being marginalized as a deficient student because of her lack of full expertise in English. However, her way of exercising her 'personal agency' (Morita, 2004: 594) was to remain silent and avoid becoming a central participant in the class, reminiscent in some ways of Michael's agency-enhancement choices in McKay and Wong's (1996) study. The student in Morita's study can also be compared with the American university student studying Chinese as a foreign language, who changed from wanting to become strongly proficient in Chinese to wanting merely to pass the course because of a clash of beliefs with her Chinese language instructor regarding how best to teach and learn a language (Lantolf & Genung, 2002). The adult students in these cases agentively 'chose' not to participate actively in formal learning contexts as acts of resistance to what they saw as undesirable identity options for themselves in these situations. These studies, along with many others (Baynham, 2006, 2011; Bourne, 2001; Deters, 2011; Duff, 2012; Gao, 2010; Menard-Warwick, 2009; Mercer, 2011, 2012; Ros i Solé, 2007; Vitanova, 2005, 2010) have greatly advanced our understanding of the role of agency in language learning. However, in many cases, such second language research implicitly or explicitly adopts a perspective toward identity, agency and language learning as occurring in a 'dialectic between the individual and the social – between the human agency of . . . learners and the social practices of their communities' (Toohey & Norton, 2003: 58).

It is this dialectic perspective that requires some unpacking. In this book, I caution against adopting a perspective of humans or learners as already agentive, with little or no recognition given to how human agency is itself thoroughly social, dynamic and co-constructed, rather than an *a priori* quality that is variously constrained or enabled when cast in opposition to external social practices, i.e. the 'dialectic between the individual and the social' (Toohey & Norton, 2003: 58). In fact, Mercer (2012: 42) has argued that learner agency is really a 'hypothetical construct like motivation or intelligence'. It is a constructed concept in that we talk it into being and/or write about it as though it were real. While the discursive framing of agency is useful in providing researchers with a slippery, though somehow still recognizable, concept by which to better understand human actions, choices, desires and values, we need to take great care to avoid treating it as an already-there phenomenon. Nearly two decades ago, Price (1996: 332) offered trenchant criticism against perspectives that treat learners as 'pre-given' subject–agents and individual's learning actions as emerging from 'individual capacities'. His critique aligns with Bakhtin's observation that 'there is no such thing as an abstract biological personality, this biological individual that has become the alpha and the omega of contemporary ideology . . . To enter into history, it is not enough to be born physically . . . A second birth, social this time, is necessary as it were'. Bakhtin adds, 'only such a social and historical localization makes man [sic] real and determines the content of his personal and cultural creation' (as cited in Todorov, 1984: 31).

In taking up Bakhtin's perspective on the social 'birth' of individuals, one quickly recognizes that defining agency is no simple matter. One does not simply *have* agency by virtue of being a 'biological individual'; it is constituted in particular social and historical locations. Joseph (2006: 239) contends that the difficulty in agreeing upon a definition is both unavoidable for a concept as complex as agency and even desirable given that researchers are better served in investigating the particulars of 'who has or who lacks it in what contexts'. Several applied linguists have problematized the dialectic model of the pre-given individual agent in interaction with and/or resisting the social world (i.e. social structure) through articulating the relevance of Activity Theory for understanding second language learning (Lantolf & Pavlenko, 2001; Lantolf & Thorne, 2006; Pavlenko & Lantolf, 2000). Perspectives informed by Activity Theory regard individuals' sense of Self (i.e. identity and/or subjectivity) and the individual mind as ongoingly shaped through one's interaction with the social and cultural worlds in which one participates. That is, by interacting with others, mediated through artifacts and symbolic systems such as language, one also appropriates and internalizes the cultural values and beliefs that render these entities as meaningful in some way. Socioculturally situated ways of seeing the world and attributing meaning to social experiences become part of who one is and form the basis for how one can act and how one sees the Self as capable of acting. For this reason, Lantolf and Pavlenko (2001: 148), pointing to language learners in particular, contend that 'agency is never a property of the individual, but a *relationship* that is constantly co-constructed and renegotiated with those around the individual and with society at large'.

This notion of the historically, socioculturally and interactionally distributed nature of agency is further promoted as Lantolf and Thorne (2006) draw on Bakhtin's notion of addressivity to argue that the socioculturally influenced expectations one has of how one's utterances will be received in a particular social situation, in fact, mediate and enable those utterances to be produced (see also Vitanova, 2010). In this way, what one typically perceives as one's 'own' utterances and actions, creations that originate from Self, are in fact social to the core. Such a perspective does not deny that individuals develop intentions or make decisions or speak in ways that defy conventions, but it does argue that all such 'individual' acts, whether performed internally in the mind or externally through visible or audible actions, are constructed in and emerge out of socially constituted realities that are 'shaped by history, culture, multimodal resources (including language) and space' (Block, 2010: 58).

I think it is important to note that the socially constituted realities through which many adult immigrants to the United States come to desire to learn English often position them as disempowered individuals. For many, the everyday reality of their lives is often marked by enormous struggle as they seek to find work, earn sufficient money to support their families, rear children in unfamiliar cultural milieus, to say nothing of contending with social discrimination. Finding the time and resources to learn English is often difficult for them. However, as I argue further in Chapter 2, being positioned as disempowered is not the same thing as having no agency. Individuals whom we might regard as less powerful in relation to dominant institutional contexts (children, homeless people or immigrants who have limited cultural and economic capital) are not necessarily lacking agency. For this reason, exploring how agency is understood and discursively constituted among a small group of adult immigrants, individuals who perhaps are regarded as less likely to 'have' it, provides an important research context for exploring this abstract concept further.

Organization of the Book

In Chapter 2, I explore the notion of language learner agency as fundamentally socially mediated. This theoretical exploration draws on the sociohistorical legacy of Vygotsky and the dialogism of Bakhtin, but not exclusively from the perspective of Activity Theory. I devote less attention to the (neo)Vygotskian interest in the development of learner language and more to a theoretical understanding of a socioculturally constructed acting Self. I incorporate Bakhtin's perspective on the ongoing dialogic construction of a languaged Self, which enables an acting or agentive Self to be constituted. I further consider these perspectives in light of contemporary sociolinguistic research, which points to the constitutive role of language ideologies and the 'agency of spaces' in enabling and constraining individual agency in particular spaces and interactional configurations (Blommaert et al., 2005a). And finally, I draw on Butler's (1990, 1997, 2010) notion of performativity in exploring how thoroughly social, ideologically constrained and interactionally contingent language learner agency takes on a semblance of permanence and essential interiority for individuals.

In Chapter 3, I describe how the study was conducted, but more importantly, I discuss the theoretical premise for treating research interviews as discourse data in analyzing how 'theories of agency' (Ahearn, 2010) are co-constructed with immigrant language learners. This discussion addresses the constructivist epistemology that infuses how the interview data and the language of discursive practices are treated in this book.

In Chapters 4, 5 and 6, I undertake varying forms of discourse analysis as I explore how the interviewees, in concert with me, talk about their experiences of learning and using English and other languages, giving particular focus to how they positioned themselves as agentive or inagentive. In Chapter 4, the analysis focuses on the subject-predicate structures of interviewees' utterances directed to topics relating to language learning and use. In Chapter 5, I analyze emergent stance positions in exploring how these individuals evaluated their actions and their capacity to learn and use language well. Chapter 6 introduces an analysis of how these interviewees performed or staged their story-world and interactional Selves through producing reported speech. In each of these analysis chapters, I examine utterance patterns across the interview corpus as well as undertake microanalysis of selected interview excerpts. I believe that these are complementary approaches to undertaking discourse analysis. Examining how utterances are patterned across the interview corpus allows one to explore discursive typicalities and to consider why interviewees appear to 'choose' (if unconsciously) particular methods for positioning themselves and others as particular kinds of story-world figures. Taking an in-depth micro-analytic approach to selective interview excerpts allows one to explore the nuanced, sometimes contradictory, but still commonsensical methods by which interviewees are co-constructed as variously agentive and responsible in relation to language learning and use.

Chapter 7 explores how these locally co-constructed ways of positioning, evaluating and performing Self as agentive or inagentive are occasions for re-constituting ideological understandings of who can and should act, when, to what ends and for whose benefit. In this chapter, I discuss my understanding of ideology and explore ideologies regarding immigrants and language learning, as well as ideologies of agency and responsibility.

Chapter 8 reviews key interpretations from the analyses and the theoretical and methodological approaches that inform them. It first addresses the constitutive role of my own work as researcher in producing an integrated, coherent account. It then provides a comparative review of the analytic interpretations from Chapters 4 to 6, showing how the language effects of the varied focal language structures overlap and support each other. It also shows how nuanced distinctions are enacted as interviewees produce language effects relating to agentive subjectivity, evaluative stance and discursive evidence. It ends by discussing a few implications of these findings for future second language research and for teacher–student relationships in language classrooms.

2 Theories of Agency and Language Learning

Agency as Socially Mediated

In this chapter, I explore the notion of agency as socially mediated and discuss how we might avoid the 'agonistic model' implicit in much second language research and, indeed, in much social science research concerned with issues of human agency. Davies (1990: 343) describes the agonistic perspective as one in which 'the individual is conceived as being in relation to "society" which acts forcefully upon the individual and against which any individual can pit themselves.' She advocates instead a poststructural perspective that views the process of becoming a 'person' as occurring through the appropriation and internalization of the discourses and practices in which one participates. Davies (1990: 343) contends that:

> embedded within discursive practices is an understanding that each person is one who has an obligation to take themselves up as a knowable, recognizable identity, who 'speaks for themselves', who accepts responsibility for their actions, that is as one who is recognizably separate from any particular collective, and thus as one who can be said to have agency.

Rather than the 'commonsensical' perspective that regards individual human beings as agentic in essence, Davies' poststructural perspective posits that we develop a *sense* of ourselves as agentic as we participate in mundane social practices. She notes that it is in such practices that we learn how to become a 'normal' person, someone who is recognized as an 'individual', separate from the collective, and someone who is assigned and claims responsibility for particular actions. Thus, how one views oneself as an agent and as an individually formed Self is not an *essential* fact of oneself, but a social construction that develops over time and through participation in human interactions and other socially meaningful discursive practices. In this way, a poststructuralist perspective provides a theoretical framework for understanding how culturally distinctive understandings of Self as agentive and/ or responsible develop 'naturally'. As will be discussed further in this chapter, such a view does not posit that there are no material, economic or political constraints existing apart from Self, that social reality is 'only' discourse or that there is no 'structure'. Rather, what I hope to address is how our understanding of 'essential' Selves, which we regard as able to perceive, choose and act on their own powers, emerge from a history of incorporating social realities into that notion of Self. In one of his later works, Bourdieu (2000: 136–137) describes it this way:

> this capacity to construct social reality, itself socially constructed, is not that of a transcendental subject but of a socialized body, investing in its practice socially constructed organizing principles that are acquired in the course of a situated and dated social experience.

One might wonder why a thoroughly social approach to learner agency is important to consider. Anthropologist Sherry Ortner (2006: 130) contends that too much focus on the agency of individuals, as individual in essence, can lead to a 'gross oversimplification of the processes of history ... the pulse of collective forces' in the constitution of 'individual' desires, decisions, values and actions. Communications scholars Gunn and Cloud (2010) view the human individual as an articulation point for agency rather than the inevitable location where agency resides. Such a perspective attempts to avoid the extremes of the humanist sovereign agent on the one hand and the determined or dominated subject on the other. I cite Gunn and Cloud at length on this point:

> Individuals do not exist in isolation, but bear the traces of other individuals, institutions, collective social relations, and histories in such a way that to speak of 'agency' as something any one person possesses ignores the interactive dynamic of material and social reality. This is not to say that an individual does not make choices that affect his or her life. Rather [one]...sees an individual only in relation to other individuals, social relations and histories. Consequently, *the individual cannot exist independent of interactivity, dialogue, and collectivity.* (Gunn & Cloud, 2010: 72, italics added)

Similarly, anthropologist Robert Desjarlais (1997: 201) warns against assumptions that 'methods of agency' are the same everywhere. That is, rather than conceiving agency as 'an essential, unchanging given and ontologically prior' (Desjarlais, 1997: 201) characteristic of all humans, agency must be approached as 'context-dependent', a capacity that arises out of 'practical concerns' as well as 'social, political, and cultural dynamics' (Desjarlais, 1997: 204).

Undoubtedly, the most widely cited definition of agency is that put forward by another anthropologist, Laura Ahearn (2001: 112), who describes it as the 'socioculturally mediated capacity to act' which, she acknowledges, is left 'deliberately underspecified'. Ahearn argues that arriving at a finalized definition that can account for agency in all cases and for all time is impossible. Further, it is important that researchers account for more than observable actions. Wertsch *et al.* (1995: 11), collectively representing the fields of cultural psychology and anthropology, point to the fact that agentive action is not merely 'sheer motion' but action that is understood as meaningful in some way. And of course the choice not to act is also an exercise of agency. I believe that second language research has much to learn from these and many other scholars from across the social sciences regarding the development and maintenance of our perceptions of ourselves and others as agentic creatures.

With respect to processes of language learning among the adult immigrants whose interview accounts are explored in this study, it is important to recognize how their sometimes imperfect facility in the locally dominant language, English is this case, is frequently regarded as developing when they, as individuals who already *have* agency, can exercise this 'pre-given' characteristic by overcoming constraints to learning or resisting unequal power structures in order to develop linguistic competence. A socially mediated perspective would argue instead that language learners' agentive capacity is 'born of a gamut of cultural, political, biological, linguistic and environmental forces' (Desjarlais, 1997: 24). As such, the 'individual' language learner's capacities to act toward various ends are understood as social to the core and as 'situated relations rather than intrinsic capacity alone' (Cudworth & Hobden, 2013: 447). And if agency is social to the core, then it is also inevitably and unavoidably constrained, historically and ideologically and materially.

In the following sections, I explore how we might understand agency as emergent and context dependent (i.e. socially mediated) with a particular focus on the relational constitution of agency for second language learning. I first discuss the influence of Vygotsky's view of semiotic mediation; I then examine Bakhtin's view of dialogism in terms of interactional mediation; next I consider the 'agency of spaces' and ideological mediation; and, finally, I explore how Butler's performativity theory allows us to bring these theoretical perspectives together in arriving at a poststructuralist understanding of socially mediated agency.

Vygotsky and Semiotic Mediation

In considering how humans develop their capacity to act in meaningful ways, that is, how they develop a *sense* of themselves as agentive, responsible individuals, this book draws on Vygotsky's concept of semiotic mediation. Lantolf and Thorne (2006: 56) regard mediation as 'the central concept of [Vygotskian] sociocultural theory', and though Vygotsky himself did not use the term agency, his notion of self regulation and its socioculturally mediated origins is instructive for understanding the development of humans' perceptions of themselves as agentive beings as well as of language learner agency more particularly. Vygotsky's sociocultural theory is now widely drawn upon in second language studies, and many contemporary Vygotskian researchers in second language acquisition focus on the microgenetic moments of socially mediated learning (i.e. language development evidenced in relatively short time frames) as learners interact with others, either face to face or through online interactions (Foster & Ohta, 2005; Swain, 2000, 2006; Thorne, 2008). Such investigations often trace particular kinds of language development to particular interactional moments, as well as to the material artifacts or other affordances that are relevantly available in given contexts.

Swain (2006), for example, describes a study with adolescent students who attended a French immersion school in Toronto. The students were asked to write a story in French, based on prompts provided by the researchers. The stories were then rewritten by an adult with the goal of maintaining the meaning of the students' stories, while using language structures that would be acceptable to a native speaker of French. When both versions of the story were returned to the students, they were asked to comment on what they noticed was different between their original story texts and the revised texts, and they were video-recorded as they did so. Finally, these videos were played back to the students, and at each point where students had commented on a difference in the two versions of their stories in the video, they were asked to elaborate on what they were thinking at those moments of noticing during the playback. Swain (2006: 98) writes, 'During the noticing stage and the stimulated recall stages, the students expressed their beliefs about the target language, often languaging themselves through to an understanding of why the reformulator had changed what they had written'. Swain notes that when these students later rewrote these same stories, many of them incorporated the substance of the language features that they had noticed and discussed. Their enhanced ability to write more target-like French forms on their own suggests that they were developing enhanced 'self regulation' in producing written French. However, such 'independent' ability could be traced back to moments of noticing and then discussing the differences between their own written productions and those produced by an expert writer of French. We can understand that these students' ability to notice and attend to such differences was mediated by the written artifacts in front of them and the researcher-structured activity in which they were engaged. In this way, Swain and other neo-Vygotskian researchers demonstrate quite vividly how language learning is mediated by social processes and language-in-use and is distributed across interlocutors and artifacts rather than an individualistic, solely in-the-brain process.

At the same time, it is important to remember that even though Vygotsky viewed language in use – and, relatedly, learning to use language – as the fundamental meditational means for development (i.e. semiotic mediation), he was primarily interested in understanding how higher mental functioning, or consciousness, develops in humans rather than in language learning per se. Tomasello (2009) provides an example of how the development of consciousness is mediated for a young child. He constructs a scenario involving a one-year-old child seated on the floor and playing with a toy. When an adult enters the room, seats himself on the floor and begins to play with the toy, the child develops an understanding of what is relevantly meaningful to 'what [they] are doing' at that moment (Tomasello, 2009: 22). Though the child may be aware of the sofa and rug in the room, these entities do not figure in the meaning-making activity constructed between the adult and the child as they play with the toy. By contrast, if the adult enters the room with a diaper in hand and proceeds to lay the child on the rug in preparation for a diaper change, the rug may become relevant to the activity and the toy becomes irrelevant to 'what [they] are doing'. Tomasello argues that in such contexts, human activities and the artifacts that help to comprise them:

> gain their identity and coherence from the child's and the adult's understandings of 'what we are doing' in terms of the goal-directed activities in which we are engaged. In one case we are playing with a toy, which means that certain objects and activities are part of what we are doing, and in another case we are changing a diaper, which brings into existence, from the point of view of our joint attention, a whole different set of objects and activities. This enables the child … to create the common ground within which [he or she comes to] understand the adult's communicative intentions when the adult uses a novel piece of language—at least partly by creating a domain of 'current relevance'. (Tomasello, 2009: 22)

Tomasello's example illustrates how participation in mundane sociocultural practices enables children to interpret, appropriate and internalize culturally appropriate ways of acting and using language, and the socially assigned meanings attached to them, as they develop as sense of Self. Referring to Vygotsky's notion of semiotic mediation in the development of human consciousness, Smolka *et al.* (1995) note that:

> [w]hen Vygotsky formulated the general law of development postulating that 'any function in a child's cultural development appears twice—first between people and then inside the individual' (1978: 57), one of his fundamental issues was, in fact, the question of the formation of a person, that is, the individual consciousness. This development of *the individual was taken as a semiotically mediated process*, with signs playing an essential role in the encounters of the person with others and in the construction of intrapsychological functioning. (Smolka *et al.*, 1995: 179, italics added)

In addition to theorizing the development of human consciousness, Vygotsky's early notions of 'volitional activity' (Vygotsky, 1987a) are suggestive of his later explorations into how children develop self-control or self-regulation of social actions and interactions (Vygotsky, 1987b), features of human action that we could refer to as agentive. When a child's actions are treated by others as meaningful, the child is likely to repeat them, and such actions become more habitual over time, allowing the child to perform these actions more and more independently over time. However, the socially mediated texture of any such self-regulated and seemingly individual action never disappears. Just as a young child first learns to count through using her fingers but then develops the ability to count 'in her head', at no point is this individual ability to count and manipulate numbers unmediated. Numerical symbolic systems, shared across individuals and contexts, always mediate such individual action. In this way, all forms of semiotic mediation that regulate meaning and supply possibilities for action may be gradually appropriated and can be understood to constitute and enable cognitive, sociocultural and linguistic development simultaneously.

As these appropriated meanings and actions become more familiar and habitual for a child, the *social* world of meaning-making forms the child's *inner* world or her 'inner speech' (Vygotsky, 1978). Holland *et al.* (1998) warn against viewing this internalization in too simplistic terms. They note that 'this traffic of social speech to inner speech is not a simple or direct process. It does not result in a facsimile of the social reproduced upon the body' (Holland *et al.*, 1998: 186). Further, the process of making the social world personal is inevitably different for everyone. Constituted in and through semiotic material and other forms of meaning-making activity, such as learning how to play with toys or learning what happens during a diaper change, each child develops in somewhat different configurations of interlocutors and contextual affordances. Cognitively mature 'independent' actors in the world are thus not mere clones of those with whom they have interacted throughout their lifetimes, though they do embody and reproduce traces of these earlier interactions.

Many mediated actions become so habitual that they scarcely seem to require thought or planning, while others continue to require conscious attention and deliberate decision making. But even habitual acts can be understood as agentive acts given that individuals need 'to recall, to select, and to appropriately apply the more or less tacit and taken-for-granted schemas of action that they have developed through past interactions' (Emirbayer & Mische, 1998: 975; see also Giddens, 1979: 58). In his ethnographic study conducted at a Chicago 'ghetto' boxing gym, Wacquant (1992: 221) demonstrates how gruelingly repetitive training requiring near-daily rounds of 'shadow-boxing, hitting the bags, speed bag, jumping rope, and stomach exercises' (Wacquant, 1992: 237), actions that initially are carefully instructed practices, lead these boxers to develop a sense of 'wholeness and "flow"' (Wacquant, 1992: 239). In other words, once-conscious and carefully instructed sparring actions become so habituated that they appear to emerge without any conscious intentions at all. Wacquant further maintains that each individual pugilist's developing ease in performing the particular actions that are relevant to boxing, what he called the 'socialized lived body' (Wacquant, 1992: 221), must be understood as socially or collectively mediated. Such an example can help us understand how increasingly habitual as well as more conscious agentive actions – such as intentionally learning a language – are always historically and socially shaped.

Meaningful agentive acts and mediating symbolic systems do not emerge just in the moment; they pre-exist child–adult interactions or boxers sparring in the ring or language learner–teacher talk and are reconstituted and sometimes transformed in these interactions. For this reason, Holland et al. (1998: 8) maintain that the 'intimate terrain' of our lives is an 'outcome of living in, through, and around cultural forms practiced in social life'. They describe this as one's 'history-in-person' and also as the 'sediment of past experiences' (Holland et al., 1998: 18), which forms the mediating material through and upon which one is able to act in and on the world, or as Emirbayer and Mische (1998: 1005) put it, 'it is the sociality of experience that drives the development of agentic capacities'.

In considering second language learning in particular, we understand that self-regulation, or the developing internalization and appropriation of socially constituted discursive practices, enable individuals to undertake and engage in the actions of learning a language, as well as to use a learned language appropriately in situated contexts. Agency in language learning encompasses the development of linguistic and communicative know-how but also the *desire* to learn a language and the *valuing* of such activity. At the same time, when individuals share a language or a culture, this does not mean that they will all adopt similar perspectives regarding their capacity to act agentively. The sociocultural 'material' by which we are enabled to act does not determine our actions. There clearly are differences among 'individuals'. And yet what can be identified as 'individual' is a socially saturated reality. As Ortner (2006: 151) argues, people are always 'embedded in webs of relations'. And for this reason, agency is understood to be 'relational all the way down' (Emirbayer & Mische, 1998: 974).

Bakhtin and Interactional Mediation

A Vygotskian approach to the development of human consciousness allows us to understand where our sense of personhood and perceptions of Self-as-agentive originate. These perceptions are not automatically attendant with person but develop as our perceptions of who we are as individuals do. Relatedly, a Bakhtinian approach allows us to understand how agency is ongoingly mediated. It is the way we live our lives. As Holland *et al.* (1998: 185) note, the differing theories of Vygotsky and Bakhtin are compatible in that they both see human consciousness and social development as 'products of the collective life' even though they attend to different aspects of human activity: Vygotsky to human ontogenetic and microgenetic development, and Bahktin to 'ongoing social struggles and the continuous social demands' of human experience. Clark and Holquist (1984: 177) contend that for Bakhtin 'activity is omnipresent' and is necessary for the Self to exist. We are not only individuals with well-developed higher mental functioning or complex consciousness that has emerged out of our participation in socioculturally meaningful actions as children. We view ourselves as 'individuals' whose sense of Self and agentive capacity is continually mediated (i.e. enabled and constrained) through interacting with the social world. In fact, Bakhtin contends that the Self *only* exists dialogically. That is, an individual person's actions from one moment to the next, and how they are interpreted, how they are made possible, is only ever possible in dialogic relation to an Other. There are no 'isolated acts . . . Being is therefore the activity of "being with" or . . . of "co-being of being"' (Clark & Holquist, 1984: 65).

It is important to reemphasize here that Bakhtin's *dialogic* Self, with its ongoingly mediated agentive capacities, is not merely engaged in *dialectic* (or *agonistic*) interactions with the social world, but is already constituted through and in the social world. This constitution occurs over time, emerging from our socioculturally based development of Selfhood (Vygotsky's semiotic mediation) and as we take the words of others and make them our own by uttering them with our own voice and from our unique perspectives (Bakhtin, 1981). Our *individual* perspectives and voices gain meaning in relation to an Other and through using the meditational means constituted by many historical Others. Bakhtin's dialogism is clearly far more encompassing than simply face-to-face interaction; it is meant to capture the sociality of all aspects of human experience. Bakhtin (1984: 138), for example, has said that 'life by its very nature is dialogic'. Likewise, Vološinov (1973), a member of the Bakhtin circle, is credited with commenting on the sociality that undergirds our sense of individuality:

> A special kind of character marks the individualistic self-experience. It does not belong to the 'I-experience' in the strict sense of the term ... the individualistic type of experience derives from a steadfast and confident social orientation. Individualistic confidence in oneself, one's sense of personal value, is drawn not from within, not from the depths of one's personality, but from the outside world ... the structure of conscious, individual personality is just as social a structure as is the collective type of experience. (Vološinov, 1973: 89)

Somewhat paradoxically, a dialogic perspective contends that it is as we participate in collective experiences and socially constructed discursive practices, over time, that we develop our sense of ourselves *as individuals* (the 'I-experience').

Contributing to this understanding of the interactionally mediated Self is Bakhtin's understanding of language as never politically neutral. That is, language is not an independent, autonomous system that one merely 'uses', but rather an assembly of words and utterances that are 'shot through' with the meanings and 'tastes' and 'accents' of others (Bakhtin, 1981: 293). He further notes that an individual's 'ideological development is ... an intense struggle within us for hegemony among various available verbal and ideological points of view, approaches, directions, and values' (Bakhtin, 1981: 346). As such, 'traces of others' infuse our utterances and our values and beliefs. For this reason, Wertsch *et al.* (1993) have noted that viewing selfhood and agency as *essentially* social and mediated does not render individuals as bearing no responsibility for their (lack of) actions. The ideological meanings that infuse all social interactions serve to assign responsibility to individuals for particular kinds of actions, and to sort the 'responsible' from the 'irresponsible'.

Agency of Spaces and Ideological Mediation

Though we typically think of agency as something uniquely human, agency can also be attributed to non-human entities. For example, agency has been assigned to spirits and/or fate as well as to machines and technologies (Ahearn, 2001). Relatedly, Blommaert et al. (2005a: 203) explore the 'agency of spaces' with respect to language ideologies and immigrant language learners in noting that space 'does something to people' when it comes to sorting those whose language expertise (Rampton, 1990) is legitimated from those whose language expertise is not. Considering the implications of such agency of spaces, Blommaert (2010: 6) describes human movement, whether relatively local or transglobal, as in the case of migration, as a 'trajectory through differently stratified, controlled and monitored spaces in which language "gives you away"'. For example, in describing relatively homogeneous 'monoglot' communities in Belgium, Blommaert et al. (2006: 53) argue that unless one speaks standard Dutch when one enters these spaces, one is 'stripped of any other symbolically valued resources' and often comes to be regarded as 'language-less and illiterate'. What has been described for Belgium could undoubtedly be said of many immigrant-receiving communities.

For this reason, Blommaert et al. (2005a) argue that instead of adopting the normative perspective that treats immigrants as linguistically deficient when they have not learned, or learned well, the dominant language of their new communities, we ought to consider how situations or spaces, and the ideologies that are constructed in making such spaces recognizable, render some forms of linguistic expertise as legitimate and others as non-legitimate. The 'situated relations' (Cudworth & Hobden, 2013: 447) of an individual to a context affords particular identities of language (in)competence to become relevant. Blommaert et al. provide an example for how to better understand this notion of 'agency of spaces' in describing a scene at a café in Ghent. A Bulgarian immigrant woman who worked at the café and who could speak Bulgarian fluently, and, they surmised, could likely communicate in Turkish and Russian as well, was identified as someone who 'spoke no language' by a group of student researchers who visited the café. The students arrived at this casual assessment given that she did not speak Dutch, English or French, their languages and the ratified languages of this public space. If one or more of the student researchers had known some Bulgarian, Turkish or Russian, and had spoken to the café employee in one of those languages, the employee's capacity to interact and to contribute to the social constitution of this space would have been enabled rather than tightly constrained by the normative expectations regarding which languages were 'common sensically' legitimated and used in the café. Blommaert *et al.* (2005a: 211) thus conclude that 'agency results from the interplay between people's situated intentions and the way the environment imposes particular regimes of languages'.

As Blommaert and his colleagues have demonstrated, language ideologies need to be considered in thinking about how agency is enabled and/or constrained for immigrants learning and using the dominant language of their new milieus. Ideologies are not floating in the 'macro' world as intangible social beliefs and values but are locally generated and (re)constituted in 'micro' interactions. Though this example might appear to conjure up the 'agonistic model' critiqued earlier in this chapter, that is, that there are external (i.e. structural) forces that constrain what the agentive individual is able to do, I would argue that a socially mediated account of learner agency assigns a different kind of ontology to agency. The circumstances in which agency emerges, as I have extrapolated from Vygotsky and Bakhtin, are historically, culturally and interactionally shaped. The mediating effects of space are constructed by people as they engage in the social practices that are legitimated in particular spaces and which in turn (re)constitute and sometimes transform these spaces. Blommaert (2010: 6) noted that 'space is always someone's space' and Pennycook (2010: 7) contends that 'what we do with language in a particular place is a result of our interpretation of that place; and the language practices we engage in reinforce that reading of place' (Pennycook, 2010: 2).

As the immigrants in my study indicated, their capacity to create workspaces in which multilingual and/or English-only interactions are valued depends to a large degree on whom they interact with in these spaces and how their interactional practices are (in)validated. For example, the small business owners who cater primarily to other immigrants can agentively co-construct spaces in which limited multilingualism is legitimated and valued, and where the need for strong English proficiency is treated as less important for operating their businesses. However, several of the small business owners who cater primarily to English-speaking customers discussed their awareness of how their use of languages other than English is often regarded as suspicious activity by their customers. Thus, these individuals' agentive capacity to interact with others must be understood as constrained by, as well as enabled in, the interactional milieu of their places of business and by the ideologies (re)produced by participants in those interactions that often render their varying kinds of linguistic expertise to be problematic – or not.

In his recent work on agency, Block (2013) contends that applied linguistics research has gone too far in the direction of the social construction of agency and has failed to theorize structure adequately. He is correct to warn against perspectives that leave the impression that 'individuals are relatively unconstrained as they make their way through intercultural experiences' (Block, 2013: 127). As he notes, an emphasis on the emergence of identity and/or agency in interaction can end up 'grant[ing] more weight to agency than to structure in the making sense of how individuals make their way through social worlds' (Block, 2013: 131). In promoting the need to consider how neo-liberal world views and economic policies 'appear to be tightening the large-scale structural organization of the world', Block contends that applied linguists and other language scholars need to provide 'sustained and detailed treatment of what is meant by structure and agency and exactly how they interrelate' (Block, 2013: 132). Though this book does not provide a detailed treatment of structure, in my exploration of interviewees' 'theories of agency', I argue that their perceptions of Self as agentive or inagentive develop *in relation to* the constraints and affordances that are integrated into ideologies of language and ideologies of agency. A socially mediated perspective thus regards the development of an individual's sense of agency as shaped by social and historical influences, which necessarily include economic constraints, political policies and the differential power and position-taking that comprise such realities. Such a view posits a world separate from Self, but it does not posit a Self as separate from the world. In promoting the notion of *habitus*, Bourdieu (2000: 152) writes, '[t]he body is in the social world, but the social world is in the body … The very structures of the world are present in the structures (or, to put it better, the cognitive schemes) that agents implement in order to understand it'. A perspective advocating agency as socially mediated maintains that the social and material (i.e. structural) worlds are remade and/or maintained as we ongoingly participate in discursive practices, what Gunn and Cloud (2010: 72) have described as the 'interactive dynamic of material and social reality'.

Norton's (Peirce 1995, 2000) early research among immigrant women in Canada led her to argue that unequal power relations often impede individuals' language learning progress when they are made to feel disempowered because of not knowing the dominant language well. She comments that:

> [t]he reality for most of the women in the study was that the outside world was frequently hostile and uninviting. Native speakers of English were often impatient with their attempts at communication and more likely to avoid them than negotiate meaning with them. The multitude

of contextual clues that they picked up were that native speakers did not like to talk or work with immigrants. (Norton, 2000: 113)

The ideologies that were reconstructed as these women interacted with native-English-speaking Canadians made it 'sensible' for expertise in English to be treated as normative and for other kinds of linguistic expertise to have no value. But not all of the women in her study yielded to this positioning by their co-workers or other native Canadians. They persisted in seeking the 'power to impose reception' (Bourdieu, 1977b: 648) and resisted being marginalized, driven, as Norton contends, by their investment in bettering their families' futures as well as their own. As she suggests, these women exercised their agency despite their lived experiences of disempowerment. Thus, one's socioculturally mediated capacity to act must not be simplistically equated with desirable subjectivity or empowered social positioning. I think this distinction is important to emphasize: empowerment and agency are not the same thing.

Someone who is treated as 'language-less', such as the café worker in Ghent noted earlier, may be unable to claim a place in an interaction if there are no, or only limited, meditational means in play that enable socially legitimated actions. Being recognized as a legitimate participant in a practice depends on the relational configurations operating in such practices and in particular spaces that have histories of assigning unequal status to different kinds of individuals and languages. On the other hand, sometimes it is through being positioned as a non-legitimate speaker or actor that one is 'recognized' as a particular kind of 'subject'. And such 'recognition' or 'interpellation' (Butler, 1997: 26) as a particular kind of subject, even if it is an undesirable kind of Self, can enable one to act from that subject position.

Performativity and Constituting the Agentive Individual

When one perceives humans' agentive actions to be socially mediated, one might wonder, along with Barker and Galasinski (2001: 45): 'if subjects and identities are the products of discursive practices, if they are social and cultural "all the way down," how can we conceive of persons as able to act and engender change in themselves and the social order?' Judith Butler's (1990, 1993, 1997, 2010) notion of performativity is helpful in bringing together the varying perspectives considered in this chapter, by giving constitutive efficacy to semiotic and interactional mediation in conjunction with the constraints and affordances produced through ideological mediation.

Proposing a view of human subjectivity as 'constituted in language', whose power to create and to act is 'derive[d] from elsewhere', Butler (1997: 16) acknowledges that 'some critics mistake the critique of sovereignty for the demolition of agency'. However, she argues strongly that 'agency begins where sovereignty wanes', and further that 'the one who acts ... acts precisely to the extent that he or she is constituted as an actor, and hence, operating within a linguistic field of enabling constraints from the outset' (Butler, 1997: 16).

Vasterling (1999), who takes up Butler's perspective on agency as performatively constituted, argues that if one is recognized as someone who speaks or acts intelligibly, then one has complied to some extent with the social conventions that serve to constitute recognizable identities and familiar practices. That said, a performativity perspective does not claim that agency is 'only language' or that personhood and selfhood are 'only discursive practices'. Packer (2011: 264) points out that we need to be careful to avoid the too-easy associations of 'constructed' or 'constituted' with something that is 'insubstantial' or 'easily changed'. Similarly, Vasterling insists that to approach social reality as 'epistemologically dependent on language' (Vasterling, 1999: 19) does not entail that everything is reducible to 'some sort of linguistic substance' (Vasterling, 1999: 18), but what it does argue is that discourse provides the 'epistemological condition' (Vasterling, 1999: 21) by which we *know* the world and ourselves, and by which 'people and things "show up"' (Packer, 2011: 11) as meaningful entities in our social worlds – as individuals who desire, value and pursue agentive acts. Performativity theory does not entail that there are not real things that exist apart from discourse, but rather it provides a theoretical perspective from or through which we can understand that our sense of Others and Self, and of how to participate in discursive practices and of how to interpret, use and relate to the real things in the world is always mediated through such practices.

Butler's (1997: 16) depiction of the 'linguistic field of enabling constraints' is problematically vague, but I regard it as one's ongoing participation in discursive practices, which depend on language, but which incorporate far more than language. These are symbolically/linguistically mediated practices with social, cultural and economic histories. Young (2009: 2) describes discursive practice as involving 'the production of meanings by participants as they employ in local actions the verbal, non-verbal, and interactional resources that they command, but [also] ... how employment of such resources reflects and creates the processes and meanings of the community in which the local action occurs'. Young (2009: 3) adds that on specific occasions of discursive practice, such interactions are both 'unique' to the situation and 'profoundly influenced by processes that occur beyond the temporal and spatial horizon of the immediate occasion of interaction'.

Kulick (2003: 140) helps us understand the difference between performance and performativity by noting that '*performance* is something a subject does. *Performativity*, on the other hand, is the process through which the subject emerges'. Locally situated performances are the means by which subjects are performatively re-constituted as they re-issue and re-sediment social conventions – always mediated by their history-in-person, the dialogic production of utterances in interaction and the social ideologies reconstructed in particular spaces. Herndle and Licona (2007: 141) note that 'the performance itself is not adequate to constitute agency', but rather agency emerges as we re-enact normative discursive practices. That is, we perform ways of being in the world, such as a gendered identity (Butler, 1997), that make 'sense' in relation to how such performances have been recognized and interpreted in other discursive practices. In this way, one is performatively constituted as male, female, homosexual, or some other gendered identity, as one re-enacts or subverts socially recognizable performances or practices of gender – often unconsciously.

Pennycook (2005) stresses the need to recognize how individuals' local interactional performances renew or repeat utterances, practices and actions, and thereby (re)produce a Self; they do not merely *animate* or *represent* an essential, foundational, ontologically prior subjectivity. Elsewhere, he paraphrases Deborah Cameron's pithy observation that instead of thinking that people talk the way they do because of who they are, a performativity perspective would argue that people are who they are because of how they talk (among many other reasons) (Pennycook, 2004). Such an orientation to language and language use treats semiotic, interactional and ideological mediation as the basis for meaningful action. Rather than approaching individuals as agents who generate actions derived from their 'own' powers, we come to understand that human actions are mediated as humans are constituted as particular kinds of actors, over time. Importantly, these performances are not free-willed or free-wheeling, emerging as ahistorical, individual acts, but are 'regulated' (Butler, 1997: 27) by past and current understandings of socially meaningful and appropriate actions, power relations, dominant ideologies, material realities and past and current encounters with an Other.

Butler (2009: *xi*) has also argued that even the desire to act has to be understood as socially generated in commenting that 'if what "I" want is only produced in relation to what is wanted for me, then the idea of "my own" desire turns out to be something of a misnomer. I am, in my desire, negotiating what has been wanted of me'. This comment evokes the notion of a mediated 'history-in-person' discussed earlier. Our 'individual' Selves have been semiotically and interactionally mediated through our participation in discursive practices so that we come to desire particular identities. With respect to adult immigrants and language learning, we can understand that they are enabled to and desire to act towards learning a language, in part, because they are 'recognized' as social beings who *should* do so. Of course, not all adult immigrants choose to learn the dominant languages of their new environments. Sometimes such 'choices' not to learn a language develop in relation to material constraints, such as childcare responsibilities and long work hours. Choosing between learning a language or putting food on the table may, in fact, not appear to be a choice at all. Individual persons are often not able to overcome the many constraints that are part of the mediating web of relations (social and material) by which their particular actions, such as learning English, may or may not be enabled. I view these accumulating layers of historical events, economic inequalities, institutional influences, political policies, as well as local familial responsibilities that often conspire to prevent any one person or even large groups of people to act in any way that they might wish, to *be part of* the mediating web of relations for (in)action. Barad (2003: n.p.), for example, refers to the 'conjoined material-discursive nature of constraints, conditions, and practices'.

And rather than view all constraints to action as inevitably or invariably problematic, Butler (2009: iv) argues that constraints, such as social norms of various types, provide 'the terms of recognition' by which an agentive subject comes into being. She notes that it is through the 'citation of existing conventions' (Butler, 1997: 33) that one is able to construct a recognized presence such as a gendered Self or a particular kind of linguistic Self. By contrast, 'to move outside the domain of speakability is to risk one's status as a subject' (Butler, 1997: 33). Furthermore, if agency develops through the repetition and re-sedimentation of Others' actions and utterances, then this also opens the possibility for transformative actions to occur. That is, even as one is constrained by the meditational means available over time and at any moment in time, one is still afforded the 'material' by which one can act in ways that are not predetermined. Further, subverting social norms is made possible because the social norms provide the 'material' or mechanisms for acting against them.

In taking a socially-mediated and performatively constituted view of agency, I contend that adult immigrants' lack of power to overcome particular barriers and a likely 'sense' that they have no agency in those cases is not evidence of a dialectic or agonistic struggle between external structures and individuals with pre-given agency, but of a dialogic interaction between an external world and a Self that is *patterned with* that world. In describing the situated agency that was constructed among people who spent much of their lives living in or near homeless shelters, Desjarlais (1997: 246, italics added) writes about the 'cultural, discursive, and political forces' that '*patterned the grounds* for what was possible in people's lives'. He adds that such patterned grounds 'shaped what residents could do, what powers they could claim, how they spoke, knew, felt, and thought' (Desjarlais, 1997: 246). Deetz (194: 193) contends that 'the individual experiences a particular world, one which is the product of socially inscribed values and distinctions like the subject itself'.

Though some have critiqued Butler's notion of performativity as undermining attempts to understand a 'historically and geographically concrete subject' (i.e. Nelson, 2010: 332), I believe that performativity provides a theoretical frame for conceptualizing how our socially mediated sensibilities of our agentive capacities are enacted, perpetuated and sometimes transformed. In a recent article, Butler (2010: 147) describes performativity as helpful for 'counter[ing] a certain kind of positivism', by 'draw[ing] our attention to the diverse mechanisms of [cultural] construction' and by 'describ[ing] a set of processes that produce ontological effects'. Her article addresses the notion of economic markets, and she notes that 'to say the market is performatively produced is not to say that it is produced *ex nihilo* at every instant, but only that its apparently seamless regeneration brings about a naturalized effect' (Butler, 2010: 149). Thus, performative moments should not be regarded as ahistorical moments in time, but as re-sedimentations and/or transformations of previous practices that involve complex relationships, histories and ideologies, and which re-signify material structures and constraints. In understanding the constitutive power of performativity, we come to see that we view ourselves as autonomous agents, as individuals who think and act on our *own* powers, as we ongoingly participate in discursive practices in which such identities are reified. That is, it is through symbolic, interactional and ideological mediation that we come to see ourselves in terms of an 'I' versus an Other and as individuals who are responsible to act in particular ways, and in some cases but not others.

Conclusion

A performativity perspective frames agency as called or interpellated into being (Butler, 1997) as individuals participate in discursive practices, over time. Material as well as social constraints and affordances, and the ideologies by which we assign meaning to particular actions, provide the means by which particular kinds of (in)action are recognized and become meaningful. For example, if immigrants to the United States take no steps to learn

English, their inaction is still meaningful and is often chastised by members of the dominant culture. By contrast, my own lack of action to learn Vietnamese while living in the United States in my particular context is not regarded as inaction. It has no social or ideological meaning. For this reason, it is important to consider how language learners' 'theories of agency' (Ahearn, 2010) are mobilized in discourse, what Pennycook (2007a: 74) refers to as the 'language effects' of discourse. A Vygotskian-informed perspective to human agency allows us to understand how personhood and beliefs about agency and perceptions of Self as agentive originate. Bakhtin helps us to understand how such perceptions of one's agentic capacities and responsibilities are continually mediated in dialogic encounters. Blommaert and colleagues point to the need to consider how some actions take on common sense status and are made possible in particular spaces, because of the normative practices and ideologies that are (re)constituted in those spaces. Human actions are mediated not just by time and interactional configurations, but by how locality and situation contribute to such meditational means. Thus, as individuals act on and through a nexus of socially produced mediating factors (Scollon, 2001), they are performatively constituted as particular kinds of human subjects.

Within second language research, performativity theory has been drawn on in relation to gendered identities and language learning (O'Loughlin, 2001; Pavlenko, 2001), language testing (McNamara, 2006), language teacher identity (Morgan, 2004) and language learner identity (Miller, 2011b), but not yet in relation to understanding the construction of language learner agency. What does one gain from working from a performativity perspective? Pennycook (2004: 8) has argued that performativity 'provides a way forward for thinking in non-essentialist terms' in applied linguistics. At the same time, Butler (2010: 153) acknowledges that 'performativity never fully achieves its effect'; it relies on practices of reiteration and re-sedimentation. If we work to avoid essentialism in relation to learner agency, then we are drawn to focus on the iterative *processes* of its constitution and can perhaps evaluate the effects and/or effectiveness of such processes and imagine ways to intervene productively.

3 Analyzing Agency Constructs in Interview Discourse

Undertaking an Interview Study

This book is built around and informed by a set of interviews with adult immigrant small business owners. In adopting a performativity perspective (Butler, 1997) to language, identity and social practice (Miller, 2011b; Pennycook, 2004, 2007a, 2010), I align with a perspective that positions my, and all researchers', explanatory theories and the analytic approaches that we use as helping to constitute our research data. Data do not speak for themselves. To some extent, that means that I have 'constructed' my research subjects. That is, in planning my study, I settled on three criteria for selecting interviewees: individuals must have immigrated to the United States after childhood, they must have learned English after childhood and they must have opened their own businesses in the United States. These are factual identity attributes true for all of the research participants, and yet, as Rosenblatt (2002) would argue, these interviewees are still my 'imagined' research subjects (see also Holstein & Gubrium, 1995). As Rosenblatt (2002: 230) puts it, 'We cannot decide on an issue to study or what data to gather without imagining the research subject'.

What does it mean to imagine a research subject? In determining the criteria by which I would select interviewees, I constructed a type of individual who could speak authoritatively to the topics of interest to me: second language learning and use in non-classroom contexts. In treating this interviewee type as a construction, I do not conjure someone out of nothing, but I do selectively 'address' and thus constitute particular kinds of speaking subjects – a kind of 'foreclosure' that both constrains and enables interviewees to speak and to act in legitimated, recognizable ways for the purpose of my research (Butler, 1997: 139). Rosenblatt (2002: 230) further notes that not only does 'the process of constructing the subject begin[] prior to the interview … it is modified during the course of an interview session, so once we begin the interview the imagined subject is co-constructed'. Interviewees too have 'hypotheses' about who the interviewer is and what he or she is doing as an interview progresses, and these perspectives influence how the interview content is constructed as well (Rosenblatt, 2002: 231). This chapter first describes the interview study and then introduces more comprehensively the theoretical and analytical approaches that I adopted in interpreting the interview talk.

When I began planning this study, I was not focusing on agency as a researchable concept. Rather, my decision to interview individuals in non-classroom contexts and in the spaces of their own small businesses was influenced by admonition voiced now more than a decade and a half ago by Firth and Wagner (1997). They advocated for less research attention to the difficulties and problems experienced by language learners, i.e. the 'learner-as-defective-communicator mindset' (Firth & Wagner, 1997: 290), and more on their communicative successes. They described such communicative successes as 'competencies through which the participants conjointly accomplish communication with the resources—however seemingly imperfect—at their disposal' (Firth & Wagner, 1997: 290). In deciding to interview adult immigrant language learners who also owned their own businesses, I perceived (imagined) these to be individuals who had experienced communicative successes in a learned language, to some extent, given that they had managed to establish their own businesses in English-dominant communities and in relatively unfamiliar cultural milieus. However, as my research interests shifted more and more to the question of learner agency, I abandoned the difficult notion of 'success' and began to focus on another slippery concept, that is, on how these individuals positioned themselves and were positioned as (non)agentive actors in relation to language learning and use.

As I talked about my project with colleagues, several told me about the adult immigrants they knew and interacted with regularly at dry cleaning shops, nail salons, hair salons and 'ethnic' restaurants. These colleagues served as liaisons for me in making contacts with potential interviewees. I also contacted all of the overtly ethnic community organizations in my region (a large city in the Southeastern United States) that had either a web-based presence or a name and number in the telephone book. These efforts led to several more interview contacts. One of those contacts owned an insurance company franchise in a shopping center where many of the shop owners are adult immigrants and non-native speakers of English. Though the insurance company franchise owner could not be included in the study given that he had immigrated to the United States as a child and thus did not conform to the criteria I had constructed for selecting research participants, he introduced me to a number of the shop owners in this shopping complex, many of whom agreed to be interviewed. Thus, my efforts to find individuals who fit my interview profile were mediated by others' contacts and their generous help. With the exception of one participant, whom I met at a coffee shop, I interviewed each of them at their place of business. With a list of guiding questions and a digital recorder in hand, I engaged in conversations seated on a dusty folding chair next to shelves stacked high with restaurant supplies, at customer tables in restaurants owned by the interviewees, in a comfortable chair in the well-appointed office of a sushi supply company owner and at an outdoor table in front of a bakery, among others. I tried to arrange these meetings when business was slow, but even so, our conversations were sometimes interrupted by customers or employees. In several cases, I turned off the recorder while an interviewee left to attend to a business-related issue, and we then resumed once she or he could return. Though it was not possible in all cases, I tried to patronize interviewees' businesses as a customer at least once.

As is shown in Table 3.1, the 18 interviewees who are included in the study come from nine different countries. These ten women and eight men speak different languages. Their home cultures differ. Their education backgrounds and socioeconomic backgrounds and reasons for immigrating to the United States differ. So one might wonder how such diverse individuals could comprise a research population. They clearly do not comprise a cohesive social group or a homogenous cultural community. What they all *can* do is speak knowledgeably about the experience of learning English as adults, about how they opened their own businesses in the United States and about using language in particular ways in their places of work. As representatives of my 'imagined subject', they provided me with specialized knowledge on these topics. Baszanger and Dodier (2004) posit that an interview study:

> aims to take stock of the dynamic relationship between the real activities of individuals with the framework of complex, normative references, which are related to the situation but are not unified. Although the arrangements framing [a narrated] action are assumed to have a historical origin and a particular distribution in space, they are not automatically assigned to a culture. (Baszanger & Dodier, 2004: 19)

In this case, the interview study aimed to explore how the dynamic relationship of action and experience is constituted in relation to normative references

Table 3.1 Interview participants

Pseudonym	Gender	Country of origin	Type of business owned
Lan	Female	Vietnam	Hair and nail salon
Kay	Female	Vietnam	Nail salon
Jin	Female	Vietnam	Facial shop
Tony	Male	Vietnam	Vietnamese sandwich shop
Don	Male	Vietnam	Restaurant supply store
Hannah	Female	China	Chinese restaurant
Joe	Male	China	Chinese restaurant
Keith	Male	China	Chinese pastry shop
Lois	Female	Korea	Nail shop
Soo	Female	Korea	Dry cleaning pick-up store
Hee	Female	Korea	Korean restaurant
Donna	Female	Laos	Dress-making shop
Dorothy	Female	Laos	Lao music and variety store
Paul	Male	Burma	Sushi supply business
Jenny	Female	Brazil	House cleaning business
George	Male	Greece	Barbecue restaurant
Ivan	Male	France	Bakery
Lou	Male	Italy	Import/export business

to language learning and use, with a particular emphasis on the topic of learning English in the United States.

In undertaking this study, I became increasingly aware that attempting to determine causes for interviewees' agentive acts would result in extremely limited and, more likely than not, often incorrect explanations. It seemed more useful to try to learn about interviewees' own 'theories of agency', as performed in the interview conversations. Ahearn (2010: 41) coined the phrase 'theories of agency' to identify people's implicit beliefs and values regarding themselves as social actors that are often made 'public' in *how they talk about* their own actions and others' actions, *how they attribute* responsibility for events, [and] *how they describe* their own and others' decision-making processes' (italics added). As individuals talk about their past and ongoing experiences, during which they position themselves as variously agentive, responsible and/or successful protagonists in their story-worlds, we can begin to understand what they treat as socially appropriate actions or as problematic ones. Orienting to the interview talk in this way changes the focus from collecting representational verisimilitude to understanding

interviewees' discursively constituted sense-making practices and enactments of social ideologies regarding who is responsible to act and in which
cases. In adopting such a perspective, one must, most simply, account for
both *what* interviewers say and *how* they say it (Holstein & Gubrium, 1995,
2003). Packer (2011: 9), in fact, contends that an interview has 'the power to
change how the world is understood.' And for this reason, he contends that
'analysis should focus on how an interviewee crafts a way of *saying* to invite
a way of *seeing*' (Packer, 2011: 9, italics in original).

Interview Talk as Discourse

In the 1990s, second language researchers began to advocate for the need
to practice greater researcher reflexivity (Canagarajah, 1996; Holliday, 1996;
Willett *et al.*, 1998). This increasing attention to the role of the researcher in
contributing to how meaning and knowledge are constructed in the process
of conducting research coincided with the burgeoning development of qualitative research methodologies in the field. As qualitative research, particularly
ethnographic and narrative studies, gained legitimacy in the field, more attention was given to the co-constructed nature of research 'data'. Undoubtedly,
the need to defend the use of non-positivist and non-experimental methods
contributed to second language researchers' enhanced awareness of the
impossibility of conducting 'disinterested' or 'objective' research. In an overview of the efficacy of narrative inquiry for second language researchers and
L2 education in particular, Bell (2002) commented that 'whether or not they
[research participants] believe the stories they tell is relatively unimportant
because the inquiry goes beyond the specific stories to explore *the assumptions
inherent* in the shaping of those stories. No matter how fictionalized, all stories rest on and illustrate the story structures a person holds' (Bell, 2002: 209,
italics added). Pavlenko (2007: 180) celebrates the narrative turn in second
language research, but also offers strong cautions to researchers not to 'disre-
gard the line between life and text reality [or] to forget that narratives constitute, rather than reflect, reality'. Pavlenko thus emphasizes the need to
account for research narratives as 'discursive constructions' and to analyze
their 'linguistic, rhetorical, and interactional properties, as well as the cultural, historic, political, and social contexts in which they were produced and
that shape both the telling and the omissions' (Pavlenko, 2007: 81).

Only recently have second language researchers begun to theorize the
constructed and non-transparent meanings that are generated in research
interviews, a somewhat different theoretical discussion from the focus on
narrative co-construction or on researchers' influence in constructing

qualitative data more generally. Talmy (2011) identifies the divide between an approach to interviews as a 'research instrument' in which interview data are meant to reveal 'truths, facts, experience, beliefs, attitudes and/or feelings of respondents' (Talmy, 2011: 26) and a 'social practice' approach to interview data that foregrounds the constructed character of the data produced in the interview context. Talmy's approach to the interview process, along with that of other second language researchers (see Special Issue on 'Qualitative Interviews in Applied Linguistics: Discursive Perspectives' in *Applied Linguistics*, 2011, Issue 1), builds on the influential work of sociologists James Holstein and Jaber Gubrium who articulated the notion of the 'active interview' (Holstein & Gubrium, 1995, 2003). Holstein and Gubrium describe the still-too-prevalent view of interview research as a 'search-and-discovery mission' by the 'social scientific prospector' who is 'bent on finding what is already there inside variably cooperative respondents. The challenge lies in extracting information as directly as possible' (Holstein & Gubrium, 1995: 2). As you might guess, they are highly critical of this perspective to interviewing activity and the interpretive work that develops from it. Drawing on earlier work by sociologists Aaron Cicourel (1964, 1974) and Elliot Mishler (1986), along with that of anthropologist Charles Briggs (1986), Holstein and Gubrium (1995: 16) argue that all interviews, no matter how structured, are always 'active' occasions for meaning making. That said, interviewees and interviewers do not create meaning from scratch in the moment of the interview exchange but draw on the biographical particulars of the interviewee, the research interests of the interviewer and 'local ways of orienting to those topics' (Holstein & Gubrium, 1995: 16).

Holstein and Gubrium thus do not discard the need to examine the content of the talk, the *whats*; after all, it is the content of the talk that motivates the research in the first place. However, they do advocate careful investigation of how such talk is generated, leading to their much cited admonition that researchers must account for both the *whats* and the *hows* of interview talk:

> Because the respondent's subjectivity and related experience are continually being assembled and modified, the 'truth' value of interview responses cannot be judged simply in terms of whether those responses match what lies in an ostensibly objective vessel of answers. Rather, the value of interview data lies both in their meanings and how meanings are constructed. These what and how matters go hand in hand ... The entire process is fueled by the reality-constituting contributions of all participants; interviewers, too, are similarly implicated in the co-construction of the subject positions from which they ask the questions at hand. (Holstein & Gubrium, 2003: 15)

Interview accounts thus cannot be regarded as unilateral achievements. Rather interviewees and interviewers jointly assemble meanings and identities in relation to each other, in relation to the topics at hand and in relation to social discourses or ideologies by which they interpret the 'sense' of their questions and answers. Researchers who align with these approaches face new challenges. Instead of attempting to minimize the interviewer's impact on how an interviewee responds (i.e. to minimize researcher-influenced bias in the data), researchers now are confronted with the need to account for how the interviewer inevitably and necessarily influences the production of knowledge and the practices used to construct the interview talk. Atkinson and Coffey (2001: 808) contend that such a perspective does not undermine the utility of interviews for gaining understanding, but requires that researchers:

> treat interviews as generating accounts and performances that have their own properties and ought to be analyzed in accordance with such characteristics. We need, therefore, to appreciate that interviews are occasions in which particular kinds of narratives are enacted and in which 'informants' construct themselves and others as particular kinds of moral agents.

On this point, De Fina (2009: 240) argues that as interviewees produce accounts, even seemingly neutral or factual accounts of what happened and when, they are in fact responding to an 'explicit or implied ... evaluative question' on the part of the interviewer. As such, exploring what aspects of an account are treated as neutral and unproblematic versus those that are treated as potentially face-threatening and thus requiring greater negotiation and explanation, allows us to begin to understand the sense-making processes that are mobilized in interview talk (Miller, 2013).

When working with interviews, one cannot make the same kinds of arguments or claims as when one works with triangulated ethnographic data, but this difference arises not merely because interview data are somehow more limited. Clifford (1986) has argued that all research data, including comprehensive ethnographic data, can only ever lead to 'partial truths', and that such partial truths are not necessarily overcome through collecting more data, but characterize the inexorably perspectival and historically framed interpretations that constitute all research endeavors. Further, whatever form of data collection we engage in, we are inevitably participating in 'invention' not 'representation' according to Clifford (1986: 2). Bringing some analytic and theoretical structure to this 'invention' process, Kvale and Brinkmann (2008: 53) identified seven characteristics of the 'nature of knowledge yielded by the research interview' when approached from a non-positivist perspective. According to them, the knowledge that emerges from interviews must be treated as: (1) produced and 'not merely found, mined or given' (2008: 54); (2) as relational or co-constructed; (3) as conversational; (4) as contextual; (5) as linguistic; (6) as narrative; and also (7) as pragmatic or 'useful' (2008: 56).

This constructivist epistemology of interview data aligns with Bakhtin's more comprehensive notion of dialogism as discussed in Chapter 2. As Holquist (1993: xii) argues, 'for Bakhtin, *the unity of any act and its account*, a deed and its meaning, if you will, is something that is never a priori, but which must always and everywhere be achieved. The act is a deed and not a mere happening ... only if the subject of such [an act], from within his own radical uniqueness, *weaves a relation to it in his accounting for it*' (italics added). In relation to a social practice orientation to interview research, Bakhtin's dialogic perspective grants social efficacy to *how* interviewees' utterances create meaning. Atkinson and Coffey (2001: 813), in fact, contend that 'in a performative view, interviews and other accounts, need not be seen as poor surrogates or proxies for unobserved activities. They can be interrogated for their own properties—their narrative structures and function'. Garfinkel (1967: 240, cited in Packer, 2011: 198) too reminds us that our mundane act of giving accounts helps constitute the very actions that are made account-able as he discusses the 'incarnate character' of such discursive activity.

For these reasons it is incumbent upon researchers to undertake disci-plined analyses of *how* meaning is (co-)constructed in interview accounts (De Fina, 2009). Madison (2008: 226) acknowledges the limitations to what researchers can know, but adds that she 'believe[s] that a delicate balance of analysis can open deeper engagement with the narrative text and unravel contexts and connections ... without the researcher acting as psychoana-lyst, clairvoyant, or prophet'. She then argues that a 'researcher points to those moments or small details that we might take for granted as "ordinary talk" or prosaic and opens us to layers of complexity and associations that we might otherwise not come to realize' (Madison, 2008: 227). Though interviewers and/or researchers can never secure a God's-eye view or arrive at a comprehensive understanding of all that is *really* going on, they are responsible for undertaking careful analyses of the social and ideological effects of how interviewees weave relationships between themselves in the here and now of the interview talk, to events and experiences from other times and places.

Mobilizing Language

In addition to approaching interview accounts as ongoingly assembled and modified, I align with a perspective toward language that treats it as semiotic material that is 'assembled as the speaker goes along' (Quigley, 2000: 31). Such a perspective rejects an understanding of language as a preexisting autonomous entity that people simply *use*, or *tap into* or *draw upon*. Rather, it treats language as becoming 'somehow more or less materialized' (Bakhtin, 1981: 299) in interaction (or in any discursive context), thereby creating semiotic contact surfaces that enable interpretations to be made and intersubjectivity to be achieved. As was argued in Chapter 2, meaning- and language-constructing discursive processes do not create something *ex nihilo*. Each of us has a history of discursive experiences, of appropriating and then re-issuing language constructs we have heard, read and used in other interactions (Miller, 2011b). And each speaker/writer/meaning maker is able to do so through the language materialized in discourse with others, a dialogically constructed discursive interface distributed across time, space and interlocutors (Bakhtin, 1986).

In contrast to the view that recurrent or patterned language forms serve as evidence of an autonomous, neutral, underlying structure, Bakhtin (1986: 213) views them as 'a prior set of norms', which are then applied in 'fluid situations'. This ability to mobilize discursive norms is what comprises language mastery; it is not knowing the rules, but knowing how to apply 'an always changeable and adaptable sign' in particular concrete contexts (Vološinov, 1973: 68). We constitute and maintain discursive systematicity through re-issuing frequently used constructs – though such systematicity remains unstable, dynamic and incomplete. Hopper (1998: 156) sees grammar as emergent from, or as a 'by-product' of, discursive practices, and Ford *et al.* (2003: 119) argue that 'linguistic structure is rooted in and shaped by everyday language use' (see also Bybee & Hopper, 2001; Du Bois, 1987; Givón, 1979; Hopper & Thompson, 1984). The notion that language systematicity results from the sedimentation of language usages can only be dealt with diachronically as Kerbrat-Orecchioni (2010: 94) points out, but she notes that when we deal with 'one particular instance of discourse-in-interaction, what we can observe is the collective and tentative construction of malleable utterances according to a set of flexible rules'.

Such an approach to language systematicity points to the socially saturated character of language production and the social effects of language use. If language systematicity is understood to emerge from and to be organized by utterances used to perform discursive practices, then we understand that language, as a meditational means for constituting subjectivity and agency, is not merely a conduit, resource or tool, it is also an effect of these same discursive processes. At the same time, these discursively constructed propensities or regularities have powerful effects. Wertsch (1998: 55) notes that when we use 'the cultural tools [such as language] provided to us by a sociocultural

context, we usually do not operate by choice. Instead we inherently appropriate the ... affordances, constraints and so forth associated with the cultural
tools we employ'. Quigley (2000) has commented that when one learns a
language, one also adopts a particular framework for schematizing experience. The interviewees in this study can be understood to create meaning
through the enablements and constraints associated with English language
patterns, which are quite different from those found in Vietnamese, Korean,
Laotian or any of the other the languages these individuals were socialized
into from childhood. Even though interviewees' English utterances display
many non-native patterns and their talk is undoubtedly constrained by their
still-developing expertise in English, I am able to explore how they schema-
tize their experiences according to a limited set of discursive potentialities
that have emerged over time, recognizable as 'English' constructs.

Analyzing Selected Linguistic Constructs

In the three analysis chapters that follow (Chapters 4–6), I explore how
particular types of discursive regularities were produced in interviewees'
accounts. These discursive constructs were selected because they are among
some of the more effective constructs that enable individuals to talk about
their and others' actions, the attribution of responsibility to Self and Others,
and their evaluations of and enactments of these aspects of themselves and
others – all useful for constituting one's 'theories of agency' (Ahearn, 2010) in
discursive practice. The analytic approach adopted in this study can be
described broadly as discourse analysis; however, the individual analysis chapters are informed by different research strands within the larger and increasingly diverse field of discourse analysis. My overall analytic project can be
compared with Kerbrat-Orecchioni's (2010: 72) approach, which she describes
as 'eclectic', relying on 'the controlled use of tools coming from different para-
digms'. Though she acknowledges that eclecticism often carries a 'perjorative
connotation' (Kerbrat-Orecchioni, 2010: 72), she also points to many influential scholars in discourse analysis who have adopted hybrid or mixed analytic
methods, among them Eggins and Slade (2004) and Wetherell (1998). In each
of the analysis chapters in this book, I provide a short literature review or
scholarly history that anchors each of the three focal discursive constructs: (a)
subject–verb predicate structures, (b) evaluative stance and (c) reported speech
utterances. My rationale for taking these three separate, though overlapping,
foci is to explore the nuanced differences, but also interesting similarities in
their interactional and ideological effects. Many research studies have explored
these linguistic constructs independently, much as my separate chapters do.

In undertaking focused attention to selected patterned constructs across the interview corpus, and then comparing their discursive effects in particular discursive contexts, I believe that one can gain a better sense of the nuanced performative effects of these language constructs that might otherwise be overlooked. Though addressing narrative research in particular, De Fina and Georgakopoulou (2008: 381) speak to the need to account for 'recurrent evolving responses to given situations while allowing for emergence and situational contingency ... [and] for an oscillation between relatively stable, prefabricated, typified aspects of communication and emergent, in-process aspects'. In examining the selected discursive foci noted above, I considered both propensities for usage across interviewees (numerical or pattern analysis based in the whole corpus) and selected excerpts from interviews (micro-analysis), striving for 'both an in-depth view and an overview of the corpus' (Van De Mieroop, 2005: 108).

The analysis chapters are not meant to serve as 'how-to' guides, though they do demonstrate varying foci to pursue and analytic methods to adopt when exploring discourse, with an eye to how interlocutors construct aspects of (non)agentive story-world Selves. The detailed micro-analyses of selected excerpts incorporate attention to the turn-by-turn development of interaction and a number of the accompanying interactional behaviors, such as intonation contours, laughter, overlapping talk and so forth. However, the micro-analysis I engage in does not align with a particular theoretical strand of discourse analysis such as conversation analysis (Sacks *et al.*, 1974) or interactional sociolinguistic discourse analysis (Gumperz, 1982; Rampton, 2001), though it is informed by these approaches and has adapted the transcription conventions first generated for conversation analysis (Jefferson, 1984; see Appendix for explanation of transcription conventions used here). Though referring to interactional sociolinguistics in particular, Rampton's (2001: 97) beautiful description below captures the essence of what micro-discourse-analysis of varied types desires to achieve: 'with its commitment to an analytic "aesthetic of slowness" (Silverman, 1999: 415)' micro-analysis can

> produce a particularly intimate view of communication as a process of negotiation, imposition, collusion and struggle in which people invoke, avoid or reconfigure the cultural and social capital attendant on lines and identities with different degrees of accessibility and purchase in specific situations.

Rampton then adds that micro-analysis can 'reach ... right up to the act-by-act unfolding of such situations' in order to explore how 'participants "have a grasp, if only tacit, of the specific contextual moments in which they act and of how various possible courses of action will fulfill or disappoint the constitutive expectancies attached to those moments"' (Heritage, 1987: 244, in Rampton, 2001: 97).

The general methodological approach I followed in recording and transcribing the interview talk is undoubtedly familiar to many readers. After consent papers were signed by interviewees at the beginning of each interview meeting, I proceeded to ask questions from a prepared list. These were semi-structured interviews, however, and thus not all questions were addressed to all interviewees and many new questions emerged in the give-and-take of the conversation. The average length of the interviews was 24 minutes, with the shortest lasting only 12 minutes and the longest 36 minutes. They were all conducted in English and audio-recorded, resulting in 430 minutes of audio files. The audio recordings were transcribed by a graduate student, resulting in 280 pages of transcribed text. I then listened to all of the interviews with the transcripts in front of me as I identified stretches of talk that addressed particular conversational topics. The stretches of talk that became part of the data analysis, both in the numerical overview of discursive constructs and the micro-level discourse analysis, were re-transcribed by me. This second round of selected re-transcription led to the incorporation of greater detail in the transcripts. Analyzing each of the focal constructs described in Chapters 4–6 required separate analyses of the entire corpus of interview talk, that is, three iterations of focused attention to three different utterance types. I found that I often focused on the same accounts in each iteration but with different analytic lenses, and in so doing I was able to identify corroboratory discursive effects as well as nuanced distinctions, discussed further in Chapter 8.

Conclusion

These analytic processes, both in the overviews of patterned usages and in the micro-analytic explorations of how such usages were mobilized in the situated contexts of the interview conversations, enabled me to begin to understand the overlapping performative effects of particular discursive constructs and to consider the role of ideologies in constituting the sense-making practices produced in these interview encounters. By that I do not mean to suggest that I somehow managed to uncover the hidden meanings behind interviewees' words or arrive at the true understanding of what was really going on. Through rereading interview transcripts and listening repeatedly to bits of the audio recordings, I developed interpretations regarding what I understood to be 'talked into being' (Heritage, 1984: 290). However, as Briggs

(2007: 552) reminds us, such researcher practices in fact 'produce subjects, texts, knowledge and authority'. Through selecting or imagining an interviewee type, producing questions and follow-up comments that helped to constitute interviewees as representatives of this type, making selections from the interview corpus, homing in on some discursive constructs and not others, and then creating a relatively tidy interpretive whole for publication, I have, in fact, constructed the research 'findings'. This is not to say that they are not true, but it does suggest that the discursive work that I believe takes place as interviewees produce accounts of their language learning experiences in the interview context is re-enacted as I produce a researcher account in the making of this book. Briggs (2007: 562) would argue that such 'recontextualization' work in the research process is inevitable and that researchers unavoidably 'co-create cultural forms' that they claim to have discovered (Briggs, 2007: 564). I thus invite readers to participate in this constitutive process as they read, critically and analytically.

4 Agency and Responsibility: Positioning Self in Subject-Predicate Constructs

Agency and Grammar

In this chapter I explore selected subject-predicate constructs that were produced in interviewees' accounts of language learning and use and analyze them for their performative effects. Such an approach requires some explanation given that grammar analysis typically posits language as a symbolic given or an already-there entity that language 'users' can draw upon, more or less expertly. However, from a performative perspective, language is understood to be 'materialized' (Bakhtin, 1981: 229) in discursive practices. That is, each speaker/writer/signer is able to create meaning with others via a dialogically constructed semiotic interface distributed across time, space and interlocutors (Bakhtin, 1986). Goodwin (2011: 183) notes that in face-to-face interactions, we act on and through 'the sign complexes made publicly available by others'. Clearly, single interactions do not create language *ex nihilo*, for as Goodwin contends, 'to build utterances, speakers do not create sentences from scratch but creatively reuse and reshape materials provided by the talk and actions of others' (Goodwin, 2011: 185). And such 'materials' have histories. They emerge from repeated occasions of use in other contexts and with other speakers as normative methods for configuring semiotic resources (Bybee & Hopper, 2001; Hopper, 1998; Miller, 2011b; Pennycook, 2010). The patterned grammatical constructs produced by the interviewees in this study are thus regarded as dynamic semiotic constructs that have accrued stability as they have been ongoingly recycled and reconstituted in everyday interactions, allowing the interviewees to configure social actors, events, stances, beliefs, and so on, in ways that are recognized as 'sensible' and, thus, often as ideologically normative.

Though such a view argues for discursive propensities or typicality in how we use and re-issue linguistic constructs, it does not in any way suggest that we can predict how individuals will construe events or experiences. One certainly finds variability in the interview accounts examined here, but one also finds patterns across interviews in how the participants organized story-world figures and events. In analyzing such materialized linguistic phenomena in interview conversations, I reuse the familiar metalinguistic terminology developed in structuralist approaches to language. I do so because of their familiarity and the related rich body of research that helps to inform these types of discursive regularities. Poststructuralist and feminist researcher, Cate Poynton (1993), in fact, argues that *post*structuralist researchers ought not overlook the linguistic means by which subjects and other social realities come to be constituted, including those

> critical aspects of representation, concerned particularly with questions of the agency of grammatical participants and the relative focus (foregrounding/backgrounding) on those participants [that] involve highly specific grammatical features at the level of the individual clause. Such 'choices' are not on the whole under conscious control, so do not imply conscious volition on the part of the individual … [They] carry significant meanings, however, concerning the shape of the habitual and hence proper relationships within [a] culture. (Poynton, 1993: 6–7)

Of course, such 'habitual' ways of using language, at the level of grammatical features, are only some of the many mediating phenomena by which we create social meaning (see Bucholtz & Hall, 2005; Muntigl & Ventola, 2010), and yet, as Capps and Ochs (1995: 54) have noted, 'attending to grammatical form is central to understanding how people create meaning through language'. Through re-issuing discursive constructs in recognizable, normative patterns, interviewees constitute themselves as variously (in)agentive. This is one of the means by which they can perform their 'theories of agency' (Ahearn, 2010).

In focusing on subject-predicate constructs and, particularly, Duranti's description of the linguistic agent in the section that follows, I want to emphasize that I am not equating the performatively realized social agent with the subject of a transitive clause. However, I do propose that as we re-issue discursive constructs when we construct our story-world Selves as linguistic agents, we produce interactional performances, and repeating such performances not only re-sediments normative ways of using language, it also enacts particular ways of *doing* identities. Such performances are not merely 'word plays' (Harissi *et al.*, 2012: 532) that one can blithely choose to engage in or not, but rather, as Harissi *et al.* (2012: 533) note, 'subjectivities are performatively realized using tools of apparent fixity'. And further, when interviewees produced accounts of their past and ongoing experiences with learning and using English, they co-constructed with me, the interviewer, recognizable social positions and subjectivities, such as learner, immigrant newcomer and business owner, among others. In the remaining text of the chapter, I first introduce the grammar constructs that were selected for analysis and then provide a numerical overview of the utterance types produced by interviewees. These are followed by a section in which I explore selected interview excerpts using micro-level analysis. The analysis includes discussion of the performative effects of these constructs in the interview accounts.

Subject-Predicate Constructs and Agent-oriented Modality in Discourse

Duranti (2006: 460) argues that there are several 'putative universals' with respect to agency encoded *in* language: (1) all languages enable agency to be construed; (2) there is variation across but also within languages in how agency is encoded; and (3) all languages have constructs or strategies that mitigate agency. Duranti adds that some linguists regard comprehensive language typologies to be based on how languages encode agency (see Foley & Van Valin, 1984; Hopper & Thompson, 1980). The linguistic construct of transitivity, a discursive regularity found in many languages around the world, including English, organizes agentive relationships among actors, actions and those entities that are acted upon in spoken and written utterances. The encoding of agency in English is understood to involve a noun phrase subject of a transitive predicate clause. Such a construct positions the subject, or linguistic agent, as acting upon a noun phrase object. The example sentence Duranti (2006: 460) provides is: 'The boy broke the window' in which the subject 'the boy' is positioned as acting upon (i.e. 'breaking') the object 'the window'.

Donzelli (2010), however, critiques linguists' continued focus on transitivity as central to understanding the encoding of linguistic agency. Working with Toraja, an Indonesian language spoken in Sulawesi, she finds that notions of 'affectedness' or 'involvement' are more central to agency constructions. That is, in Toraja, the linguistic agent appears to be more affected by an action than a grammatical object, and further, it seems that transitivity is 'mitigated' and that linguistic objects are 'background[ed]' in such Toraja constructions (Donzelli, 2010: 214). This non-transitive encoding of agency in Toraja leads Donzelli to caution that the:

> general association of the notion of agency with the ideas of active-ness, voluntarism, and creativity is probably owing to its tacit assimilation with conceptions and notions derived from Western semantic and linguistic theory, such as that of transitivity as a property of a clause which describes an action 'which is carried over or transferred from an agent to a patient ... [and] which is typically effective in someway'. (Hopper & Thompson, 1980: 251, cited in Donzelli, 2010: 214)

However, as already demonstrated in Duranti's (2006: 463) 'universal' characterization of the encoding of agency as necessarily involving variation across and within languages, in which 'there are a number of (sometimes conflicting) factors conspiring toward making no grammatical system perfectly coherent from the point of view of the encoding of agency', the irrelevance of transitivity in some languages does not undermine its functionality in others when it comes to recurrent constructs that signal agentive relationships. Even so, Donzelli's caution is important. Sedimented constructs in English enable and constrain how we organize actors or story-world figures in relation to each other. The interviewees in this study, in other contexts and speaking in other languages, may well perform their theories of agency somewhat differently.

Another discursive regularity that can be used to constitute social beings as differently agentive is the production of 'agent-oriented modality' (Bybee *et al.*, 1994). Agent-oriented modality, as a grammatical construct, has been described as 'report[ing] the existence of internal and external conditions on an agent with respect to the completion of the action expressed in the main predicate' (Bybee *et al.*, 1994: 177). These modal constructs include 'have to', 'got to' or 'need to', what Bybee *et al.* (1994) have labeled as obligation or necessity modality, which can position a story-world figure as someone who is compelled to act in order to constitute or maintain an identity of someone who acts responsibly. The performative effects of producing utterances with constructs such as 'have to' can, according to Scheibman (2007), serve to (re)establish social normativity as language producers implicitly (and in most cases unconsciously) appeal to societal belief systems or ideologies in their interactions with others. That is, when interlocutors construct an action as a (social) obligation, they often subtly reconstitute value systems at the same time as they position themselves as responsible, 'moral' and aware of these value systems.

One might well argue that obligations and necessities are imposed on individuals and thus an individual's actions, constructed as performed under these conditions, ought not be treated as agentive. However, if agency is not regarded as free-willed, individualistic or solely self-motivated action (Duranti, 2006), then it seems that even imposed expectations for action can be understood to function as enablements for agentive action. That is, in many cases, because one believes one *must* act, one *does* act. Further, it is often the case that as socially constituted norms become internalized, they come to be regarded by individuals as arising from their *own* beliefs concerning desirable behavior. In this way, one's lack of action in some situations comes to be regarded as personal failure, just as taking action in those situations comes to be regarded as personal achievement. The socially constituted sense of 'individual' agentive actions is particularly relevant in regards to language learning and use. Though sociocultural theorists have shown that learning is a socially distributed activity, influenced by one's history and one's status and participation in varying communities of practice (Lantolf & Thorne, 2006; Lave & Wenger, 1991; Pavlenko & Lantolf, 2000), long-held views of language learners as discrete individuals who learn, more or less well, owing to internal and/or individual variables, continue to function as the default view in everyday discourse as well as in much scholarly research.

Duranti's (2006) recognition of intralanguage complexity and Donzelli's (2010) caution regarding interlanguage diversity with respect to agency constructs in language, are important considerations for the analysis of grammar constructs undertaken in this chapter, particularly for considering the relationship between linguistic agency and social agency. The agency constructs produced in human utterances can help (re)constitute particular identities and be used to position story-world Selves as particular kinds of social beings in the world, but they can never be regarded as direct proxies for social agency in human experience as noted earlier (see also Quigley, 2001). On this point, Duranti (2006: 466) notes that researchers who explore transitive utterances in languages, such as English, must examine both how information is encoded (e.g. the agent of an event) as well as the 'type of persons and the type of world that speakers build through their typically unconscious but nevertheless careful choice of words'. It is this performative effect, constituted through the situated performances of particular utterances, that I want to foreground in this chapter through examining selected grammatical constructions produced in interviewees' accounts. In considering the effects of such utterances, I draw on Duranti's (2006: 453) three-part 'working definition' of agency in language: (a) agents are entities constructed as having 'some degree of control over their own behavior', (b) whose actions affect others and sometimes themselves and (c) whose actions can be evaluated in terms of responsibility for an action and its outcome.

Discursive Agency: An Overview of the Interview Corpus

In this section, I explore how the interviewees in my study positioned themselves as variously agentive through their production of subject-predicate constructs as well as selected modal verb constructs. Duranti (2006) follows the distinction implemented by other linguists (Fillmore, 1968; Jackendoff, 1990) in treating transitive constructs with noun-phrase subjects and objects as encoding agency. However, among researchers who have analyzed written and/or spoken discourse, agency constructs are less rigidly defined. In many cases this is because utterances in interactional discourse tend to be mostly intransitive, with no linguistic agent (see Du Bois, 1987, 2003; Scheibman, 2002; Thompson & Hopper, 2001). De Silveira and Habermas (2011: 9) use the term 'narrative agency' to identify utterances that position the speaker as the 'acting I' who 'goes' or 'says' or 'thinks' or 'does' something. In these utterances, there is not necessarily an object of a transitive verb, but rather a subject-predicate construct that creates 'an agentic meaning' (De Silveira & Habermas, 2011: 9). Similarly, Wertsch (1998) incorporates subjects of intransitive clauses and copula clauses along with subjects of transitive clauses in his analysis of agency constructions in written texts.

I have chosen to use the term *discursive agency* to name the focal subject-predicate utterance types that emerged in the interviews as well as to capture their performative efficacy. That is, as interviewees mobilized utterances in which they indexed themselves as story-world figures through using first-person pronouns such as 'I', 'me' or 'we', and sometimes inclusive 'you', and positioned these pronouns as predicate subjects or objects, they discursively constituted their story-world Selves as particular kinds of (in)agentive social beings. I follow Du Bois (2003) in counting such utterance types across the interview corpus. He argues that in order to make a claim regarding 'recurrent tendencies in discourse' one needs to provide a 'numerical accounting', an approach that he notes has long been a 'hallmark of discourse and grammar studies' (Du Bois, 2003: 55) (see Du Bois, 1980, 1987; Fox & Thompson, 1990; Givón, 1979, 1983; Thompson & Hopper, 2001).

Subject-predicate utterance types

In analyzing and counting utterance types, I included subject-predicate constructs in which an interviewee's story-world Self was not overtly uttered as an 'I' but was readily recoverable as such from the discourse context (see

De Fina, 2003, for a similar approach). For example, George, a Greek man who owned a restaurant commented:

(1) *'go* home and uh read the book, so what's different you know, Greeks and English.'

In this instance I counted his utterance as one example of an agentive construct given that it was clear from the context that he was speaking about himself: *'(I) go* home and read'. In another example, Hee, a Korean female interviewee commented:

(2) *'I dig dig* in dictionary … and always *I reading* aloud … so *I do* and slowly I understand it'.

In this case, I counted three agent-of-action predicate utterances ('I dig dig … I reading … I do'), but I did not treat utterances such as 'I learn English' (Don, Vietnamese restaurant supply store owner) as an agentive construct given the ambiguous sense of 'learn' with respect to agency. In some cases, 'learn' seems to serve as a synonym for 'study', an agentive action, but in others, it seemed to position the subject more as an experiencer of the action than an agent of it. Given this ambiguity, I chose to count 'learn' utterances separately.

When interviewees positioned their story-world Selves as the objects of others' actions, they are constructed as inagentive Selves, such as in the utterance produced by one Chinese female, Hannah, as she comments on her English-language tutor:

(3) 'and then he *teach me* you know'.

And finally, I counted utterances that used agent-oriented modality, particularly the modal verb phrases 'have to', 'got to' and 'need to', which position interviewees' story-world Selves as obligated or needing to act in particular ways. For example, Keith, who never studied English formally in the United States, noted that:

(4) 'but you want to living over here *you got to* be able to. Kind of *have to* learn [English]'.

Six of the interviewees produced such modal verbs when speaking about their early efforts to learn English in the United States, thereby positioning their story-world protagonists as aware of their responsibility to study and use English while living in the United States. In responding to my questions regarding their learning of English, three interviewees indicated that they had never studied English in the United States, and nine others explicitly indicated that they stopped studying English or attending English-as-a-second-language classes at some point after they immigrated to the United States. All 12 of these interviewees supplied accounts for why they could not study English at all or for why they had to give up attending English classes and five of them used the obligation/necessity modality when describing their need to stop learning or their inability to ever attend classes, casting such lack of learning activity as due to other more powerful obligations outside of their control. Most frequently, these obligations included the need to work all day, sometimes until late at night, as noted by Soo:

(5)   'I *have to* you know overtime, like until ten o'clock'.

The other most common obligation that constrained them from studying English was their need to take care of their family as recounted in Hannah's utterance:

(6)   'no time. I have three children. I *got to* work hard for them'.

In my numerical accounting of recurrent discursive constructs, I only counted utterances that directly addressed topics regarding interviewees' experiences in: (1) their early learning of English; (2) their use and continued learning of English at work; and (3) their use and learning of languages other than English at work. Additional example utterances are shown in Table 4.1, organized so that a sample utterance type (i.e. figure as agent of action predicates) is matched with a particular account topic (i.e. use and continued learning of English at work).

Though individual interviewees varied in the number of utterances produced on any given topic and thus also in the number of focal linguistic constructs related to each of these topic areas, a numerical accounting allowed me to gain an overview of the more typical and patterned ways interviewees constructed socially recognizable story-worlds in which individuals act or are acted upon. As demonstrated in Tables 4.2 through 4.4, the constructs produced by interviewees that had the highest number of utterances and the largest percentage of total utterances, positioned their story-world Selves as subjects of action predicates, and thus as agentive to some degree, across all three topics. One can further see that the interviewees were far less inclined to cast their story-world figures as inagentive (see 'Story-world figure as object of others' actions' in each Table).

All of the interviewees in this study share the experience of immigrating to the United States, learning English and opening their own businesses,

Table 4.1 Examples of interviewee's subject-predicate utterance types by topical category

	Topical categories		
Utterance types	*Early learning of English*	*Use and continued learning of English at work*	*Use and learning of languages other than English at work*
Figure as agent of action predicates	*I go* school night time like two hours Tuesday and Thursday.	*I use* mostly English with American.	*I teach* them Vietnamese.
Figure as subject of 'learn' predicates	First few years *I learn* speak in uh broken English with a lot of Americans.	*I still learning* English every day.	Spanish *I learn* from them.
Figure as object of predicate action	I had one Brazilian girl *she teach me.*	*My customer help me* a lot.	*They teach me* a little bit of [Lao].
Figure as agent of necessary or obligatory action	So there *have to be* effort *by myself.*	*I need to write* oh I'm sorry I broke something.	So *you* kind of *have to* learn some.

but they also have quite different histories with respect to kinds and levels of education, economic advantage, family life, work histories, political and institutional influences, as well as languages and cultures. And yet, despite their markedly different histories, we see that the interviewees displayed striking similarity in their 'preference' for positioning their story-world

Table 4.2 Number of utterances directed to 'Early Learning of English'

Utterance type	*Number of utterances*	*% of total*
Story-world figure as agent of action	68	52%
Story-world figure as learner	31	24%
Story-world figure as object of others' actions	7	6%
Story-world figure as agent of obligatory/necessary action	24	18%
Total	130	100%

Table 4.3 Number of utterances directed to 'Use and Continued Learning of English at Work'

Utterance type	Number of utterances	% of total
Story-world figure as agent of action	63	61%
Story-world figure as learner	16	15%
Story-world figure as object of others' actions	12	11%
Story-world figure as agent of obligatory/necessary action	13	13%
Total	104	100%

Table 4.4 Number of utterances directed to 'Use and Learning of Languages Other than English at Work'

Utterance type	Number of utterances	% of total
Story-world figure as agent of action	26	63%
Story-world figure as learner	6	15%
Story-world figure as object of others' actions	7	17%
Story-world figure as agent of obligatory/necessary action	2	5%
Total	41	100%

Selves as agents of learning and using English and other languages as shown in the tables. However, the fact that the interviewees in this study positioned themselves as both inagentive and agentive when addressing the same topic and in the same stretch of interaction, also indicates that interview topics did not determine their choices absolutely though they do perhaps motivate particular kinds of social beings to be constituted in the talk.

The greater likelihood for interviewees to produce agentive constructions can, in part, be understood as a feature of conversation with an auto-biographical focus (Scheibman, 2002). However, speaking about oneself in interview accounts does not always predispose individuals to construct themselves as agentive figures. McCollum (2002), for example, found in interviewing middle-class Americans that these participants positioned themselves very differently depending on whether they were discussing how they came to be in their current professions (agentive) versus whether they were discussing how they fell in love with their current romantic partners (inagentive). As he argues, this contrast in how these interviewees positioned themselves 'is deeply rooted in interpersonal and other important socialization experiences from early childhood' (McCollum, 2002: 113). For this reason, he contends that interviewees rely on culturally normative sense-making procedures, such as the use of (non)agentive subject-predicate constructions, to 'make presuppositions about what can be taken as expected, what the norms are, and what common or special belief systems can be used to establish coherence' (Linde, 1993: 3, cited in McCollum, 2002: 116). Likewise, the interviewees' accounts in my study cannot be taken as direct reports of agentive actions, but rather as ideologically sensitive accounts that construct interviewees' 'theories of agency' (Ahearn, 2010).

In order to understand how such subject positioning emerged across interviews, I next examine how these agentive and/or inagentive positionings were accomplished locally. The act of directing questions to these individuals constrained interviewees as needing to speak in order to be regarded as cooperative interlocutors, even as it enabled them to speak through creating an interactional space in which they could construct their story-world Selves as knowledgeable and responsible (Miller, 2011a). Even the lexical items uttered in my questions have both enabling and constraining influences on the interviewees' responses. On the one hand, they supply semantic material on which a cooperative response can be built, but at the same time they may predispose interviewees to construct their protagonist Selves in relation to the actions entailed in my questions. Clearly, these are not unilateral achievements but rather fully co-constructed. However, such co-construction is not limited to what two individuals at one time and in one space produce jointly. It also builds on social relevancy and the ideological 'sense' regarding what can be presumed or considered appropriate in the situations that they discuss. As Busch (2012: 509) argues, following Butler (1997), the 'discursive, performative power of language' can be attributed to its 'normativity', that is, what is regarded as 'sayable and what is not'. These performative effects require particular scrutiny.

Subject-Predicate Constructs in Discursive Practice: A Micro-Analysis

Early learning of English

Jenny, a Brazilian woman who owned a house cleaning service, varies between positioning her story-world Self as agentive and inagentive in Excerpt (7). In the moments preceding the talk displayed below, Jenny informed me that she had learned English from an English language tutor, and I followed up on this information by asking how she had found her teacher (line (1)). In responding, Jenny positions herself as the agent of the action of 'telling' of her need for a teacher while simultaneously positioning herself as the object of this sought-after teacher's instruction: '(I) *told* I needed one teacher *to teach me* English' (4). Jenny continues to move between positioning her story-world Self as the agent of actions which then led to her finding an English teacher and as the object of others' actions, 'some Brazilian people', who contributed to this goal. She positions herself agentively in noting 'and then *I called*' (11), which set in motion the continued visits of the English tutor to her house (13). In this way, even though she indicates that some other Brazilians in the community informed her of a teacher and gave Jenny the teacher's telephone number, thereby positioning herself as the object of their actions, these same actions were set in motion by Jenny's agentive act of announcing her need for a teacher and were culminated through Jenny's agentive act of calling the teacher (11).

(7) *Jenny calls an English teacher*

   1. **Int:**   How did you find you- your English teacher.
   2. **Jen:**   I was already here,
   3. **Int:**   Okay [okay.
   4. **Jen:**   [and told I needed one [teacher to teach me English,
   5. **Int:**   [Yeah okay.
   6. **Jen:**   and the:n I found some- some Brazilian people
   7.   *oh I know someone,*
   8. **Int:**   Uh huh.
   9. **Jen:**   and gave me the number,
  10. **Int:**   Okay.
  11. **Jen:**   and then I called=
  12. **Int:**   =Super=
  13. **Jen:**   =and she started to come to my house.

Throughout this brief segment of talk, Jenny and I orient to the normative turn-taking procedures of interview talk in that I initiate questions, Jenny supplies responses, and I typically insert minimal utterances ('okay', 'uh huh') to signal my acceptance of her responses (Mishler, 1986; Ten Have, 2004). These minimal utterances also signal that I continue to yield the floor to her and thereby contribute to her production of an extended account regarding her efforts to learn English. I orient to Jenny's account of her actions taken to learn English as socially appropriate and even as unsurprising, in part through producing 'neutral' minimal receipt tokens such as 'okay'

(Miller, 2013). Our co-constructed production of doing 'being ordinary' (Sacks, 1984) can thus be regarded as ideologically normative. In Laihonen's (2008: 683) analysis of interview talk, she contends that 'normality is connected to morality'. The exception to the neutral stance enacted by myself as interviewer, is my very positive receipt token 'super' (12) uttered without a pause immediately after Jenny reported on her agentive action of calling the English tutor (11). Though it is not clear why this action should be selected over Jenny's other actions for special acknowledgement, it is clear that an agentive action is treated as worthy of praise in this context. If Jenny had instead reported that she ended up being too busy to call the tutor, or if she had supplied some other socially acceptable rationale for being unable to follow-up on the contact information provided to her, it is highly doubtful that I would have produced such a strongly positive receipt token at that point in the interaction.

Similar to what was demonstrated in Jenny's account, variation in the agentive positioning of the Self as story-world figure can be found in Excerpt (8), taken from an interview with Hannah, a Chinese female restaurant owner. As was the case in all interviews, early in our conversation, I asked her if she had ever gone to an English class (1). In using the verb 'go', my question positions Hannah as a potential agent of the action of attending English language classes, and indeed she recycles the verb from my question in her response, 'Yeah. And *I going* to adult school ... for two hour a day' (2, 4), activity that she indicates continued for about four years (6). In analyzing these constructs, I treated her use of 'going' and 'learning' in lines (2) and (6) as main verbs of the predicates, rather than verbals, given that they are the only verb entities in these utterances. However, Hannah does not simply recycle the vocabulary options introduced by my questions when she appends another example of how she learned English, this time without my direct elicitation. She adds that she '*pick* an American friend' (10–11), someone who also knew Chinese, to be her English teacher. This highly agentive construction of her protagonist Self is followed by an utterance in which Hannah positions herself as the object of this friend's instruction: 'he *teach me* you know' (15).

(8)   *Hannah picks a teacher*

   1. **Int:**   Yeah yeah. Did you ever go to an English class?
   2. **Han:**   Yeah. And I going to adult school?
   3. **Int:**   Yeah.
   4. **Han:**   yeah for two hour a day,
   5. **Int:**   Oh?

6. **Han:**   and then uh and then and then learning about four years?
7. **Int:**   Wow.
8. **Han:**   Uh huh.
9. **Int:**   Good for you.
10. **Han:**   Uh huh. And and about ho- how many years. And then I pick
11.   American friend?
12. **Int:**   Yeah.
13. **Han:**   He's uh speak really good English. Chinese. [He's a teacher.
14. **Int:**   [Ah ah ah
15. **Han:**   And then he he teach me you know.
16. **Int:**   Okay.
17. **Han:**   Yeah.

As was true in my interview with Jenny, I co-construct our interaction as interview talk through producing questions and supplying minimal receipt tokens following Hannah's responses. But I also break from interviewer 'neutrality', uttering 'wow' (7) and 'good for you' (9) after Hannah reports that she attended 'adult school' (2) for 'about four years' (6). This shift to a strongly positive acknowledgment occurs when Hannah reports on her effortful and sustained actions to learn English, i.e. Hannah's positioning of herself as highly agentive. Though agentive actions taken to learn English are treated as normative, invoked in part through the form my question takes ('Did you ever *go* to an English class' (1)), I appear to treat some actions as demonstrations of exceptional effort and thus as particularly worthy of commendation.

In these two excerpts, one can see my influence as interviewer in discursively mobilizing agentive positioning for the interviewees through uttering verbs such as 'go' (Hannah) and 'find' (Jenny) when asking these women about their early experiences learning English. Such questions presuppose that Jenny and Hannah engaged in some type of effortful action that initiated their language learning processes. Even so, both interviewees did more than merely re-issue my verb choices and produced additional subject-predicate constructs, which positioned them as agentive figures in pursuing the learning of English while also, in other utterances, positioning themselves as the object of others' actions in relation to being taught English. Thus we find that the topic of learning English did not lend itself to a singular performance of Self as agentive. And yet, as was noted earlier, interviewees' most typical positioning of their story-world Selves with respect to their early learning of English presupposed some degree of control over their behavior, i.e. as agents of action predicates (see Table 4.2). Other interviewees spoke of scheduling and/or attending classes, buying English language books or watching television, guided by their desire to learn English rather than to engage in mere passive entertainment.

More intense demonstrations of effortful agentive actions were effected through interviewees' use of agent-oriented modality. In Excerpt (9), George, a Greek restaurant owner, establishes very firmly that immigrants who 'come this country' (1) can 'throw out' English (2), which I interpret to mean that they can choose not to bother with learning the language. George rejects this as irresponsible behavior and contrasts it with responsible actions, marked by intention and effort through his use of agent-oriented modality in his repeated comments that 'you *have to* try' (5, 10, 13) and in his comment that one has to work hard even when it is not easy (16).

> (9)   *George: You have to try*
>
> 1. **Geo:** See any any- anybody come this country and if you want
> 2.   to throw out English they can do that. I don't see why
> 3.   I don't see no reason,
> 4. **Int:** Mmhm.
> 5. **Geo:** but you have to try.
> 6. **Int:** Mmhm.
> 7. **Geo:** Or if you want your own business or if you do anything
> 8.   really you know,
> 9. **Int:** Yeah.
> 10. **Geo:** you have to try.
> 11. **Int:** Yeah.
> 12. **Geo:** You can't sit at home and say you know learn English.
> 13.   You know here you have to try go to school or some,
> 14.   but you have to try yourself.
> 15. **Int:** Yeah.
> 16. **Geo:** And work (your) hard, this not easy now this is not [uh
> 17. **Int:**   [Yeah.
> 18. **Geo:** you know.

In constructing actions taken to learn English as an obligation and/or necessity through the use of the modal 'have to', George constitutes the agents who take such actions to be responsible, in contrast to those who take a more dilatory approach and simply 'sit at home' (12). In using 'you' as the agentive subject in his utterances, George's assessment of responsible language learning behavior is generalized beyond himself, though it simultaneously implicates his own actions as desirable and responsible. The 'general truth' that George constructs is treated as legitimate by me, the interviewer, in that I produce only minimal receipt token turns throughout the interaction. As such, I do not treat his account as exceptional, but rather as a 'sensible' account of what individuals need to do in order to learn English.

Kay's account in Excerpt (10), however, demonstrates the push and pull of her recognition of the need for and the desire to act toward learning English, but also the constraints that can curtail such efforts. In narrating her language learning history, Kay constructs her actions to learn English as developing out of a series of cause–effect events. She indicates that after she arrived 'here' in the United States (5–6) she recognized that she needed to practice more English and 'that's why' (8, 19) she decided to attend a community college ('CPCC'). However, in lines (24–27), Kay uses the obligation/necessity construct in uttering 'I *have to* work daytime and night- nighttime go to school'. The upshot is that she saw college as 'too much' (27) for her, and she finally had to give up on school.

(10)   *Kay has to work*

1.	**Kay:**	I learn English in our country before I came here, yeah,
2.		like I learn in my uh high school and I learn in college
3.		in our country,
4.	**Int:**	Okay okay.
5.	**Kay:**	and after that you know we came here, and after I came
6.		here, I know I have to practice more and more,
7.	**Int:**	Yeah.
8.	**Kay:**	and uh that why I went to CPCC school,
9.	**Int:**	Okay.
10.	**Kay:**	to learn a-
11.	**Int:**	And was that mostly conversational English at CPCC?
12.	**Kay:**	Uh yeah.
13.	**Int:**	Okay, and probably in high school and college it was mostly
14.		reading [and writing?
15.	**Kay:**	[Yeah
16.	**Kay:**	Because before I plan I back to school like uh finish college
17.		[in here,
18.	**Int:**	[Yeah.
19.	**Kay:**	that's why I try get back to CPCC [learn about English.
20.	**Int:**	[Yeah.
21.	**Kay:**	And I I took several uh uh class you know like math
22.		[or something like that?
23.	**Int:**	[Uh huh.

24. **Kay:**   But after a while I think it's hard because I have to
25.   [work daytime and
26. **Int:**   [I understand yeah.
27. **Kay:**   night- nighttime go to school and college is too much for me
28.   you know [and finally I give up?
29. **Int:**   [I know.

In this interaction, Kay is positioned as someone who not only had the wherewithal to go to school to learn English, but also as someone who had the background for and aspirations to finish college in the United States. However, in attributing her inability to continue going to school to the understandable and socially recognized difficulty of juggling work and school simultaneously, Kay positions herself as someone who cannot be held responsible for not finishing college or continuing to take English classes. That is, if her inaction cannot be helped then she cannot be held responsible for it. I co-construct the sense of this by abandoning interviewer neutrality, constructing myself as an understanding and sympathetic interlocutor in commenting, 'I understand yeah' (26) and 'I know' (29) with respect to her need to stop taking English classes in order to attend to work and family (see Hak, 2003: 203, on 'appreciative interviewer discourse'). In addition, my responses overlap with her turns (26, 29), also signaling a stance of alignment or solidarity with her (Tannen, 1990).

In treating Kay's report of her need to stop attending English classes differently from her reports of actions taken to attend community college (sympathetically versus neutrally), I orient to and reproduce the ideological effects of her discursively constructed story-world figure. That is, her actions to continue learning English are treated as normal and thus positive though not necessarily exceptionally so (in contrast to my more strongly positive response to Hannah's report of going to English classes for four years). As such, her inability to continue learning English is treated as undesirable, even though it is simultaneously treated as excusable and understandable given that acting to fulfill family and work obligations is also socially normative and desirable. The discursive work Kay and I engage in to preclude her being positioned negatively (perhaps as irresponsible) points to the social values that are attributed to individual agentive actions in relation to learning English. As Kay establishes reasons or causes for her need to retreat from acting to learn English, I orient to these utterances as requiring some face maintenance (Arundale, 2010). In this way, we both display our sensitivity to normative expectations for desirable subject positioning.

Constructing a spatially positioned self: Performative effects

In the four Excerpts (7–10) examined, the interviewees constructed their protagonist Selves as agents or benefactors of actions taken toward learning English in particular (though sometimes ambiguously identified) spaces. Jenny, in Excerpt (7), for example, comments that 'I was *already here*' (2) when she launched her efforts to find an English teacher. George, in Excerpt (9), indicates that in *'this country'* (1) and when *'here'* (13), one has to try to learn English, while Kay, in Excerpt (10), indicates that it was 'after I came *here*' (5–6) that she came to realize that she needed to learn more English. Unlike George's reference to 'this country', the deictic references to 'here' are somewhat ambiguous in that they may reference the United States as a whole or perhaps interviewees' adopted American cities. However, in all cases, they construct their local contexts (whether national or community-level) as self-evidently spaces where English usage is normative. In addition, Hannah's reference in Excerpt (8) to 'pick[ing] an American friend' (10–11) who could also speak Chinese to be her English teacher, seems to constitute an American identity as self-evidently one that is also an English-speaking identity. In producing these utterances, these interviewees simultaneously constitute their story-world Selves as not from 'here', and by constructing their English language learning as necessary, or precipitated by their location 'here', these interviewees, in collaboration with me the interviewer, reconstitute the legitimacy of English as 'naturally' and 'commonsensically' used in American spaces.

The performative effects of such unremarkable positioning moves can serve to reconstitute the 'regimes of language' (Blommaert *et al.*, 2005a: 211), which sediment the legitimacy of English for 'this' space. In their discussion of Billig's (1995) book-length exploration of 'banal nationalism', Dixon and Durrheim (2000: 33) note that 'banal' language constructions 'including deictic references to the national homeland (e.g. *"this* country")' serve to 'locate' narrators and other individuals according to the 'ideological traditions that sustain relations of domination'. The fact that the United States has never been solely English speaking (Miller, 2009; Pavlenko, 2002; Potowski, 2010; Ricento, 2005) or that the American cities where these interviewees lived at the time of the interviews were marked by robust language diversity points to the problematic construction of 'here' as manifestly English speaking. At the same time, the perceived normative 'imposition' of the need to use English when spatially positioned in the United States, can also be understood to enable the learning of English.

Davies (2000: 56) discusses the ways in which 'we are spoken and speak ourselves into existence', which involves, in part, the 'discursive placing of responsibility' upon ourselves through constructing our 'agentic acts as purely individual acts'. Both the interview questions and interviewees' responses contributed to such an orientation in these accounts, as interviewees constructed themselves as self-evidently having the capacity to act to learn English and as commonsensically 'choosing' to do so when they arrived in the United States. Thus, what is left to be determined are the details of when and how. In this way, interviewees' agentive orientations in constructing their story-world Selves can be understood as socially and ideologically motivated rather than emerging solely from *within* individuals. Butler has argued that the 'paradox of subjectivation' (Butler, 1993: 15) is that the constraints that are imposed at a given moment in time (and, I would add, in discursively constructed spaces) simultaneously enable a subject to act meaningfully. Elsewhere, she notes that one's capacity to speak/act is mediated exactly because of being 'addressed' or 'recognized' as a particular kind of subject, in which 'agency becomes possible on the condition of such foreclosure' (Butler, 1997: 139). In being addressed or recognized as immigrant residents in the United States, who commonsensically have chosen to learn English, the interviewees are positioned in an interactional and ideological space 'both of restrictions and potentialities' (Busch, 2012: 509). That is, they must constitute themselves as responsible, agentive Selves in the interview talk to be recognized as desirable interlocutors given my orientation to them as language learners (restrictions), but in so doing, they *can* constitute desirable subjectivities for themselves by showing themselves to be ideologically responsive (potentialities). In the section that follows, I explore how interviewees constructed their story-world Selves as English language users and learners in their business spaces somewhat differently with respect to agentive acts.

Using and continuing to learn English at work

In considering how the participants constructed their protagonist Selves when responding to questions regarding their use and continued learning of English at work, one finds that they continued to exhibit a 'preference' for agentive constructs involving themselves as protagonists (see Table 4.3), though a close analysis of these interactions suggests that these story-world Selves tended to be less strongly agentive. For example, in Excerpt (11), Jin, a Vietnamese female owner of a facial salon, indicates that she rarely has difficulty understanding English (1, 3) but that when she encounters 'some word' (5) that she does not understand when placing an order with a supplier, she solves the language problem by consulting an online dictionary (8). Though an agentive action on Jin's part, her choice to consult an online dictionary is not one that requires persistence or forethought. This action occurs *in response to* a moment of language difficulty and is treated as an easily 'fulfillable' action (Miller, 2010: 479).

(11) *Jin goes to the Internet*

1. **Jin:** I'm I'm most the time I'm understand.
2. **Int:** Yeah. So it's not-
3. **Jin:** I'm understand [I don't have any problem.
4. **Int:**   [Turns out not to be a problem.
5. **Jin:** Yeah, but some word if I don't understand for the
6.   supply, to order?
7. **Int:** Yes. Yes.
8. **Jin:** and we go to Internet to find our dictionary to to um
9.   explain you know.
10. **Int:** Yeah.

In a similar fashion, Chinese restaurant owner Hannah in Excerpt (12) describes the actions she takes when she has difficulty understanding English while interacting with her customers. She repeats examples of the clarification requests that she directs to her customers (2, 4–5). In this way, Hannah positions herself as agentively taking the initiative to negotiate for meaning, but she also downgrades the degree of effort or difficulty this action entails in using the 'depreciatory qualifier' (Kishner & Gibbs, 1996) 'just'; i.e. Hannah 'just' (1) tells her customers that she does not understand them. As with Jin, Hannah's agentive acts are cast as non-onerous and responsive to contingent moments of language difficulty.

(12) *Hannah asks for clarification*

1. **Han:** We don't understand sometime, and uh just I tell you
2.   *I not really understand that.*
3. **Int:** Yeah, so they just say it again.
4. **Han:** Yeah yeah and then uh *can you repeat again*? or uh *can*
5.   *you write down for me*? or something yeah.

In yet one more example, in Excerpt (13), Tony, a Vietnamese sandwich shop owner, describes moments when he is unable to understand his English-speaking customers. In doing so, he positions himself as agentive in that he indicates that he directs his customers to slow down when they speak (3). He notes that when they do, he is able to 'catch up' (5) with them in the English language interaction.

(13) *Tony tells customers to slow down*

1. **Tony:** Sometimes I cannot understand,
2. **Int:** Yeah.
3. **Tony:** And I tell my customers *slow down* and they slow down,
4. **Int:** Okay.
5. **Tony:** And I can catch up.

The presupposition in these three scenarios is that linguistic misunderstandings are undesirable and that responsibility for dealing with them lies with the immigrant business owners. The actions described by Jin, Hannah and Tony in managing their use of English at work can be understood as agentive rather than unconscious or purely reactive behaviors. However, these are not cast as highly effortful, but rather as responsive acts that are contingent upon co-present interlocutors or other mediating entities (i.e. an online dictionary). I co-construct the sense of this easy agency through my minimal receipt tokens in all three of these interview excerpts, but also in my affirmation to Jin that her occasional misunderstandings 'turn[] out not to be a problem' (Excerpt (11), line (4)), as well as to Hannah in affirming that moments of misunderstanding are easily alleviated when customers 'just say it again' (Excerpt (12), line (3)).

The apparent ease by which some of the interviewees manage to continue learning English at work is further highlighted in Excerpts (14) and (15), as both Ivan, a French bakery owner, and George, the Greek restaurant owner, claim that they are able simply to 'pick up' English while at work. We see this in line (1) in Excerpt (14) and in lines (3) and (8) in Excerpt (15).

(14) *Ivan 'picks up' English*

1. **Ivan:** I think English is an easy language to pick up,
2. so what's important to me is to be able to just
3. communicate what I want to say.
4. **Int:** Right.

(15) *George 'picks up' English*

1. **Geo:** Everyday uh everyday I working with my waitress,
2. **Int:** Yeah.
3. **Geo:** uh I pick up something for customers from waitress everyday.
4. **Int:** Yeah okay.
5. **Geo:** Yeah working uptown for like eight nine years whatever.

6.   Some nights, sometimes the place used to be 24 hours,
7. **Int:**   Wow.
8. **Geo:**   and I just pick up everyday something.

These accounts of language learner Selves who effortlessly 'pick up' English contrast sharply with how Ivan and George described their early learning of English. Ivan, for example, described his dislike for learning English when he was a high school student and recounted that he decided to spend a semester in England at that time to prove to his parents that he was motivated to learn the language, but that his study abroad experience only seemed to further de-motivate him from learning it. His relationship with the language changed only when he met an American woman who eventually became his wife. At that point, he began to study the language intensively using books and tapes to learn it on his own. Such actions point to an intentional and effortful agentive Self, much as the protagonist constructed in George's accounts of someone who worked hard to learn English after coming to the United States. As was seen earlier (Excerpt (9)), he emphasized repeatedly that one 'has to try' to learn the language.

In line with the 'easy agency' constituted in interviewees' accounts of learning and using English while at work, there were relatively few cases of obligation/need modality produced. One such example is found in Excerpt (16), in which Ivan, the French bakery owner, describes how he managed to learn English at work after moving to the United States. He and his American English-speaking wife both worked at the same restaurant, he as a cook and she as the pastry chef. Ivan notes that he could benefit from his wife's language assistance during the day when she could translate for him, but during the evening dinner shift he comments that he *'had to* deal with waiters one on one' (13, 15) in English. Though this obligation/need modal construction points to Ivan's difficulty in interacting with the English-speaking waiters, he seems to suggest that because he was interacting with them one on one when taking orders (establishing a cause–effect relationship through his use of 'so' (15)), his ensuing workplace learning of English 'became progressively more fluent' for him (15, 17). In constructing his continued learning of English in this way, he constructs himself as an experiencer of learning, more than as someone who agentively pursues it; that is, rather than intentionally seeking out ways to learn English, the learning process is constructed as happening *to* him; his English simply *became* more fluent.

(16) *Ivan becomes more fluent*

1. **Int:**   I mean do you have any kind of memory at all of how that
2.   learning process happened during that time?

3. **Ivan:**   Yeah, I guess so, you know um at work basically,
4. **Int:**   Yeah.
5. **Ivan:**   uh because I worked the dinner dinner shift, so my wife
6.   was the pastry chef there.
7. **Int:**   Okay.
8. **Ivan:**   So we worked together.
9. **Int:**   Yes.
10. **Ivan:** So that was helpful, during the day she was here to translate
11.   if I needed help,
12. **Int:**   Yes.
13. **Ivan:** in the evening, I had to deal with waiters=
14. **Int:**   =Yes.
15. **Ivan:** one-on-one, I got orders, so it became progressively=
16. **Int:**   =Okay=
17. **Ivan:** =more fluent for me=
18. **Int:**   =Yes=
19. **Ivan:** to be comfortable.

Relatedly, in the following interaction in Excerpt (17), Keith contrasts two opposing obligations/needs, which complicate individuals' responsibility to learn English. He comments that if you want to 'living over here' in the United States then you 'kind of *have to* learn (English)' (6–7), but he then counterbalances that obligation with the comment that 'you kind of *have to* work' (11) as well. Working in order to survive and to support oneself and one's family are obligations/needs that often trump the obligation/need to learn English (see Kay's account of her giving up going to college, Excerpt (10)). In pursuing the topic of how Keith had managed to learn English, given these constraints, I asked whether he 'just learned' English while at work (12–13), to which Keith responded, 'just yeah just learn by work' (14).

(17)   *Keith just learns at work*

1. **Int:**   When did you uh first learn some English.
2. **Keith:** Oh. Well uh when I- When I first come here, I don't know,
3. **Int:**   Yeah. You'd didn't know any=
4. **Keith:** =I don't know anything.
5. **Int:**   Wow.
6. **Keith:** But but but I I you want to living over here you got to,
7.   kind of have to learn-
8. **Int:**   Did you go to an English-
9. **Keith:** Uh no because when we come it's kind of already,

10.	**Int:**	Yeah.
11.	**Keith:**	you kind of have to work.
12.	**Int:**	Yeah, so you- the English you know you just learned
13.		by- at work?
14.	**Keith:**	Just yeah just learn by work.

In using the depreciatory qualifier 'just' in the phrase 'just learn' (12, 14), both Keith and I downgrade the agency required for such action and construct this language learning as a byproduct of the situated social practices of his work-place. As noted earlier in the chapter, the use of 'learn' is less informative with respect to the constitution of agency given that it can suggest an experience that simply 'happens' to a story-world figure though it can also suggest more agentive efforts by that figure. The kind of learning that Keith engaged in is not unpacked in this interaction. However, the use of the mitigative qualifier 'just' positions this learning activity as more incidental than intentional.

When thinking about language learning, whether in classrooms or 'incidentally' in workplace spaces, one could argue that these individuals are doing the same thing. That is, they are learning English. Interviewees' story-world figures in their workplace accounts can still be understood to be per-forming agentive acts when they explicitly request their English-speaking interlocutors to repeat their utterances or to slow down when they speak; that is, they are constructed as having some degree of control over their own behavior, which suggests that they could have acted otherwise (Duranti, 2006). But in treating these acts of learning as mostly unmotivated acts, dependent on unplanned contacts with other English-speaking interlocu-tors, interviewees also are simultaneously constructed as less responsible for these actions. If the necessary mediating factors are not present, their actions to learn English may not happen either. Such attenuated agency is even more pronounced in interviewees' accounts of using and learning non-English lan-guages in their places of business.

Using and learning languages other than English at work

I was particularly curious about interviewees' use of non-English lan-guages at work and whether they found their native languages useful or whether they found it necessary to learn other non-English languages in order to conduct their work successfully. More than half of the participants indicated that they did not use a language other than English in their work-places. Some of them even seemed to be somewhat confused by my ques-tions to that effect. Out of the 18 participants, only seven spoke about their active use of non-English languages in their workplace.

One of these participants, Tony, the Vietnamese sandwich shop owner, produces an enthusiastic agreeing response 'Oh yeah' (Excerpt (18), line (2)) when I query him about whether his customers ever learn Vietnamese from him. He then constructs a narrative account of how 'Laos customer[s]' (4) come to his shop and ask him about his language as they order sandwiches (6, 8). He positions himself as an agentive figure in commenting '*I teach* them a little bit, then *I ask* them about their language' (10–11). Tony treats such interaction as an everyday kind of exchange, one that does not require great effort. It seems to happen almost spontaneously in such language contact situations. Tony also positions himself as the object of others' actions in adding that his customers teach him 'a little bit' (13, 15, 21) of Lao, Thai and Hmong (15, 17, 19).

(18)   *Tony teaches and learns a little bit of language*

1.	**Int:**	Do do customers ever learn any Vietnamese from you?
2.	**Tony:**	Oh yeah.
3.	**Int:**	Yeah?
4.	**Tony:**	Some uh Laos customer,
5.	**Int:**	Okay.
6.	**Tony:**	they come they come to order my sandwich,
7.	**Int:**	Yeah.
8.	**Tony:**	and they ask me about my language.
9.	**Int:**	Yes yes.
10.	**Tony:**	And I teach them a little bit, then I ask them
11.		[about their language.
12.	**Int:**	[Yes.
13.	**Tony:**	They teach me a little bit.
14.	**Int:**	Excellent.
15.	**Tony:**	They teach me a little bit of Laos?
16.	**Int:**	Uh huh?
17.	**Tony:**	And Thai?
18.	**Int:**	Uh huh?
19.	**Tony:**	And Hmong?
20.	**Int:**	Yeah.
21.	**Tony:**	A little bit. Yeah.
22.	**Int:**	Very good.

In this interchange, I respond very favorably to Tony's account, producing 'yeah' continuer tokens as well as strongly positive assessments: 'Excellent' (14) and 'Very good' (22). Though Tony mitigates the significance of these teaching–learning interchanges as leading to 'just a little bit' of language knowledge, my enthusiastic responses, in addition to more neutral minimal turns, treat these actions as desirable and laudable.

Like Tony, a female Vietnamese owner of a hair salon, Lan, too suggests that multilingual interactions are commonplace in her shop and even necessary for developing good relationships with her immigrant customers. As shown in Excerpt (19), in asking her about this activity, my question presupposes that such multilingual interactions are a relatively recent development ('you *now* have customers who come in who speak Spanish' (1)) and in some cases surprising ('you *even* have some customers who speak Arabic' (2)). Lan, however, denigrates the significance of these interactions in much the way Tony did, commenting that such multilingual activity was 'just some small little bit' (4). I follow this downgrade with a truncated question: 'But like how do you-' (5), which requests clarification of how such activity occurs. Lan answers matter-of-factly, 'Because I asked them' (6) and adds that when a customer 'sit my chair' (6–7) she will then ask them how to say 'hello' (9) or how to say 'come here' (11) in their language, just to make some conversation. She sums up this language learning activity by noting, 'they told me so I remember' (11). Like Tony, Lan treats these everyday language learning encounters as easy, mostly spontaneous interactions. Though I produce minimal receipt tokens in response to Lan's description of these encounters, my question constructs these events as somewhat extraordinary actions.

(19) Lan makes conversation

1.	**Int:**	You now have customers who come in who speak Spanish
2.		and you even have some customers who speak Arabic who
3.		come to your store,
4.	**Lan:**	Oh yeah just some small little bit.
5.	**Int:**	But like how do you- so I mean-
6.	**Lan:**	Because I asked them I asked them you know when I sit
7.		my chair you know,
8.	**Int:**	Yeah.
9.	**Lan:**	conversation I say *how how speak hello:* you know,
10.	**Int:**	Yeah.
11.	**Lan:**	*how to so say come here* and they told me so I remember.

There were only two cases of obligation/necessity modality produced when participants spoke about their learning of non-English languages while at work. On one occasion, Jin, the Vietnamese owner of a facial salon, produced such a construction when speaking about her need to sometimes write in Vietnamese, but only as a confirmation of what I as the interviewer asked. In attempting to ascertain how she used languages other than English, I uttered, 'so you just *have to* write in Vietnamese' with rising, question intonation. Jin responded with 'I *have to* write Vietnamese'. In this case, Jin's use of the obligation/necessity modal mirrors the linguistic construction in my questioning utterance. The only other occasion in which this modality is used occurred during my interview with Keith, when he described learning bits of various Asian languages from his customers. When I ask Keith if he asks his customers how to say phrases such as 'thank you' in their languages (Excerpt (20), line (11)), he replies immediately with 'of course' and then appends 'so you kind of *have to* learn some' (12–13).

(20) *Keith kind of has to learn some English*

    1. **Keith:** Uh huh because over here it's [most-
    2. **Int:**   [Yeah.
    3. **Keith:** mostly the Asian people, [like uh Thai, Laos,
    4. **Int:**   [Yeah.
    5. **Keith:** Vietnamese, you know, Chinese? You know,
    6.   Asian people.
    7. **Int:**   Yeah.
    8. **Keith:** So when they come, we know uh (1) here more,
    9.   so you will know what i::s [ha ha
  10. **Int:**   [Like do you do you
  11.   ask them? Like *how do you say thank you*.=
  12. **Keith:** =Yeah. Uh of course if you ask the:m, ha ha ha
  13.   so you kind of have to learn [some.
  14. **Int:**   [Yeah yeah yeah.

Given the minimal detail supplied by Keith, it is difficult to tell whether he views the learning of his customers' languages as necessary to conduct business interactions or merely to establish good rapport with his Asian customers. But even when constructing such language learning as necessary, Keith downgrades this as learning only 'some' (13) of his customers' language. A lack of effortful action for such multi-language learning and interaction was implicated in comments by other interviewees, such as when Joe noted that business at his Chinese restaurant had dropped off considerably owing to the economic downturn in 2008 and added that he now no longer has 'much *chance*' to learn bits of his customers' languages (Korean, Vietnamese, Thai, Japanese and 'even German') as he once did. When such opportunities did arise, interviewees sometimes treated them as merely playful interactions, such as when Don, a Vietnamese restaurant supply store owner, commented that he and his Spanish-speaking employees 'just learn and ... joke'. Although these brief language learning encounters do seem to be regarded as a means for creating good rapport with customers and/or employees, and thus engaging in language learning and teaching with the people one encounters at work can be consequential for business success, they are not treated as consequential for interviewees' identities as responsible language learners.

Constructing a less agentive Self in space: Performative effects

In contrast to the more generalized constitution of space when interviewees talked about their early efforts at learning English (use of 'here' to index their location in the United States, or American cities and local communities), it is not surprising that when they discussed their use and learning of English and other languages in their small businesses, they discursively positioned themselves more particularly and concretely within such spaces. Interviewees enacted that positioning through locational phrases such as 'at work' or '[in] my [salon] chair'; through work-related terms such as 'supply', 'order', and 'dinner shift'; and through work-related identity categories such as 'customers', 'clients' and 'waitresses'. Interviewees' use of reported speech, such as Lan's demonstration of what she asks her customers ('how how speak hello', Excerpt (19), line (9)), further served to position interviewees as located in particular spaces in that they perform 'authentic' workplace utterances, thereby recreating those moments in the here-and-now of the interview talk.

The unproblematic nature of the teaching and learning interchanges between business owners and customers or suppliers, both in using and continuing to learn English as well as in learning non-English languages, is mobilized in part because of their agentive capacity to open their own businesses. Their 'performative competence' (Canagarajah, 2013: 174) is practiced as they actively align with their interlocutors in their particular business environments, and it seems they are able to use English and other languages with enough ease and expertise to carry on their business interactions comfortably. Though they never stated so in their interviews, it is possible that they sought out businesses in which complex English-language interactions would not be required. They undoubtedly had limited employment options because of their still-developing expertise in English. If so, then we must also recognize that their agentive capacities are *patterned with* the constraints they need to contend with. Many of the interviewees indicated that the kinds of language exchanges they engaged in tended to be simple and repetitive. Soo noted 'So we'd talk not much, just "Hi how are you" and "How's it going", something like that. So it's not difficult'. With the exception of Paul, who indicated that he had to do extensive email writing to conduct his sushi business, the rest of the interviewees indicated that they did very little writing or reading in English or in any language. Keith reported reading only telephone and order numbers. Some said they only wrote when faxing orders. Kay adopted a confiding tone when she told me, 'I tell the truth, most people do nail, I don't mean to say their English is poor, but some Vietnamese people do nails, they they don't speak English like really good'. She went on to say that they were able to work with American clients only because of the good quality of their work. So it is possible that their seeming success in using English at work was enabled in part because of the limited English language literacy practices that were required and the often ritualized texture of their service encounters with customers and suppliers.

In all these cases, they refer to co-present mediating entities that enable such learning to take place. Jin interacts with the internet to find word meanings, whereas Hannah, Tony, Ivan, George and Kay make use of clients or employees who can correct them or provide language constructs for them to 'pick up' or who will slow down when speaking, so that the immigrant business owner can follow and understand their English-speaking interlocutors. Their actions to learn English and other languages are necessarily spread across other individuals and entities and are dependent on such contingent social arrangements. They also are cast as mostly responsive rather than willful, intentional actions. Kockelman (2007: 397) who regards agency as 'distributed, graduated, and dimensional and hence inherently communal' argues that for this reason 'agency will be shown not to necessarily (or even usually) inhere in specific people' (Kockelman, 2007: 376). And if action is distributed, then responsibility no longer 'inhere[s] in specific people' either. Kockelman (2007: 387) adds that in construing agency 'in different ways … [we] may thereby license others to attribute different degrees of accountability' to such actions.

Conclusion

A subtle paradox emerges from interviewees' differently agentive orientations to their past and their more current language-learner Selves. That is, in constructing themselves as more agentive through undertaking effortful actions in relation to their early learning of English, these interviewees are simultaneously constituted as having contended with difficult constraints.

For example, finding an English teacher required that Jenny consult with other Brazilians in her community and then call a potential tutor, and though not included in the excerpts here, elsewhere Jenny commented that she could only meet with the tutor at 11:30 at night given her full work schedule (see Chapter 5, Excerpt (1)). In contrast, in their workplace spaces where language use and learning were constructed as requiring reduced agency, the interviewees also are positioned as interacting with reasonable ease and relatively comfortable language competence. Emirbayer and Mische (1998: 1008) suggest that 'the capacity to draw, when needed, upon different forms of *routinized* relationships … underlies[s] [our] ability to gain greater control and directivity over the various contexts in which [we] act'. Hitlin and Elder (2007) further argue that routinized behavior is no less agentic than novel actions and contend that 'agency occurs in the flow of responses to situational exigencies. Routine identity enactment involves a different form of agency than does novel action' (Hitlin & Elder, 2007: 185).

When one can manage to just 'pick up' language or to construct language learning opportunities with one's customers or employees on the fly, in the ebb and flow of workplace interactions, the focus shifts 'away from the individual to the inter-subjective and relational dimension of … agency' (Cornwall, 2007: 43). In treating some types of learning as easily fulfillable actions (Miller, 2010), and even as merely good fun, interviewees' agentive acts are constituted as bearing a different relationship to responsibility, with different consequences for identity accounting. That is, in constructing themselves as responsive, tactically agentive actors who act on and through mediating affordances when learning and using English or other languages in their workplace environments, these interviewees are no longer cast as responsible Selves in the same way as when they constructed their story-world Selves as *individuals* who find or 'pick' language teachers, who attend classes – sometimes for several years – and who 'have to try' when it comes to learning English. Though none of the interviewees contested the obligation or need to learn English while living in the United States and actively positioned themselves as agentively responding to such obligations, they did not seem to find it necessary to produce reasons or 'excuses' for their not learning (better) English or other languages while at work. If they could get by reasonably successfully, they generally did not seem to find it relevant to construct themselves as ongoingly undertaking effortful actions to learn English or other languages.

Of course, the interviewees (and I as interviewer) did orient to a notion of responsibility that is assigned to specific people when they talked about their past efforts to learn English. As was noted at the beginning of the chapter, all 12 interviewees who indicated that they were either never able to attend English classes or had to give up attending English classes owing to other obligations, supplied accounts for why they could not (continue to) study English. And when they commented on their workplace language interactions as relatively simple rather than complex usage situations, the interviewees orient to such language usage as having less social capital through mitigating their significance. Thus, their ways of constructing their story-world Selves suggest sensitivity to normative ideologies. That is, the interviewees appear to construct versions of agentive Selves that are *patterned with* the constraints and affordances of their social and material worlds and that display sensitivity to how various languages and degrees of language expertise are valued differently in their current contexts, a notion that is explored more fully in the following Chapter 5.

5   Stance and Subjectivity: Evaluating Agentive Capacity

Agency and Stancetaking in Discourse

This chapter addresses the discursive performance of evaluation or stancetaking, a fundamental feature of all talk and texts (Du Bois, 2003; Jaffe, 2009), with a focus on how interviewees constructed evaluative stances towards aspects of their language learner Selves and/or learning actions. Duranti (2006: 466) contends that there is a need to 'expand' current research on agency in language to incorporate speakers' stance or 'point of view'. Just as the positioning of Self as (in)agentive is ubiquitous in talk given English language users' reliance on subject-predicate constructs (see Chapter 4), so evaluative stancetaking permeates narrative accounts. Jaffe (2009), for example, argues that adopting a neutral, seemingly non-evaluative stance is still a case of stancetaking. That is, treating phenomena as neutral, objective and non-controversial entities is as much a discursive construction as producing a clearly evaluative stance in relation to such phenomena. These phenomena are not inherently neutral or objective; they are constructed as being so. More importantly, when we produce evaluative stances with respect to ourselves and other individuals, social practices, events and entities in the world, whether positive, negative or neutral, we also reconstitute, contest and/or transform social norms (Quigley, 2001).

Despite, or perhaps because of, the ubiquity of stancetaking in discursive practice, researchers vary widely in how they analyze stance. Recent reviews of the broad-ranging research that has explored stancetaking note that there is no 'monolithic' definition of stance (Englebretson, 2007: 1; see also Jaffe, 2009; Thompson & Hunston, 2000). That said, much of this research construes stance according to two broad categories, as cases of either epistemic or affective stance (Biber & Finegan, 1989; Cook, 2011; Ochs, 1993). Epistemic stance refers to displays of knowledgability and the degree of certainty and/or commitment to the truth that a speaker expresses with respect to the propositional content of his or her utterances (Chafe & Nichols, 1986). Affective stance refers to displays of one's attitudinal or emotional point of view toward a given phenomenon (Ochs & Schieffelin, 1989).

Kockelman (2007) explored the historical shift from Jespersen's (1965/1924) notion of grammatical mood, i.e. 'certain attitudes of the mind of the speaker towards the contents of the sentence', to current perspectives on stance, and notes that linguists have moved away from an emphasis on the 'private, subjective, and psychological (attitude) to an emphasis on the public, intersubjective, and embodied (stance)' (Kockelman, 2007: 131). In promoting this social basis for stance, Du Bois (2007: 141) notes that stance is 'simultaneously a linguistic act and a social act' and defines stance most simply as 'the smallest unit of social action' (Du Bois, 2007: 173). At the same time, Du Bois offers a more comprehensive definition of stance:

> a public act by a social actor, achieved dialogically through overt communicative means, of simultaneously evaluating objects, positioning subjects (self and others) and aligning with other subjects, with respect to any salient dimension in the sociocultural field. (Du Bois, 2007: 163)

In this study, the discursive acts that position interviewees as they evaluate aspects of their language learning Selves, actions and successes help to constitute their story-world Selves as moral entities in the world. To Du Bois's definition, I would add that the 'public' and 'overt' actions that comprise stancetaking can simultaneously function as covert or implicit actions that reconstitute ideologies in mundane interactions.

Though often hardly noticed in the interactional give-and-take of conversational evaluations, stancetaking must be understood as highly consequential for constructing locally relevant identities, for creating and maintaining the interpersonal texture of conversations and for reconstituting social ideologies – even in the most mundane moments of interaction. In the sections that follow, I first explore the notion of stancetaking as dialogically achieved with an emphasis on evaluative stancetaking performances. I then discuss the patterns of stancetaking that emerged in the interview corpus. This is followed by a close examination of the dialogical construction of stancetaking as it emerged across turns of talk in selected excerpts of interview interaction and its performative effects.

Dialogic Construction of Evaluative Stance

Given the growing recognition that stance is consequential for establishing intersubjectivity in interaction, research on stance has increasingly emphasized its co-constructed or dialogical production (Cortazzi & Jin, 2000; Damari, 2010; Du Bois, 2007; Jaffe, 2009; Kärkkäinen, 2006; Scheibman, 2007; Verhagen, 2005). Du Bois (2007) can, perhaps, be credited with advancing the dialogical approach to stance most fully. Stancetaking, as he contends, necessarily involves processes of (dis)alignment among interlocutors towards each other, but we can also engage in dialogic processes of stancetaking with non-present interlocutors, such as when we produce reported speech in narratives (Trester, 2009; see also Chapter 6), or when engaged in the solitary act of producing written texts by anticipating and responding to (imagined) readers.

These studies also indicate that evaluative stance can be constructed at nearly every level of discursive production, from one's lexical choices, to the syntactic organization of one's utterances, to the structure of whole texts (Thompson & Hunston, 2000). Cortazzi and Jin (2000: 107), for example, comment that evaluative stance 'can appear anywhere in a narrative and may be realized by any level of linguistic structure (phonological, lexical, syntactic, discoursal)'. They further add that to interpret stance 'a hearer or analyst may have to use contextual or cultural knowledge' (Cortazzi & Jin, 2000: 107). Such a perspective does not deny the value of highly focused studies on particular linguistic structures or particular stance effects, but it does suggest that arriving at a comprehensive taxonomy of stance structures and their functions may be unattainable, in part, because of the ubiquity of stance in discursive practice, but also because of the inescapable reliance on context in interpreting stance forms and functions.

Of particular interest for this study is the understanding that 'every act of evaluation expresses a communal value-system, and every act of evaluation goes towards building up that value-system ... [which] in turn is a component of the ideology which lies behind every text' (Hunston & Thompson, 2000: 6). Jaffe (2009: 5) adds that stancetaking 'invokes moral and social orders, systems of accountability, responsibility, and causality'. This is not to suggest that such value systems are equally shared by all interlocutors in an interaction; however, they are often treated as normative, unquestioned givens by interlocutors, sometimes even when competing values are indexed. A focused examination of interactions on particular occasions with particular interlocutors is necessary for understanding how local interactional moments contribute to maintaining or disrupting social ideologies (Miller, 2009), which, in the context of this study, involves ideologies of language learning and immigrant identity. Examining moments of seeming collusion or contestation of values enables us to better understand how individuals performatively constitute processes of sense-making with respect to themselves, in relation to others and to social ideologies. Understanding the connection between the local and individual to the social and ideological remains contested terrain among scholars, but most analysts agree that the local is never *just that.*

Analyzing Stance: An Overview of Patterned Constructs

In this section, I analyze the production of evaluative stancetaking in relation to the same interview topics considered in Chapters 4 and 6; i.e. interviewees' use and learning of languages. In analyzing patterns of evaluative stance within single interview interactions as well as across interviews, I found that the quantitative approach I adopted in analyzing subject-predicate constructions (found in Chapter 4) and in counting reported speech utterances (found in Chapter 6) was not feasible. Hunston (2007: 35) too has argued that 'quantifying stance is problematic because there is no simple correspondence between words on the one hand and stance functions on the other, so the attempt to count evaluative stance by counting particular words is likely to be unsuccessful'.

I follow Hunston and Thompson's (2000) lead in orienting to affective stancetaking along a continuum of positive-to-negative evaluations. That is, stancetaking is understood to occur when one produces a positive (to varying degrees) evaluation, a negative (to varying degrees) evaluation or a neutral 'non-evaluative' stance with respect to some discursively constructed entity. In particular, I examined how each interviewee performed negative and/or positive evaluations toward the outcomes of their language learning actions (i.e. their language learning capacity). For example, I treat Hee's 'negative stance' toward her capacity to learn and use English well as a single analytic category even though this stance category is comprised of several linguistic constructions, such as the use of a negative marker + evaluative (adverb functioning as) adjective ('My English *not* very *well*'), an adverb + verb (in commenting that her learning of English '*never* end') and an intensifier + evaluative adjective (in proclaiming that English is '*very difficult*'), produced over the course of the interview.

As shown in Table 5.1, I analyzed the kinds of evaluative stances (negative, positive and neutral) displayed by all interviewees towards their agentive capacity: (a) to learn English after arriving in the United States;

Table 5.1 Number of interviewees adopting stance types regarding their language learning and use

Type of stance	Object of stance A	Object of stance B	Object of stance C
Negative stance only	**12**	2	0
Positive stance only	1	1	**6** (mitigated)
Negative AND positive stance by same interviewee	0	**14**	1
No positive or negative stance displayed (neutral)	5	1	—*

Object of stance A – capacity to learn English after arriving in the United States.
Object of stance B – capacity to continue learning English and using it at work.
Object of stance C – capacity to use and learn languages other than English at work.
Numerals indicate number of interviewees who adopted this stance.
*Nine interviewees said nothing about object of stance C.

(b) to continue learning it and using it at work; and (c) to learn and use languages other than English at work (see Object of stance categories listed in the caption below Table 5.1). Though there was anticipated variability among interviewees, there were three situations in which interviewees displayed robust commonality in their stances toward each of the three selected objects of stance.

One pattern that emerged is identified in the top left corner of Table 5.1 by the bolded numeral 12. This indicates that 12 of the interviewees produced negative evaluative stances with respect to their capacity to learn English (well) upon arriving in the United States (five produced neutral stances in relation to this topic). I use Du Bois's (2007) stance diagram model in order to better represent the relationship between the stance subject and the stance object, as well as the words used to produce the type of evaluation being performed. The plus (+) and minus (–) symbols represent the type of evaluation as positive or negative. As displayed in Stance Diagram 1, Ivan constructs a negative stance toward his capacity to learn English by uttering, 'I really lousy in English. As lousy as I can be' in relation to his early difficulties in learning the language. Two others, Donna and Hee, both evaluated the learning process as difficult. Only one interviewee constructed a positive stance toward her competence and learning ease. Lan proclaimed, 'I learn quick. English to me is easy'. (The words in parentheses in the stance diagrams indicate the unspoken but implicit references.)

Stance Diagram 1 Stancetaking with respect to interviewees' capacity to learn English after arriving in the United States and/or to Self as learner

Speaker	Stance subject	Evaluates	Stance object
Ivan	I	really lousy (–)	in (learning) English
Donna	(Donna)	not easy (–)	to learn it (English)
Hee	(Hee)	very difficult (–)	(learning English)
Lan	I	quick (+)	learn (English)

It is possible that, with the exception of Lan, the interviewees were consciously positioning themselves as modest regarding their success in learning English given that they were speaking to a native speaker of the language. As such, in producing these stance acts, they were also positioning themselves in relation to their interlocutor. While it is true that none of the interviewees produced error-free English utterances, the non-native-speaker quality of their English production does not by itself explain why the interviewees should display such marked similarity in their stancetaking on this topic. After all, Lan's English-language utterances were no more native-speaker-like than those of many of the other interviewees.

Furthermore, an interesting paradox emerged when they discussed their continued learning of English in the workplace and their capacity to use it for accomplishing workplace communication with customers and/or suppliers as discussed below. As indicated by the bolded numeral in the center column of Table 5.1, 14 individuals produced evaluative utterances in which they produced *both* negative stances and positive stances toward their capacity to continue learning English and using it in their places of business. Again, using Du Bois's stance diagram, one can see the relationship between stance subject, stance object and type of stance taken in the utterances produced by George and Soo in Stance Diagram 2. George commented, 'It's hard to communicate with people just just believe it or not. It's not easy now'. But only moments later he commented, 'I'm fine for business for my own business' when discussing using English at his restaurant. Soo said, 'So little bit have a problem but I don't I don't have a problem with communication with customers. So it's not difficult'.

As Stance Diagram 2 demonstrates, Soo and George evaluate their own capacity to communicate with others in their workplaces in English both negatively ('hard', 'not easy', 'little bit have a problem') and positively ('fine', 'don't have a problem', 'not difficult'). Like George and Soo, most of the interviewees acknowledged that their interactions in English were sometimes problematic *because of* the difficulties posed by needing to use English, but no one treated the need to use English as a persistent negative issue.

Stance Diagram 2 Stancetaking with respect to interviewees' capacity to continue learning English and using it at work

Speaker	Stance subject	Evaluates	Stance object
George	(George)	hard (–)	communicate with people (in English)
George	(George)	not easy now (–)	it (communicating with people in English)
George	I	am fine (+)	for business (communication in English)
Soo	(Soo)	little bit have a problem (– mitigated)	(Soo communicating with customers in English)
Soo	I	don't have a problem (+)	with communication with customers
Soo	(Soo)	not difficult (+)	it (communicating with customers)

Rather, nearly all of them directly commented on the ease with which they could do their business communications in English. Interestingly, a few minutes after Soo commented that she did not find it difficult to communicate with customers, she noted, 'Sometime we have a problem ... but you know, we okay each other', and then added, 'We don't need a lot of talk you know' regarding the service transactions at her dry cleaning pickup store. Soo's last comment regarding the minimal talk needed to conduct business seems to have been the case for many of the other interviewees as well. Interviewees indicated that they could simply fax orders to suppliers, or recite order numbers over the telephone, and so on, rather than engage in complex talk.

A third patterned stance production emerged among the interviewees who commented on their use and/or learning of languages other than English in their places of business (languages that are not in their native repertoires), indicated by the bolded numeral in the right-most column of Table 5.1. Only seven interviewees indicated that they used non-English languages in their workplace. Of these, six interviewees adopted mitigated positive stances toward their capacity to learn and use new languages and to teach their customers some of their own languages as shown in Stance Diagram 3. I treated interviewees' utterances in which they constructed themselves as understanding or knowing the language ('I understand ...'; 'I know ...') as positive evaluative stance acts produced in relation to their linguistic capacity and achievement rather than epistemic stance acts, since these utterances do not express their commitment to the truth of a proposition so much as an assessment of their linguistic capacity. It is important to note that each of these six interviewees downgraded his or her multilingual competence using noun phrases such 'a little bit' as in 'But *I know **a little bit*** of their languages' (Joe) or using the adverb 'just' as a depreciatory qualifier (Kishner & Gibbs, 1996) as in Lan's '*I understand **just a little bit*** Spanish'.

Stance Diagram 3 Stancetaking toward interviewees' capacity to learn and use non-English languages in their workplaces

Speaker	Stance subject	Evaluates	Stance object
Joe	I	know a little bit (+ mitigated)	their languages (customers' non-English languages)
Lan	I	understand just a little bit (+ mitigated)	Spanish (which her customers speak)

Lan was the only interviewee to produce a nuanced contrastive evaluation of the different languages she used and learned in her hair salon, taking a mitigated negative stance to Arabic ('Arabic's kinda hard'), which she followed with a positive stance to Chinese ('Chinese is easy'). Lan also constructed a subtle contrast when describing her capabilities in using Spanish with her customers. She commented, 'Just like Spanish [customers] come in now, you know. I know how to communicate with them, you know. You get by'. In this utterance, she adopts a positive stance toward her own capability, 'I know how to communicate with them', but then adds, 'you get by', suggesting that her Spanish-language capabilities are still limited, good enough to manage the exigencies of these service encounters while also suggesting that her repertoire would be inadequate for complex interactions.

In considering these stancetaking patterns produced by the participants in my study, I find Bucholtz and Hall's (2005: 595–596) reference to ideology helpful. They comment that 'linguistic forms that index identity are more basically associated with interactional stances … which in turn may come to be associated with particular social categories'. They add that the accumulation of similar stances that contribute to the construction of more 'durable structures of identity' can emerge in a 'bottom-up fashion' and develop as 'interactional norms for particular social groups' or may be 'imposed from the top down' and as such 'imposed indexical tie[s] may create ideological expectations among speakers and hence affect their linguistic practice' (Bucholtz & Hall, 2005: 596). On this same point, Du Bois (2011) contends that:

> [s]tance invites analysis as social action because it entails asking how the dialogically engaged structures of evaluative action in discourse contribute to organizing the joint construction of both the enduring cultural frames that organize our lifeworld and the local ephemeral moments of intersubjective alignment that motivate our affective engagement with it. (Du Bois, 2011: 55)

These perspectives emphasize the historical, social and ideological dimensions of stance. I thus posit that although the interviewees in this study are each speaking about their individual language capacities, these are not merely individually generated stances, but need to be treated as historically, socially and ideologically mediated stances leading to the construction of socially recognizable identities. Given that evaluation presupposes an orientation to some kind of sociocultural norm, originary responsibility for the stance displays that emerged across these individual conversations in relation to topics regarding language learning and usage cannot be assigned solely to 18 individuals in interaction with an interviewer, but must be recognized as part of the normative, mundane discursive material for meaning making. Again, I want to emphasize that by treating individual stance acts as indexes of social meanings, I do not want to suggest that all immigrant language learners are likely to adopt the same stance in relation to these topics, that everyone agrees with these stances or that such stances are ideologically determined and thus predictable. Indeed, even in this relatively small body of interviewees, Lan stands out as someone whose stancetaking acts often did not conform to the patterns produced by the others, particularly in her strongly positive evaluation of her capacity to learn English well. However, as I explore below, it seems that when these interviewees produced such individual stance acts, they simultaneously reconstituted or sedimented prevailing common sense understandings regarding how some individuals' learning actions and related competences can be commonsensically evaluated. This is not to say that these same individuals were incapable of resisting or transforming such common sense understandings, but rather that in the relatively formal context of the interview, none of them 'chose' to perform oppositional stances. The ideological effects that are performatively realized in these mundane, non-controversial evaluations thus require some unpacking.

In order to better understand the patterned productions in this particular body of interactions as ideological indexicals, we need to explore their dialogical production more carefully. As Du Bois (2007) notes, using stance diagrams helps to make explicit who is producing a stance utterance as well as the words used to overtly express or index the relationship constructed between the stance subject and the stance object. However, these diagrams do not capture the intricately co-constructed aspect of stancetaking, the fact that stancetaking 'cannot be a matter of subjectivity in isolation' (Du Bois, 2007: 157). What we need instead is to understand the 'stance utterance *with its dialogic context*' (Du Bois, 2007: 58, italics in original).

Stance in Discursive Practice: A Micro-Analysis

Stance toward capacity of story-world Self to learn English after arrival in the United States

In my interview with Jenny, a young Brazilian woman who had started her own housecleaning business, I opened the interview interaction by asking her when she had first started to learn English (Excerpt (1), lines (1–2)). She responded with an account that provided details regarding the place and time of her English tutoring, as well as some negative evaluations regarding her capacity to learn English.

(1) *Jenny doesn't speak good English*

1.	**Int:**	Um, okay so first question um (...) when did you first
2.		start learning English.
3.	**Jen:**	Mmm I think two years ago::: because when I got here
4.		I start to to learn English?
5.	**Int:**	[°That's amazing.°
6.	**Jen:**	[But it's really difficult because it's completely different
7.		my language.
8.	**Int:**	Yeah.
9.	**Jen:**	[because it's-
10.	**Int:**	[You didn't study any English in Brazil.
11.	**Jen:**	No. Not at all. Just here. [Ha ha ha ha
12.	**Int:**	[Ama::zing. That's very impressive.
13.	**Jen:**	And uh some Brazilian people speak good English
14.	**Int:**	Mmhmm.
15.	**Jen:**	and then I paid someone to go to my house um twice a week?
16.	**Int:**	Mmhmm.

17. **Jen:**   And they start to teach me at 11:30 and finish at midnight.
18.   (2)
19. **Int:**   °Oh my goodness° because you were working?
20. **Jen:**   Yes, all the time [I work
21. **Int:**   [Oh
22. **Jen:**   I have a short memory? Because of that I don't speak good
23.   English.

In line (6), Jenny evaluates the learning of English as 'really difficult'. She produces a negative evaluation of her capacity to learn English in lines (22–23) in commenting 'I have a short memory. Because of that I don't speak good English'. In negatively evaluating her ability to remember well, Jenny also negatively evaluates an aspect of herself that is treated as important for her language learning capacity. And finally, in evaluating her speaking of English as not 'good' (22), Jenny directly evaluates one fundamental component of her English language capabilities.

At the most mundane level, Jenny's stancetaking acts are tied to my questions and responses. By asking when Jenny first started to learn English, I create an interactional context in which a chronological accounting of Jenny's language learning is made relevant, though such an account does not necessarily require evaluative utterances regarding her language learning capacity. I treat Jenny's initial 'neutral' report that she began learning English two years prior to the interview as 'amazing' (5). This positive evaluation is upgraded in line (12), when I produce an even stronger positive evaluation after Jenny confirms that she never studied English in Brazil, only during the two years she has spent in the United States. Implicit in my positive evaluations is the understanding that Jenny's language learning accomplishment is 'amazing' and 'impressive' given the limited amount of time she has devoted to learning the language.

Even though Jenny and I produce quite different evaluations of her English language learning capacity, these are not disaligning moves. In negatively evaluating her English language learning capacity, Jenny constructs herself as modest and self-deprecating while interacting with a native speaker of the language who is explicitly querying her about her actions taken to learn English. Such actions can be understood as face-maintaining moves (Arundale, 2010) for Jenny. She may have wanted to avoid presenting herself as too boastful or too confident in her English language capacities, in this context, with this interlocutor. At the same time, by positively evaluating Jenny's language proficiency, I treat Jenny's learning accomplishments as something admirable, an action that can be interpreted as a face-supporting move (Arundale, 2010). In this way, both Jenny and I seem to orient to the

co-present Other by avoiding being regarded as boastful and by complimenting the achievements of the other. The dialogic co-construction of stance
emerges as one person's utterance elicits another person's utterance, but also
in relation to how relevant identities are construed and constituted in the
intersubjective dynamics of the interview interaction (Miller, 2013).

But why should it matter to delimit who took what stance? Du Bois
(2007: 173) argues that 'responsibility for the stance act is serious business,
with potentially profound consequences for the relationships of social actors
with their dialogically co-responsible partners and with their expanding networks of social relations along wider horizons of time and space'. In looking
at Jenny's and the other interviewees' negative evaluations of their capacity
to learn English well, I argue that they are not merely being modest about
their non-native-like proficiency with me, a native speaker of the language.
They are also displaying themselves to be responsible individuals. We can see
that even as Jenny negatively evaluates her English capacity in Excerpt (1),
she also provides causal explanations and narrative framing for her still
imperfect English. For example, in line (6) she contends that learning English
is really difficult for her because it is 'completely different' from her native
language Portuguese. She also describes the extreme effort she took to learn
English, which included paying a tutor to come to her house between 23:30
and midnight. This unorthodox schedule was cast as necessary because she
was working such long hours. Thus, Jenny's negative evaluations of her
English achievement are incorporated into an account of highly agentive,
responsible efforts to learn the language. In this way her still-limited English
can be explained and even legitimately excused, and perhaps more importantly, her discursive behavior displays her sensitivity to normative values
with respect to language learning and responsibility.

Both Jenny and I treat the need for Jenny to make the efforts toward
learning English as normal, as an unquestioningly obvious action to take.
Indeed, the content of the interview questions constructs such actions as
something Jenny can be held accountable for. However, when Jenny reports
that she hired a tutor to come to her house at 23:30, a two-second pause
elapses (18) before I utter a quiet 'oh my goodness' (19), thereby treating
Jenny's reported actions as surprising and unusual. My orientation to
Jenny's efforts as beyond normal expectations and thus surprising presumes
the normative value assigned to her having taken some agentive actions to
learn the language.

In asking Jenny and the other interviewees about learning 'English' very
generally, with no specification of where or with whom or for what purpose
they use the language, I do not clarify what kind of 'English' I am asking
about. The standard against which they negatively evaluate their own

language proficiency is thus not identified, and yet the interviewees and I as interviewer do not treat this lack of clarification as problematic. When Jenny comments on the 'good English' of 'some Brazilian people' (13) and negatively evaluates her own ability to 'speak good English' (22–23), she orients to an abstract notion of 'good English', undoubtedly something akin to 'native-speaker-like', standard (American) English. But determining what constitutes good English is inherently political and perspectival. As Park and Wee (2008: 245) have argued, 'specific ideologies operating in the linguistic market ... strongly influence the kinds of symbolic values assigned to particular instances of performativity, that is, how attempts at linguistic appropriation are received and evaluated'. They refer to 'ideologies of competence' rather than to objective measures of linguistic proficiency for determining how language users' linguistic capacity is evaluated (Park & Wee, 2008: 245). In another reference to 'ideologies of competence', Park (2010: 23) notes that even though 'cultural concepts of [language] competence clearly vary from one context to another' we tend to treat language competence as an objective quality that self-evidently belongs to an individual speaker.

The ideological basis for the view that native speakers serve as objective measures of good language usage (see Doerr, 2009) is further demonstrated when we contrast the interviewees' evaluations of their English capacity with speakers of Lingua Franca English (LFE), who would typically be regarded as 'non-native' speakers of English. These LFE users, in interaction with other LFE speakers, seem to escape being constituted as 'poor' users of 'English' even though their linguistic productions do not conform to native-speaker practices. Canagarajah (2007: 926) describes LFE speakers as individuals in linguistic and cultural contact situations in which 'a kind of suspension of expectations regarding norms seems to be in operation'. They are not learning and using English with the goal of becoming more native-like. Rather, they negotiate mutual understanding with their LFE interlocutors and construct their own norms *in situ* as they work to achieve their immediate communicative goals. Canagarajah contends that for LFE speakers, creating alignment with their interlocutors is more important than attaining some putative native-speaker linguistic norms.

In negatively evaluating their capacity to learn English well, the interviewees in this study are not diminishing their agentive Selves. After all, they construct themselves as responsible individuals who actively pursued the learning of English. Rather, their stancetaking indexes how such actions and efforts are understood to be valued, both locally in the interaction and more broadly. If one feels compelled to supply an account for why one has not been successful in achieving a particular outcome, such as the ambiguous goal of learning 'good English', this presupposes that success in this case is valued. The utterly normal negative evaluations by interviewees towards their capacity to learn English well, or easily, or quickly, position them as orienting to a socially recognized value system. Though it seems that the interviewees, in concert with me, implicitly orient to a 'good English' abstraction in negatively evaluating their own ability to learn English, it also seems that the norms become more fluid and more situated when they assess the success of their work place interactions in English as explored in the following section.

Stance toward capacity of story-world Self to continue learning English and using it at work

This section explores an excerpt from an interview with Hannah, a Chinese female who owns a Chinese restaurant and catering business. The excerpt begins with my question regarding whether she needs to do much reading or writing in English (Excerpt (2), lines (1–2)) in running her business.

(2)   *Hannah understand English on the telephone*

1.	**Int:**	Okay, um so for your work here do you have to do very
2.		much reading or writing in English.
3.	**Han:**	Uh yeah only the mail I read you know.
4.	**Int:**	Yeah.
5.	**Han:**	Some some (xxx) I just leave to the my bookkeeper to
6.		take everything yeah.
7.	**Int:**	Yeah okay okay.
8.	**Han:**	I just understand but I'm I read okay I understand but
9.	**Int:**	Yeah.
10.	**Han:**	I not talk really well you know.
11.	**Int:**	I think you're [doing really well.
12.	**Han:**	[ha ha ha ha ha ha
13.	**Han:**	Because you know I'm don't have the chance go college
14.		you know.
15.	**Int:**	Yeah.
16.	**Han:**	No time. I have three children. I got to work hard for them.
17.	**Int:**	Yeah.
18.	**Han:**	Yeah.
19.	**Int:**	Yeah, I think when I was here on Sunday I saw you were
20.		talking on the telephone? Maybe taking an order?

21. **Han:** Yeah.
22. **Int:** Is that more difficult than conversation like this or-
23. **Han:** Uh yeah it the telephone I understand yeah.
24. **Int:** Yeah?
25. **Han:** Uh huh.
26. **Int:** Well that's good because-
27. **Han:** Take a order yeah.
28. **Int:** Many people find the telephone more difficult.
29. **Han:** Yeah yeah I understand the phone yeah. They talk yeah.

In responding to my question, Hannah downgrades the amount of reading she does, i.e. 'only the mail' (3) and indicates that she leaves other documents (not decipherable) to her bookkeeper to take care of (5). She follows this weakly negative evaluation of her capacity to read in English with a mitigated positive evaluation in noting 'I just understand' (8) and then with a more strongly positive stance in commenting, 'but I'm read I read okay I understand' (8). However, this utterance is followed by a negative assessment of her ability to speak in English (10). I respond to Hannah's negative stance toward her speaking capacity by commenting, 'I think you're doing really well' (11), in this way displaying an orientation to Hannah's face needs. Had I produced a minimal receipt token ('yeah' or 'okay') at that moment, I would have positioned myself as aligning with Hannah's stance and thus agreeing with the negative assessment regarding Hannah's speaking capacity that was then on display in the here-and-now of the interaction. Hannah follows her negative stance act with a causal account for her 'not talk[ing] really well' (10). She comments, 'because you know I'm don't have the chance to go college. No time. I have three children. I got to work hard for them' (13, 16). In this way, Hannah, like Jenny in Excerpt (1), shows that her limited speaking capacity can be accounted for. It is owing to constraints over which she had no control (i.e. no 'chance' to go to college) and to responsibilities that take priority over language learning (i.e. taking care of children and working to support them). Here her negative evaluation of her English capacity is embedded in an account that positions her story-world Self as inagentive in relation to the material constraints that prevented her from going to school to learn English.

I then comment that I observed Hannah talking on the telephone when I had visited the restaurant as a customer the day before and ask if speaking on the telephone is more difficult than face-to-face conversations 'like this', the one Hannah and I were engaging in at the moment (19–20, 22). Hannah's evaluations of her telephone speaking capacity are all positive: 'the telephone I understand' (23) and 'Yeah yeah I understand the phone yeah' (29). This positive stance endures even as I displayed a moment of skepticism in utter-ing 'yeah?' (24) with rising, questioning intonation, and produced the gen-eralizing statement that 'many people find the telephone more difficult' (28). In producing a generalization regarding the greater difficulty many people (i.e. language learners) experience when using their second language in tele-phone conversations compared with face-to-face conversations, I construct a norm against which Hannah's reported language capacity can be compared. In this way, I appear to treat Hannah's confidence regarding her capacity to understand telephone conversations in English as unexpected and even doubtful, this despite my compliment to Hannah regarding her speaking capacity in line (10).

Like nearly all of the other interviewees, Hannah produces both positive and negative stance acts when evaluating her use of English in her business space. What really matters in these situations is that small business owners, such as Hannah, manage to communicate successfully with others and accomplish the necessary transactions for operating their businesses. Hannah indicates that she can 'understand' most of what she reads in English and when talking with customers on the telephone. According to such highly contextualized 'norms' or situated cases of adequacy, Hannah evaluates her language capacity quite positively. Though many of the interviewees com-mented on occasions when miscommunication occurred in workplace inter-actions or on situations in which they experienced difficulty understanding others or making themselves understood, more frequently, when referring to specific kinds of interactions, interviewees produced positive evaluations of their English usage. Their purported ease in conducting their business inter-actions is undoubtedly influenced by the contexts in which they occur. As discussed in Chapter 4, it seems that by opening their own businesses, an outcome of their agentive efforts, these interviewees have constructed work-place spaces where the interactions that emerge are less dependent on 'good English'. More specifically, it seems that the evaluative measure of their English usage shifts from an ambiguous native-speaker norm to one validat-ing 'good-enough English' by which they can accomplish the specific func-tions of their business. As such, their English language capacity is reframed in these stancetaking acts.

Kramsch (2008: 400) refers to this capacity as 'symbolic competence', which she describes as 'the ability not only to approximate or appropriate for oneself someone else's language, but to shape the very context in which the language is learned and used'. Blommaert et al. (2005b: 213) acknowledge that 'functionally specific and limited/truncated' forms of the dominant language often 'unfold[] in the contingencies of situated activity' involving multilingual immigrants, and while such truncated forms may carry little prestige for these individuals outside of the local interaction, they enable them to get on with the business at hand. Unlike the LFE speakers described by Canagarajah (2007), the interviewees in this study *do* orient to native-speaker norms when evaluating their 'general' English language proficiency, but like LFE speakers, they too are able to achieve 'successful communication' through 'aligning the linguistic resources [that they] bring[] to the social, situational, and affective dimensions operative in a context' (Canagarajah, 2007: 928). It seems that the interviewees in this study tend to assess their capacity to use English with respect to actual, situated moments of language use in their workplaces more positively.

Stance toward capacity of story-world Self to use and learn other languages at work

Similar to their more positive stance acts in relation to their capacity to use English well (enough) in their workplaces, interviewees also produced positive stances in relation to their capacity to learn and use non-English languages in their businesses, though these were nearly always downgraded stances with depreciatory qualifiers such as 'just', 'only' and 'a little bit'. Lan, a Vietnamese hair and nail salon owner, produces positive stance acts, shown in Excerpt (3), towards her multilingual teaching and learning activity with her customers. In giving an account of how she interacted with a repeat Spanish-speaking customer who 'hardly speak much English' (2), Lan comments that she has 'no problem' interacting with such customers (1) and adds that she 'still can communicate with Spanish' (4) though she indicated elsewhere that her Spanish proficiency is very limited. In Excerpt (3), she describes one interaction with a male client who came to her shop to have his hair colored. Lan describes how she was able to determine what color he wanted for his hair by bringing the book of color samples to his chair and asking him, 'That what you want?' (11). She indicates that she then asked him to tell her how he would say it in Spanish and added 'And then you can learn from them' (15). In this constructed case of 'easy agency' (see Chapter 4), Lan frames the event with three stance acts. The first is her positive evaluation regarding her interactions with her multilingual clients ('I have no problem' (1)). Towards the end of this episode of talk, she then constructs a positive stance toward her ability to learn some Spanish through interacting with her clients ('And then you can learn from them' (15)), and finally she constructs a positive stance regarding her capacity to guide this client, who speaks little English, through the necessary transactions for accomplishing a hair coloring appointment ('I can get him through it' (17–18)).

(3) *Lan has no problem*

1.	**Lan:**	I have no problem like this morning I got one guy I been
2.		doing it for for fifth time. He hardly speak much English.
3.	**Int:**	Mmhm.
4.	**Lan:**	But I still can communicate with Spanish. And him all
5.		he does all he does like last time I put a little bit little
6.		bit lighter this time he wanted he wanted black. I said
7.		*no problem.*
8.	**Int:**	Ha ha ha ha
9.	**Lan:**	You know what you do is take the book around, you said
10.	**Int:**	Ah.
11.	**Lan:**	*That what you want?*
12.	**Int:**	Uh huh. Uh huh.
13.	**Lan:**	And then *you tell me how you how you say that* you know.
14.	**Int:**	Uh huh.
15.	**Lan:**	And then you can learn from them.
16.	**Int:**	Yeah. That's really great.
17.	**Lan:**	But uh he hardly speak any English, but I can get him
18.		through it, you know.

As Lan produces this account of learning and using Spanish with one of her hair salon clients, I produce minimal receipt tokens, typical for interviewer discourse, with the exception of one strongly positive evaluative utterance ('That's really great' (16)). This utterance follows Lan's summary comment 'then you can learn from them' (15). In confirming the desirability of Lan's actions, I co-construct, with Lan, an orientation to 'truncated' multilingualism as a positive social value. But even as Lan produces a positive evaluation of her capacity to learn and speak the languages of her clients, she also refers to her knowledge of Spanish and Arabic as 'just some small bit', and twice more over the course of her entire interview, she comments that she knows only 'a little bit' of the multiple languages her clients speak. This downgraded positive stance toward multilingual learning and usage in interviewees' workplaces was also discussed in Chapter 4 (Excerpt (19)), in describing Tony's comments regarding how he and his customers teach each other 'a little bit' of each others' languages. Kishner and Gibbs (1996) coined the term 'depreciatory "just"', exhibited in Lan's utterance '*just* some small bit', and noted that its production serves 'to minimize an event, action or situation, usually in comparison to some other event, action or situation that is often not explicitly mentioned' (Kishner & Gibbs, 1996: 23).

Lan, Tony and at least five of the other interviewees appear to have been able to construct interactional spaces where not only is the need for native-speaker-like English lessened, but 'truncated' multilingual repertoires have become locally normative and validated. They do not need robust proficiency in these non-English languages in order to achieve success in business interactions, and it seems that the use of bits of multiple languages can function to establish a degree of solidarity and intersubjectivity between business owners and customers or employees. Otsuji and Pennycook (2010) contend that multilingualism and monolingualism ought not be regarded as dichotomous or even 'opposite ends of the spectrum', but rather as 'symbiotically (re) constituting each other' (Otsuji & Pennycook, 2010: 244). That is, multilingualism is understood to be a particular kind of linguistic activity and is constituted as such because monolingualism is part of its semiotic 'apparatus' (Otsuji & Pennycook, 2010: 244) or part of how it acquires meaning. It seems that as Lan and the other interviewees provide accounts of their multilingual interactions in their workspaces, their descriptions of learning 'just a little bit' of language gain meaning as trivialized linguistic facility in relation to interactions in which language learners exercise more robust proficiency and possibly in relation to native-speaker expertise.

Blommaert *et al.* (2005b) discuss the emergent, contingent and conditioned kind of multilingual activity in locations with large immigrant populations and dense multilingualism. In their study, they observed frequent occasions of cross-language interactions and displays of 'truncated competence' occurring at various locations throughout the Ghent, Belgium, neighborhood they studied – in coffee shops, at bus stops, in newspaper shops and on street corners. Such multilingual interactions, from the most structured and formal (Arabic in a mosque or Dutch in a primary school) to the most unplanned and emergent (Turkish at a bus stop), orient to particular 'regimes' of language that the authors describe as a 'normative, taken-for-granted dimension which regiments situated understandings of language' (Blommaert *et al.*, 2005b: 213). They add that when examining moments of actual language use in particular locations and with particular interlocutors it becomes clear that 'multilingualism is not what individuals have or lack, but what the environment, as structured determination and interactional emergence, enables and disables them to employ' (Blommaert *et al.*, 2005b: 213).

The same authors cite an example from an internet advertisement for a 'fast language learning program', which features an English-speaking international businessman who can derive 'confidence' from learning the languages of the cities where he visits and works (Blommaert *et al.*, 2005a: 204). The kinds of language usages the advertisement purports the language program will teach the business traveler include utterances such as 'Take me to the hotel, please' and 'keep the change', along with 'tasteful anecdotes from [one's] evening escapades' in the city, and greetings (Blommaert et al., 2005a: 204). The 'local' native speakers are constructed as responding positively and acceptingly to these bits of language in the context of the advertisement. It seems the truncated competence of the imagined Anglophone businessman is evaluated as neither trivial nor embarrassing, but something to be celebrated, and indeed, such achievements are constructed as sufficiently desirable that individuals should be willing to pay money to buy the language program. As such, the 'just some small bit' of multilingual competence practiced by the immigrant small business owners in this study versus the truncated competence of such hypothetical Anglophone business travelers needs to be understood as differently scaled, regimented and valued resources involving power differences 'that connect the larger social order to micro-interactional processes' (Blommaert et al., 2005b: 213). Elsewhere, Blommaert (2010: 12) argues that 'what counts as language in particular contexts' depends on 'what is ratified and recognized as a valid code for making oneself understood . . . [or] the indexical value that particular linguistic resources have in certain spaces and situations'.

In this study, the immigrant interviewees downgrade the significance of their capacity to learn and use the non-English languages of their customers and/or employees, even as they produce positive stances in relation to this multilingual activity. As such, they construct an evaluative norm that is different from that constructed in relation to 'full' or 'good English' linguistic capacity. It seems that even as some of the shop owners in this study have managed to create contexts in which it is regarded as desirable to engage in multilingual teaching and learning activities, they still display sensitivity to normative values regarding which languages count (more) in this context and often performatively reconstruct the ideological effects regarding 'good English'.

Conclusion

The performative effects of interviewees' stancetaking acts do not emerge out of a dialectic of social structure impinging on or determining the individual, but rather through the co-constructed meaning making work of socially and already dialogically constituted 'individuals' as they orient to ideologies of language or different 'regimes of language' (Blommaert et al., 2005a). Du Bois (2011: 76) puts it his way: 'in the memory and practice of dialogic modes of discourse you carry an intersubjective array of voices that partakes of both personal subjectivation and generalized systems of sociocultural value'. He then adds:

> the discursively socialized individual lays down her own autobiography in the inscription of stances taken, … [and this] fundamentally dialogic self [is] based on the sedimentations of co-opted intersubjectivity. In return the processes of dialogic production that mediate the socialization of the self can be recycled and projected outward again into the arena of public discourse. (Du Bois, 2011: 77)

In constructing evaluations of their language learning capacity and of their ability to use their learned languages (i.e. their agentive capacity for learning English and the success of their agentive actions), the interviewees, in collaboration with me, produce local performances that performatively (re)construct social values related to different languages and to varying degrees of language proficiency. Through exploring the co-constructed emergence of subtly different stances performed in Lan's, Hannah's and Jenny's accounts of learning and using English and other languages, depending on context of use, we can better understand how their 'doing of language' (Harissi *et al.*, 2012: 530) performatively effects desirable local identities (i.e. 'responsible' or 'appropriately modest'), while simultaneously re-sedimenting social values regarding the desirability of mastering native-speaker-like English proficiency. That said, the social values that were performed and produced in these conversations are not monolithic. Not everyone would share a positive orientation to multilingual language use and learning as practiced in some of the interviewees' shops; not everyone would agree that these interviewees' English proficiency is good enough in the context of their work interactions; but it is also true that not everyone would agree that their English language learning is lacking in any way (i.e. LFE speakers). Thus, performatively effecting ideologies of language and identity through such local evaluative performances of their agentive efforts to learn and use English and other languages develops in the relational intersection of interlocutors, and the displayed and legitimated social values that are invoked and constituted in particular spaces.

6 Performing Agency and Responsibility in Reported Speech

Agency and Reported Speech

This chapter investigates yet another interactional feature commonly produced in interview talk: utterances typically identified as 'reported speech'. Johansen (2011: 2858) views reported speech as a 'central phenomenon for investigating how the dimensions of agency and responsibility are negotiated in interactional processes'. Likewise, De Fina and Georgakopoulou (2012: 169) comment that reported speech is the discourse feature most clearly related to the discursive construction of morality and agency. Many scholars who have investigated reported speech as a mechanism for construing agency have examined how interlocutors manage to deflect or reduce their own agency by assigning responsibility elsewhere. That is, if one is simply the reporter for, or a conduit of, an Other's utterance, then responsibility for its content and its manner of production can be assigned to this Other as well (Clift & Holt, 2007; De Fina, 2003; Hill & Zepeda, 1993; Johansen, 2011). In addition, much of this research has focused on the construction of reported speech in narrative account giving (Holt, 1996, 2000; Labov, 1972; Lucy, 1993). Couper-Kuhlen (2007) and Clift (2007) were among the first to examine the interactional effects of reported speech utterances in non-narrative contexts, described as 'deployed fleetingly by a speaker in the course of an exchange with another' (Clift, 2007: 120) and as 'isolated quotations in conversation' (Couper-Kuhlen, 2007: 81). Both scholars found that such utterances are often integrated into assessments and accounts 'as a means of heightening evidentiality' (Couper-Kuhlen, 2007: 82).

Expanding on their contributions, I examine how the reported speech utterances, attributed to both Self and Other(s), produced by interviewees as isolated quotations as well as in extended narratives, constitute a way to supply 'evidence' for past agentive actions, intentions or decisions related to language learning and use. These reported speech utterances supply such evidence through enacting alleged assessments of interviewees' language capacity, as well as through re-enacting 'normal' interactions conducted in English, among other functions. I discuss how these performances constitute displays of interviewees' 'theories of agency' (Ahearn, 2010) and help to performatively materialize particular story-world Selves, as well as mobilize ideologically normative expectations and values assigned to immigrants' learning and use of English in the United States.

Researching Reported Speech

Many researchers have noted that the production of reported speech in interaction is a component of stancetaking, in that it demonstrates speakers' attitudes or stances toward the purported original speaker and/or to the words spoken, often evinced through the prosodic character of the utterance (Holsanova, 2006; Holt, 2007; Mathis & Yule, 1994). As discussed in Chapter 5, stancetaking is ubiquitous in interaction, infusing all utterances. By contrast, reported speech, though commonly produced in talk, can be dispensed with. As a somewhat marked feature of talk, reported speech has been the focus of research across a broad spectrum of disciplines over a number of decades, including sociology, philosophy, literary theory, discursive psychology, as well as linguistics (see Holt, 1996). Clift and Holt (2007) point to the three central foci adopted by researchers over these decades: the linguistic forms of reported speech, the authenticity or accuracy of reported speech with respect to what is purported to have been said on a prior occasion and the pragmatic functions of reported speech – the latter being the focus of most contemporary research.

Among contemporary researchers who investigate the linguistic forms of reported speech, many have explored the development of new quotative verbs, such as 'tell', 'go' and 'like', as in the use of 'he goes' or 'they're like' preceding a reported speech utterance (Macaulay, 2001; Romaine & Lange, 1991; Tagliamonte & Hudson, 1999). Yet others have found that many reported speech utterances are not accompanied by a quotative verb (Klewitz & Couper-Kuhlen, 1999; Mathis & Yule, 1994; Tannen, 1989). In such cases, speakers often rely on a marked shift in voice quality or prosody to distinguish their narrator voice from the quoted speaker's voice, functioning, in a sense, as quotations marks do in written dialogue (Klewitz & Couper-Kuhlen, 1999). Such prosodic shifts can also allow the speaker to reproduce the ostensible voice quality of the quoted author and can thereby serve to construct an implicit evaluation (i.e. stance) toward the reported utterance and/or its original speaker (Günthner, 1999, 2000; Holsanova, 2006; Holt, 2000). As Levey (2003) notes, the use of prosody 'facilitates the re-enactment of a past personal drama but also enables reporting speakers to contextualize their own attitudinal alignment towards the reported dialogue' (Levey, 2003: 311, in Relaño Pastor, 2004: 95). These studies indicate that prosodic marking is common in the production of reported speech, with or without quotative verbs; however, as Klewitz and Couper-Kuhlen (1999) show, prosodic marking should not be considered an inevitable identifying feature. They identified prosodically unmarked cases of reported speech in their data and suggest that speakers may choose not to produce special voicing if they want to construct these speakers as 'behaving in a normal "unmarked" way' (Klewitz & Couper-Kuhlen, 1999: 12).

In seeking to establish a theoretically grounded basis for the analysis of reported speech, many researchers have drawn on Goffman's (1974, 1981) concept of footing and participation frameworks. Footing refers to the process by which interlocutors signal their alignment with their interlocutors and their stances toward the utterances they produce in the ongoing development of an interaction. Though interaction is incessantly dynamic and continually negotiated, by taking footing into consideration, researchers can temporarily stabilize such fluidity and identify how different speaker roles are often laminated onto a single utterance. The *animator* role is constructed by the one whose speaking voice is used to produce the utterance in an interaction, and in this study, the animator is always the interviewee. The *author* role is constructed to signal who produced the original utterance, whereas the *principal* role is constructed to indicate who is socially responsible for the content of the utterance. One can also use reported speech to construct *oneself* as having uttered particular words on prior occasions, thereby claiming authorship and/or principalship for oneself while also performing the animator role. However, an animator often constructs the author and/or principal of the utterance to be someone different from herself or himself. It is this possibility for shifting in and out of speaker roles that enables a speaker to deny responsibility for utterances by attributing them to a different author and/or principal.

A more fundamental theoretical basis for considering the role of reported speech in interaction was developed in the 1920s by Vološinov, a member of the Bakhtin Circle. For Vološinov (1973), reported speech provides a clear exemplar of Bakhtin's notion of dialogism, exemplified in Bakhtin's (1981: 293) oft-cited contention that 'language for the individual consciousness, lies on the borderline between oneself and the other. The word in language is half someone else's. The word becomes one's own ... when he appropriates the word, adapting it to his own semantic and expressive intention'. Bakhtin also noted that 'the word does not exist in a neutral and impersonal language (it is not, after all, out of a dictionary that the speaker gets his words!), but rather it exists in other people's mouths, in other people's contexts, serving other people's intentions: it is from there that one must take the word and make it one's own' (Bakhtin, 1981: 294). Drawing on this dialogic understanding of language in theorizing reported speech, Vološinov (1973) wrote:

> We have conducted an inquiry into the chief forms of reported speech. We were not concerned with providing abstract grammatical descriptions; we endeavored instead to find in those forms a document of how language at this or that period of its development has perceived the words and personality of another addressor. The point we had in mind throughout was that the vicissitudes of utterance and speaking personality in language reflect the social vicissitudes of verbal interaction, of *verbal-ideological communication*, in their most vital tendencies. (Vološinov, 1973: 157, italics added)

Though numerous scholars have commented on Vološinov's exploration of reported speech and his insistence on the constructed nature of reported speech by a current speaker (i.e. in opposition to the mere *reporting* of another's speech) (De Fina, 2003; Günthner, 2000; Holt, 1996; Tannen, 1989), few have commented on how his interest in reported speech was not in the phenomenon per se, but rather in the phenomenon as an overt demonstration of the dialogism that he understood to be true for all utterances and as demonstrations of 'verbal-ideological communication'. This view of reported speech (and of all speech) as inherently dialogical and ideological deserves greater attention.

Given my alignment with Bakhtin's dialogic perspective in relation to language production, I need to explain my use of the term 'reported speech'. Many contemporary researchers have pointed to the fact that reported speech is rarely an accurate word-for-word representation of what was actually said in previous talk (e.g. Mayes, 1990) and that any time an utterance is produced in a new context, with different conversational participants, it cannot be the 'same' utterance. For this reason, Tannen (1989) replaced the term reported speech with 'constructed dialogue', arguing that this phenomenon 'represents an active, creative, transforming move which expresses the relationship not between the quoted party and the topic of talk but rather the quoting party and the audience to whom the quotation is delivered'

(Tannen, 1989: 109). An animator of an utterance never simply 'reports' what was said on a prior occasion, but actively constructs a scenario for the current discursive situation. Other terms recommended to replace reported speech include 'represented speech' (Banfield, 1993) and 'demonstrations' (Clark & Gerrig, 1990). Though I fully agree with these scholars' orientation to reported speech as constructed rather than monologic reports, I have elected to continue using the term 'reported speech' because of its broad recognizability. My focus in this chapter is on the performative effects of reported speech as evidentiary displays in relation to the discursive constitution of agentive story-world Selves.

Producing Reported Speech as Evidence

As noted earlier, narratives appear to be a favored activity type for the production of reported speech, perhaps because reported speech utterances help to dramatize an account and invite recipient involvement in the story-telling activity (Haakana, 2007; Holt, 1996, 2000; Labov, 1972; Lucy, 1993; Tannen, 1989). Reported speech is also regarded as an economical way to create a scenario in the here and now (Holt, 1996). That is, individuals may forgo summarizing events, which often requires more talk and more sophisticated language, and simply perform them through reporting who said what, an interactional affordance that non-native speakers may find helpful in re-constructing past events or experiences for current interlocutors. However, Tannen (1995) contends that the most fundamental effect of reported speech is that interlocutors:

> tend to take literally the act of what is accordingly called 'reported speech'. That is, they assume that when quotations are attributed to others, the words thus reported represent more or less what was said, the speaker in question being a conduit of objectively real information for which the quoted party is the principal, the one responsible. (Tannen, 1995: 200)

As such, it appears that for many speakers, a taken-for-granted feature of reported speech is that it serves to provide evidence of a 'real' discursive event that transpired on a prior occasion.

Generally, one is regarded as having epistemic rights to know and comment on 'facts about [one]self' (Goffman, 1971: 28), and in interview contexts, the purpose for interacting is typically based on an understanding that information about oneself is within the control of the interviewee who agrees to divulge relevant information of his or her past experiences to the interviewer. Importantly, what we claim to know and what we produce as evidence to support our interactional stances is 'normatively organized' according to Stivers *et al.* (2011: 3). These authors add that 'as in any normatively organized system, we can and do hold one another accountable for justifiably asserting our rights and fulfilling our obligations with respect to knowledge' (Stivers *et al.*, 2011: 3). And as Heritage and Raymond (2005: 36) argue, 'the regulation and sanctioning of such rights is no trivial matter' as interlocutors negotiate what they can justifiably claim to know. Enfield (2011: 293) points to an important distinction between 'claiming and demonstrating' what it is that we know. That is, not all *claims* one makes regarding what one knows one has said or done or witnessed will be received as legitimate; one needs to produce evidence (i.e. *demonstrate*) that it is interactionally legitimated. At the same time, Altheide (2008: 143) cautions that 'people in everyday life seldom focus on evidence per se; they just say and do what seems appropriate for the situation at hand. In this sense, evidence is very pragmatic and very interactionist; if it works with an audience at a specific place and time, it is not likely to be challenged'.

Given the interactional expectation that interlocutors will supply sufficient and appropriate evidence regarding what they can legitimately claim to know, Couper-Kuhlen (2007) notes that reported speech is one resource that can be used to authenticate one's claims. By reporting the alleged 'actual' words spoken at another time and place, one gives the appearance of supplying 'testimony of an independent and objective witness' (Couper-Kuhlen, 2007: 100). She also notes that the use of self-quotation can be used to justify past actions and adds that reporting past thoughts produced by Self can be used to portray one's actions as 'having been undertaken rationally and deliberately at the time' (Couper-Kuhlen, 2007: 103). Holt (1996: 119) too argues that reported speech can attest to the '"historicity" of an action or thought'. By re-enacting past utterances (or thoughts) in vivid detail in the here and now, such performances come to be treated as plausible authentic representations of what more or less 'actually' was said.

In this study, I explore how interviewees' performance of reported speech utterances serve as evidence to *demonstrate* that they have taken action and have acted responsibly with respect to their agentive pursuit of learning English. By re-enacting past experiences through reporting what others or they themselves said on those occasions, interviewees construct evidential authenticity. For example, in this study, interviewees' claims to have worked hard at learning English may be perceived as simply humoring me, the interviewer, or their claims to have continually worked to improve their English may be heard as merely responding contingently to questions and topics as they emerged in the interview talk in order to save face or to position themselves as aligning with dominant ideological norms. However, if they can produce 'an assemblage of performances' (Enfield, 2011: 293) in support of the veracity of such claims, then interviewees can *demonstrate* that they have taken advantage of opportunities to act responsibly, according to the normative social expectations for someone with their particular status or identity – in this case, as immigrant language learners. In the analysis that follows, I first examine the reported speech utterances produced by interviewees as monologic utterances in order to arrive at an understanding of the patterned production of these reported speech performances across the interviews. I then explore these utterances as interactionally contingent and co-constructed performances that fulfill particular interactional purposes in the micro-analysis of selected excerpts from the interview corpus, and, finally, I discuss their relevance as interactional sites for performatively constituting desirable story-world Selves.

Analyzing Reported Speech: An Overview of Patterned Usages

In this chapter, I only examine cases of direct reported speech as opposed to indirect reported speech. The distinction between direct and indirect reported speech often becomes somewhat blurred in natural interactions (Holt, 1996), but the difference is based on what interlocutors purport to be doing: directly reproducing someone's actual words as in 'I tell my customers *Slow down*' (Tony) or indirectly summarizing the gist of what someone has said as in 'Everybody said they like the food' (Hannah). I also only analyzed utterances that related to some aspect of interviewees' language learning and use, following the analytic focus maintained in Chapters 4 and 5. In the corpus of 18 interviews, I found that three of the participants never produced reported speech utterances and one did not produce any in relation to the focal topics of language learning and use. Unlike the unavoidable need to use subject-verb constructions (Chapter 4) and the inevitable production of evaluative stance (Chapter 5) in one's talk, reported speech, though common, is neither unavoidable nor inevitable. Thus, it is not surprising that I found fewer instances of it, nor that there was greater variation among participants in how frequently they produced exemplars of reported speech. The average number of reported speech utterances relating to the focal topics of language learning and use, per interviewee, was 5.6.

I identified and counted individual reported speech utterances using the following criteria. An utterance was counted as a single reported speech exemplar when it was constructed: (a) as a case of direct reported speech; (b) as though it had originally been produced by a single individual or a single, collective source and as a single turn of talk; and (c) as related to the focal topics of language learning and use. For example, I identified the following as a single reported speech utterance. In narrating an incident that occurred at the Department of Motor Vehicles (DMV) office where she was attempting to obtain her driver's license, Donna attributed the following utterance to the DMV officials.

(1)   'They said, *well that's it. You need to go learn some English.*'

In this exemplar, the reported speech utterance is comprised of two clauses but is counted as a single utterance given that it is constructed as having a single set of authors, was produced in a single turn by Donna, is prefaced with a quotative pronoun + verb, thus rendering it a case of direct quotation, and is related to a focal topic.

The following example produced by Dorothy was counted as two utterances given that she constructs the reported speech as attributable to two different authors/principals. She related that she had never been able to take formal English classes but instead learned by watching cartoons on TV. In telling this account, Dorothy produced the following dialogue.

(2)   'Everybody ask me *how can you speak English because you no- you not even go to school.*'
    '*TV.*'

She constructs these utterances as produced by different speakers and as two turns of talk in the original dialogue, in part through her prosodic delivery. She uses a breathy voice in uttering the first reported speech utterance, thereby constructing the generalized authors' ('everybody') voice quality as displaying surprise and even awe at Dorothy's achievement. Her prosody shifts to a slightly lower pitch and she uses flat intonation as she utters '*TV*', signaling that it was produced by a different speaker (herself in this case), and performing directness and confidence. The question–answer format of the two utterances also indicates that these are two utterances that are produced by different speakers. In this case, Dorothy's utterances *demonstrate* or provide *evidence* to support her claim that she was able to learn English through watching cartoons on television. Given that others have asked about and commented on her language learning strategies prior to the interview conversation, she circumvents the possibility that the interviewer may hear it as an empty claim regarding how she learned English. Of course, the fact that this interview was conducted in English, as was true for all of the interviews, supplies implicit evidence that Dorothy and the other interviewees have learned English. However, such implicit, generalized evidence becomes personalized by interviewees as they produce accounts of their own actions and interactions.

In categorizing the reported speech utterances produced by interviewees when talking about learning and using English, as well as other languages, I first considered whether interviewees constructed them as Other-generated or Self-generated. As shown in Table 6.1, there were more utterances attributed to Self than to Other(s): 41 to 31 (or 57% to 43%). Isolating reported speech utterances in this way is admittedly problematic given that they are never unilateral, monologic mobilizations in interaction. However, this snapshot overview of interviewees' utterances suggests that they were finding such talk useful for establishing the authenticity of their claims through supplying evidence of their *own* previous utterances (Couper-Kuhlen, 2007; Holt, 1996).

I also categorized the reported speech utterances according to the kind of evidence, broadly construed, that they conveyed. I found that interviewees' utterances typically served to demonstrate evidence: (1) of their prior agentive actions or intentions to learn English (or other languages, in some cases), all as Self-attributed reported speech; (2) of their 'normal' interactions with clients or employees in English by which they implicitly show that their English language learning has been sufficiently successful for them to carry out such everyday purposeful talk; (3) of assessments of their English language capacity, produced by Self and Others; and (4) of Other-attributed negative comments on their use of non-English languages, which functioned to position interviewees as aware of and sensitive to ideologies of language. There was a small number of 'Other' utterances, usually constructed as parts of a dialogue, which fit none of these categories (see Table 6.1).

Table 6.1 Number of reported speech utterances relating to language learning and use

Type of evidence supplied	Self-attributed	Other-attributed
Past agentive actions in learning/using English	20	0
Normal interactions in English	14	9
Assessments of English language capacity	6	9
Complaints regarding non-English language use	0	9
Other	1	4
Total	41 (57%)	31 (43%)

Reported Speech in Discursive Practice: A Micro-Analysis

Reported speech as evidence of past agentive actions in learning/using English

In the excerpt displayed below, Hee, a Korean restaurant owner, responds to my question regarding whether she finds some conversations in English more difficult than others (1–5) by describing two difficult situations. Hee first constructs a scenario that involves talking with a lawyer and then one that involves talking with a doctor. In first demonstrating how she manages the difficulty of talking to a lawyer, she constructs a reported speech utterance in which 'they' tell her to '*go talk to the lawyer*' (8). Though she is cast as the object of this advice, attributed to a generalized Other ('they'), and the situation as she describes it accentuates her own limitations in English ('I don't understand' (11)), she does not treat the generalized 'they' or the content of their alleged command as positioning her negatively. The unmarked prosodic delivery of this reported speech utterance, embedded in her longer turn, constructs it as neutral content (Klewitz & Couper-Kuhlen, 1999). More importantly, in narrating this scenario, she positions herself as acting agentively by demonstrating what she habitually tells lawyers in such situations. She indicates that she instructs the lawyer to '*open [her dictionary] for [her]*' ((12), see also (8–9)), presumably to the word or words the lawyer has just used so that she will understand what has been said. She follows this up by noting, 'Then I read [the dictionary]' (14), suggesting that this strategy allows her to deal with language difficulties as they emerge. Hee performs the same agentive quality when she constructs a scenario with a doctor and casts herself as someone who bluntly asks the doctor '*what's that*' (24) when she does not understand something. These reported speech utterances position her as taking the lead in making sure that she understands what is being said and in this way she supplies evidence of an agentive Self who attends to English language gaps and manages them responsibly. Her story-world Self is positioned as taking advantage of co-present others and artifacts (the dictionary) in order to manage such emergent language difficulties.

Hee summarizes the gist of these narratives as demonstrations of her desire 'to be very detailed' (28), noting that that is why she 'keep asking' (30) questions when she does not understand the language produced by doctors and lawyers. After I offer positive follow-up assessments to Hee's reported comments (32, 34), Hee performs one more typical scenario at the lawyer's office. She constructs this third narrative as a demonstration of why she needs to be so detailed and persistent in asking her lawyer questions. It is because she has to sign papers (37–38, 41) and pay them money (41). In this scenario she casts the lawyers in a negative light through her prosodic delivery of a reported speech utterance attributed to them. Hee notes that 'they say' to her *'here sign'* (38). This reported speech utterance is produced more rapidly than the surrounding talk and with a shift from medium to low pitch on the word 'sign'. The effect is that 'they', the lawyers, are cast as hurriedly, even dismissively, commanding her to sign documents (with no additional information regarding what she is signing). Hee then constructs her story-world Self as agentively instructing the lawyer to *'explain'* it to her (42) and as telling them that she will bring *'somebody [to] read it'* (43), suggesting that this third party would translate the documents as needed for her. There are prosodic cues that mark these as reported speech utterances, a brief pause before the utterance (42) and a slight pitch upgrade at the onset of the reported speech (42, 43), but these utterances attributed to herself as author and principal are produced in her 'normal' voice, with no change in tempo or voice quality, casting these as confident, matter-of-fact discursive actions (Klewitz & Couper-Kuhlen, 1999).

(3) *Hee agentively manages language difficulties*

1.	**Int:**	Mm hm. Are there different kinds of either conversations (..)
2.		yeah conversations, that you find are more difficult than
3.		others, that you sometimes have misunderstandi::ngs with
4.		people you speak to::. Does it depend on the person you're
5.		talking to:::, what you're talking about=
6.	**Hee:**	=Okay um little uh difficult lawyer.
7.	**Int:**	Yeah.
8.	**Hee:**	You know law, they say *go talk to the lawyer*? I always
9.		take with me my dictionary,
10.	**Int:**	Good for you.
11.	**Hee:**	yeah, then, I don't understand, I always tell them (.)
12.		*open for me.*
13.	**Int:**	Yeah.
14.	**Hee:**	Then I read it,
15.	**Int:**	Good for you.
16.	**Hee:**	that seems to be always a little difficult.
17.	**Int:**	Yeah.
18.	**Hee:**	Then uh then sometimes doctor?
19.	**Int:**	Yeah.
20.	**Hee:**	When I go see doctor, but I don't know about the a::ll

21. **Int:**   All the-
22. **Hee:**   all the (xx)
23. **Int:**   I don't either. ((laughter))
24. **Hee:**   Yeah, so I say (.) *what's tha::t.*
25. **Int:**   Right right.
26. **Hee:**   You know.
27. **Int:**   Okay.
28. **Hee:**   So then I want to be very detailed.
29. **Int:**   Yes.
30. **Hee:**   Ask, keep asking you know.
31. **Int:**   Yes.
32. **Int.**   You're very careful.
33. **Hee:**   Very careful.
34. **Int:**   You want to have every word,
35. **Hee:**   Yes.
36. **Int:**   You want to understand [every word.
37. **Hee:**   [Because yeah you have si::gn.
38.   The lawyer thing always sign. They say >*here sign.*< (.)
39.   But I don't kno::w.
40. **Int:**   Yeah.
41. **Hee:**   If I have to sign, I have to pay to do something. So I
42.   always ask lawyer (.) *explain to me.*
43. **Hee:**   Or I tell lawyer *I bring with me the (xxx) somebody read it.*
44. **Int:**   Yeah.
45. **Hee:**   Then then also I have time to reading by myself, (.)
46.   research it.
47. **Int:**   Yeah.

In this narrative triptych involving Hee's interactions with lawyers and doctors, Hee does not deny her English language limitations, but through her production of reported speech utterances she supplies evidence of her agentive, careful, responsible actions to manage these limitations. In dramatizing these difficult moments for my benefit, Hee supplies vivid details of who says what and how, thus demonstrating what 'actually' happened and thereby rendering plausibility and authenticity to the narrated events. Her utterances function as an implicit claim to be received as a responsible and ideologically responsive individual with respect to taking advantage of opportunities to learn English and as able to manage her language limitations appropriately. That is, the reported speech utterances help to provide evidence that her comments in the interview are not merely here-and-now comments to placate me, the interviewer, but have historical authenticity (whether or not the narrated events really happened or happened as they were described here).

In the following brief excerpt, Ivan, owner of a French bakery, is more explicit in pointing to how normal interactions in English can serve as language learning moments. He notes that starting his own business was 'a huge way of learning a lot of jargons' (1, 3), and then adds that one can also learn 'jargon' in the normal course of everyday encounters, such as when one goes to the dentist or takes yoga classes. In demonstrating what one can learn, he uses reported speech to imitate what a dentist will typically say to a patient: *Open wide. Turn to the left* (6). He produces a second example, demonstrating what a yoga instructor is likely to say: *Use your (xx) pose* (7).

(4) *Ivan shows how he learns jargon*

1.	**Ivan:**	I think starting the business was a <u>huge</u> way of learning
2.	**Int:**	[Yeah.
3.	**Ivan:**	[a lot of jargons.
4.	**Int:**	Yeah yeah.
5.	**Ivan:**	Think about it. Going to the dentist you're learning
6.		jargon. Like (.) *open wide. Turn to the left*. Uh learning
7.		yoga (.) *use your (xx) pose*.
8.	**Int:**	Right.
9.	**Ivan:**	Every experience.

Altheide (2008: 138) comments that 'evidence is bound up with our identity in a situation'. In both Hee's and Ivan's performances of reported speech they supply utterances that can be heard as appropriate for the contexts being described and the identities that are in play in these narrated situations. Their utterances thus serve as plausible demonstrations of actual past interactions and thus as evidence that their 'reports' are credible.

Reported speech as evidence of capacity to engage in normal interactions in English

In this section I examine an excerpt in which Hannah, a proprietor of a Chinese restaurant, produced Self-attributed reported speech by which she demonstrated how she interacts with customers who hire her to cater their parties. As shown below, I ask Hannah if she thinks her customers, whom she had described as friendly and loyal, 'understand' how much effort she has put into learning English or how hard it is to do so (4–9). Hannah responds with a strong 'yes' (10); however, it is not entirely clear whether she understood the question. Hannah comments that 'they know' (10) but then adds that 'sometimes they not understand' (11). It is possible that Hannah interpreted the question to be about whether her customers 'understand' her when she speaks in English. In any case, she indicates that they usually just talk about the food (13, 15) and that 'all of the food [talk] I understand' (17).

A few turns later, I ask (through producing an utterance with rising intonation) whether Hannah needs to do a lot discussion when she caters parties (24, 26). In response, Hannah performs how she handles such situations, relying, in part on reported speech utterances to demonstrate how she interacts with her customers. In this case, her reported speech utterances display no shift in prosody, but rather she produces them in her 'normal' voice, thereby performing these utterances as typical, unmarked discursive acts. Their unmarked quality indexes their everyday utility and serves as a representation of how she goes about handling mundane aspects of her restaurant and catering business, such as when she outlines the choices her catering clients have ('*You got the choice of that, that*' 31) and asks them relevant questions so that she can determine how many people to prepare for and the kind of cuisine to prepare ('*How many ki:ds, how many adu:lt people, American or Chinese or Korean*' 33–34). In performing these reported speech utterances, she positions herself as agentive, in charge, and knowledgeable and she then adds, 'and then I deciding, and then I tell them whatever' (30–31) and also 'and then I know this is what kind of food for the country people like. And then I just deciding, and then they like it' (34–35, 37).

(5)   *Hannah manages her catering business talk*

1.	**Int:**	It sounds like you have a good um a good relationship
2.		with your customers. They like to come back.
3.	**Han:**	Yeah.
4.	**Int:**	Do you think you- the American people who come, do-
5.		do you they understand how much work you put- or how
6.		much effort you put into doing this. In other words,
7.		you're doing it in a language that is not your first language,
8.		in what (..) <u>used</u> to be a new culture, do you think people
9.		understand how hard it is maybe to do-
10.	**Han:**	Oh yes. They they know that and they and they uh (..)
11.		sometimes they not understand right?
12.	**Int:**	Yeah.
13.	**Han:**	But usually they come, and just talk to the food.

14.	**Int:**	Yeah.

14. **Int:** Yeah.
15. **Han:** Talk to the food.
16. **Int:** Yeah.
17. **Han:** And and then but all of the food I understand.

. . . .

24. **Int:** So you do a lot of catering for parties,
25. **Han:** Yeah yeah.
26. **Int:** and you have to do a lot of discussion the::n? [to decide-
27. **Han:**   [Uh huh
28. **Han:** Uh just decide they tell how many people,
29. **Int:** Yeah.
30. **Han:** and maybe how many o::rder, and then I deci::ding, and
31.   I tell them whatever. *You got the choice of that, that.*
32. **Int:** Yeah
33. **Han:** I ask them *how many ki:ds, how many adu:lt people,*
34.   *American or Chinese or Korean or-* and then I know then
35.   this is what kind of food for the country people like.
36. **Int:** Yeah yeah yeah
37. **Han:** And then I just deciding, and then they like it. Yeah.

In this excerpt, Hannah, demonstrates how she competently and agentively interacts with customers who hire her to cater parties for them. The unmarked manner in which she performs the reported speech utterances points to the unremarkableness of these interactions and suggests that English usage for her on these occasions is not problematic. In his discussion regarding the difference between *claiming* and *demonstrating*, Enfield (2011: 293) comments that if he claims to be a marksman, he can 'use mere words' to claim that he is a marksman 'or even words supported by a lucky shot. But to demonstrate that I am a marksman I have to produce an assemblage of performances that would not be possible were the claim not true'. In Hannah's case, 'mere words' supply the necessary evidence; i.e. they demonstrate what she can do in English and how she manages business transactions capably.

Further, given that she deems this account to be 'tellable' and likely to be received as appropriate to the interview context points to how such mundane account telling helps to 'normalize, naturalize, and moralize' (Langellier, 1999: 130) ways of being in the world. Hannah's capacity to manage her business interactions successfully in English is treated as desirable though not particularly extraordinary. The apparent neutrality of the workplace interactions as described by Hannah indexes the power of ideologies regarding who accommodates whom in situations involving speakers with different language histories and proficiencies, in that Hannah is the one who commonsensically accommodates to the language of her customers (Wiley & Lukes, 1996). Through recreating this state of affairs as normal, natural and thus morally desirable, Hannah and I performatively reconstruct ideologies of legitimate language dominance, but just as importantly, such mundane sense-making simultaneously enables Hannah to constitute herself as an agentive and responsible individual.

Reported speech utterances as assessments of interviewees' English language proficiency: Self-attributed assessments

Of the 24 reported speech utterances that functioned as assessments of interviewees' English proficiency, the six that were attributed to Self all performed negative assessments. However, these do not appear to be produced merely as modest protestations, to guard against a perception of boastfulness. In Excerpt (6), Kay's negative assessments of her English capacity through reported speech utterances simultaneously enable her to perform a strategic demonstration of her agentive efforts to continue to learn English through her everyday interactions at work. She produces utterances that she purportedly has addressed to her clients, such as commenting that her English is 'not really well' (12), that she thus 'want to learn more and more' (13) and given these language limitations, she requests that they 'please correct [her]' (16). She follows these utterances with a string of representative questions that she allegedly has posed to her clients when she does not understand something they say in English ('_What_ does it mean', '_what_ is it' and 'I _think_ you said like that is it right? or not?' (27–28)). The analytic separation of reported speech utterance types according to those that supply evidence of past agentive actions taken to learn English versus those that assess interviewees' English capacity (see Table 6.1) is less relevant when one considers their turn-by-turn construction in stretches of talk. One can see that Kay produces both types in this interaction.

(6) *Kay asks her clients to correct her*

1.	**Int:**	Do you remember any things that you learned about
2.		English?
3.	**Kay:**	Oh uh u:m actually you know some in too many ways,
4.	**Int:**	Yeah.
5.	**Kay:**	while you talk with your client
6.	**Int:**	Right.
7.	**Kay:**	you learn a lo:t, honey,

8. **Int:**   Mmhmm.
9. **Kay:**   because most American people really nice.
10. **Int:**   Yeah?
11. **Kay:**   Eh when you talk to them and you told them like oh
12.   um *my English I think you know not really we:ll,*
13.   *I want to learn more and more,*
14. **Int:**   Mmhmm.
15. **Kay:**   or *something I sa:y, if you think it not ri:ght, you*
16.   *please correct me,*
17. **Int:**   Mmhmm.
18. **Kay:**   you just tell your client like that
19. **Int:**   Yeah.
20. **Kay:**   and you know they pay attention and they see something
21.   wrong they correct you.
22. **Int:**   Oh yeah?
23. **Kay:**   Or something they say you don't understand=
24. **Int:**   =Yeah.
25. **Kay:**   exactly, or you not for sure, you asking them.
26. **Int:**   Yeah.
27. **Kay:**   *What does it mean*, or *what is it*, or *I think you said*
28.   *like that is it right? or not?* You know? You learn a
29.   lot from clients that one way.

Kay both introduces and closes this stretch of talk with an upshot comment. In lines (5) and (7), Kay comments that 'while you talk with your client, you learn a lot [of English]' and she closes this scenario with a similarly phrased utterance: that one can 'learn a lot [of English] from clients that one way' (28–29). In performing how such learning occurs through her use of reported speech utterances, attributed to herself as author and principal, Kay demonstrates herself taking charge of her learning through being pro-active with respect to her lingering limitations in using the language. In this way, she constructs herself as agentive and deliberate in this pursuit.

Reported speech utterances as assessments of interviewees' English language proficiency: Other-attributed assessments

The reported speech utterances attributed to Others supplied both positive and negative assessments of interviewees' English language proficiency. Producing self-praise is delicate terrain in interaction and the interactional preference against self-praise has long been recognized (Pomerantz, 1984).

Interviewees such as Kay, who produced reported speech exemplars that enacted both negative and positive assessments of their English proficiency, produced only Other-attributed utterances when constructing positive assessments of that proficiency. In so doing, Kay and others assigned responsibility for compliments to Other authors or principals and constructed themselves as mere animators of such words and could thus avoid responsibility for producing self-praise. As shown in Excerpt (7), in response to my question regarding whether customers have ever talked about how she speaks English (1–2), Kay produces three turns with Other-authored reported speech utterances (by her clients), all of which are constructed as compliments regarding her English language capacity. The first of these utterances, *'your English really we:ll'* (4), is prefaced by a breathy laugh and the actual utterance is produced with a laughing voice, marking and simultaneously down-grading the potential interactional trouble that accompanies the production of self-praise. Potter and Hepburn (2010: 1552) suggest that laugh particles such as this 'display trouble with the action at the same time as doing it' and add that laughter serves to 'modulate potentially problematic actions'. Following the second reported speech compliment, *'You speak English goo:d'* (7), Kay produces a heavily laugh-inflected disclaimer, 'I don't know if they tell the truth or not', which displays a shift from the narrating talk to the local interactional context and positions her as sensitive to the risky business of producing self-praise with respect to her English language capacity in conversation with me, the interviewer. Kay then produces a multi-clause utterance reporting positive assessments regarding her English language capacity, initiated in line (13) and delivered in (15) and (16) (*'I think you live here lo::ng right? I think your English very we:ll. You speak English very goo:d.'*). She ends this utterance with another somewhat self-deprecating utterance in which she voices an awareness that she still needs to 'learn more and more' (20–21), thereby balancing the Other-authored praise of her English capacity with her own more modest and self-critical assessment of her language capacities.

(7)   *Kay's customers praise her English*

    1. **Int:**   But have customers talked about how you speak
    2.   English?
    3. **Kay:**   .hhhha (breathy laugh) I think we're lucky. Most
    4.   clients say (.) *your English really we:ll*
    5.   ((laughing voice for reported speech clause))
    6. **Int:**   Yeah.
    7. **Kay:**   *You speak English goo:d, or something*
    8. **Int:**   Yeah so-

      9. **Kay:**   Something like- I don't know if they tell the
     10.   truth or not ((heavily inflected laughing voice))
     11. **Int:**   ha ha [ha ha ha ha ha ha ha
     12. **Kay:**   [ha ha ha ha ha ha
     13. **Kay:**   but most clients told me that, *seems you you-*
     14. **Int:**   Yeah.
     15. **Kay:**   *I think you live here lo::ng right? I think your*
     16.   *English very we:ll. or you speak English very goo:d.*
     17. **Int:**   Yeah.
     18. **Kay:**   Most of the time I heard like that.
     19. **Int:**   Yeah.
     20. **Kay:**   But to me I still think I have to learn more and
     21.   more ha you know.

It seems that by using Other-attributed reported speech to convey positive assessments of her capacity to learn and use English well, Kay was able to align with the interactional preference against boasting by assigning authorship and principalship for these compliments elsewhere (Speer, 2012). Further, her demonstration of how Others have commented on her English, prior to the current interview conversation, provides evidence of her implicit acceptance of the ideological valuation that is placed on *her* learning English and on *her* making the effort to learn sufficiently well to communicate easily with her clients. At the same time, being positioned as someone who must actively and responsibly take advantage of opportunities for learning English, she is also entitled to Others' positive assessments of these efforts and their outcomes.

However, not all Other-attributed assessments regarding interviewees' English capacity were positive. Several interviewees produced Other-attributed reported speech utterances that highlighted and negatively evaluated their English proficiency. In some cases, interviewees still managed to cast these as evidence for past agentive acts, as Paul does in Excerpt (8). He commented that he sometimes notices the mistakes he makes in English himself (1), but that sometimes someone 'beside [him]' tells him *'that's not the right way'* (3–4). Rather than treating such a correction as interactionally awkward or face threatening, Paul indicates that such Other-initiated repairs enable one to learn English by oneself (6), perhaps without the need to attend formal language classes as he never was able to do.

(8) *Paul learns from Others' corrections*

      1. **Paul:**   Someti::me uh (.) I notice myself.
      2. **Int:**   Yeah.

3.	**Paul:**	Sometime you know somebody beside me telling
4.		me *that's not the right way*,
5.	**Int:**	Okay.
6.	**Paul:**	And that's how you should learn yourself.

Whether or not Paul is indeed so sanguine and receptive to corrections, or even whether or not he actually hears such comments, we can never know, but in this context, by constructing the reported speech utterance in this way, Paul demonstrates that he is a responsible language learner who takes advantage of 'instruction' however it happens. The performance of Other-attributed negative stances toward interviewees' language usage, through reported speech utterances, generally emerged in complaint accounts, such as the one analyzed in the following section.

Reported speech in complaint accounts regarding interviewees' non-English language use

In the interview corpus, there were very few complaint accounts reporting on what Others said about interviewees' use of non-English languages in their workspaces – in the form of negative assessments – possibly because of the somewhat formal nature of the interview. Only three interviewees produced such accounts. In one of these, displayed in Excerpt (9), Lan positions herself as highly agentive in responding to hair salon clients who tell her that she and her employees need to '*speak English*' (1) and to one client in particular who complained about the fact that she spoke Vietnamese to an employee at her hair salon. Lan begins her narrative with a reported speech utterance in which she performs a typical kind of utterance spoken by 'some' people (1). Though the attribution is vague, she provides a vivid dramatization of what 'some' of these people say to her: '*you need to speak English ba ba ba ba*' (1–2). In performing the utterance, she speaks quickly and shifts into a raspy, breathy voice by which she enacts an undignified, unreasonable persona, a speaker who lacks control of her or his emotions. This type of speaking persona is enhanced through Lan's production of an 'adjunctive extender' ('ba ba ba ba'). Overstreet (1999) coined this term and noted that interlocutors tend to produce adjunctive extenders when doing reported speech to indicate one could say more but that it is of little value and so can be summed up in nonsense syllables.

Lan then performs the specific event that occurred in her hair salon by describing how a male client went home and complained to his wife about Lan and her employee's use of Vietnamese while he was present in the salon. Lan adopts the same raspy, breathy voice quality in reporting the alleged words of this customer: '*You speak uh Vietnamese ak aka ak ba baba*' (9). Lan shifts back to her normal conversational voice in providing additional narrative details regarding the development of events in this situation and when revoicing the words of this customer's wife who later called Lan to complain directly to Lan about the incident (13, 15–16). In this case of chain reporting, the customer's wife 'reported' to Lan what her husband had said to her (15–16), and Lan then 'reports' that same utterance to me. Lan then revoices her response to the caller, again, maintaining her normal voice quality but also slowing the production of her words slightly. Her measured words, produced in such non-dramatic fashion, allow her to construct herself as controlled and unintimidated by the caller in allegedly responding to her client's wife: '*if I want to talk about him, I can talk any time I want to. But I don't talk about him*' (17–18, 20). She summed up the irrationality of the complaint in commenting to me, 'You know, nothing to talk about' (22), thereby dismissing the complainant as uninteresting, someone who is unlikely even to elicit gossip among her and her employees.

Lan further develops her 'reasonable' story-world persona in commenting that she would not 'feel right' talking about customers in Vietnamese right in front of them (24–25) and that she understands how customers might feel uncomfortable if they do not understand the language being spoken around them (31–33). She then performs a seemingly hypothetical reported speech utterance attributed to her generalized English-speaking customers ('they' (36)) who say that she is '*rude*' because she speaks Vietnamese when she should speak in English at her shop (36). Lan follows that reported speech utterance by voicing an alternative perspective, constructed as a response to the allegation of rudeness: 'but what happen to that person [her employee] doesn't know how to speak English' (37–38) and rebuts the negative appraisal of 'rudeness' by adding 'that not rude at all' (41–42). She notes that she would like for her employees to speak English so that 'you', indexing me and perhaps all of her English-speaking interlocutors, can understand them (44–45). However, given the reality in which her employees 'cannot communicate' in English (47), she positions herself as obligated to meet the needs at hand by translating for them (49, 51), a sensible response to an unavoidable, if undesirable, state of affairs.

Throughout this narrative, I strongly affirm Lan's positioning of herself as someone who brokers such conflictual multi-language scenarios through my positively valenced receipt tokens ('good for you', 'yeah, exactly', 'right' (19, 21, 34, 50)) and in longer response turns (39, 43). As such, I co-construct the legitimacy of Lan's complaint tale and her displays of agentive action, and the non-neutral quality of my utterances treat Lan's narrative rendering of her actions and attitudes as morally consequential.

(9) *Lan rebuts a client's complaints*

1.	**Lan:**	I mean I have some that >*you need to speak English*
2.		*ba ba ba ba*< you know? Even I work down here, I
3.		deal with a lot of professionals. And uh and I
4.		have to- I usually have the one Vietnamese guy, and he
5.		speak with me, he hardly speak much English at all,
6.	**Int:**	Mmmm.
7.	**Lan:**	so I have to translate for him.
8.		And I had a customer come in, and he got mad.
9.		He said, *you speak uh Vietnamese ak aka ak ba baba.*
10.		He get home and tell his wife,
11.		and his wife called me,
12.		and then his wife tell me,
13.		*well uh, Chris say that you know* uh uh
14.	**Int:**	Tsk °oh for heavens' sake.°
15.	**Lan:**	uh *my husband that you know you speak English,*
16.		*make him uncomfortable.*
17.		I say, *if I want to talk about him, I can talk any*
18.		*time I want to.*
19.	**Int:**	Ha ha ha good for you.
20.	**Lan:**	*but I don't talk about him.*
21.	**Int:**	Yeah, exactly.
22.	**Lan:**	You know, nothing to talk about.
23.	**Int:**	Yeah.
24.	**Lan:**	Nothing to talk about you know. I don't feel right
25.		you talk about you know customers like that. I don't
26.		know. Huh uh. Not me.
27.	**Int:**	Yeah.
28.	**Lan:**	You know why should I talk in front of him like that
29.		you know because he can ask me some few questions.
30.	**Int:**	Yeah.
31.	**Lan:**	You know what I mean? But I understand that how
32.		they feel uncomfortable, they talk, you don't understand
33.		it, you know, like-
34.	**Int:**	Right.
35.	**Lan:**	if I talk with them and you be here, (pause) s- certain and
36.		they say *oh you rude, you should speak English with me.*
37.		But what happen to that person doesn't know how to speak
38.		English.
39.	**Int:**	Exactly, because they [do it all the time as English speakers

40.	**Lan:**	[You see what I'm saying? I mean
41.		you can't- and then they think I'm rude, but if not, that not
42.		rude at all, you know. That's the way I look at it.
43.	**Int:**	No I- I think you're so right
44.	**Lan:**	But- I- I would like for them to speak English so you can
45.		understand too what they talking about,
46.	**Int:**	Yeah.
47.	**Lan:**	but that person cannot communicate,
48.	**Int:**	Right.
49.	**Lan:**	you know so I have to.
50.	**Int:**	Right, yeah.
51.	**Lan:**	Just translate for them.

The descriptive details as well as the reported speech utterances in Lan's complaint account provide a lively dramatization of the narrated event. Further, through reporting the alleged 'actual' words that the customer and his wife said to her and her own responses to them, Lan constructs evidential authenticity that this event actually occurred and that it occurred in the manner in which she retold it. In revoicing the words of her customer as he (allegedly) said them, Lan can avoid being positioned as someone who merely claims to have experienced discriminatory comments and can demonstrate they have in fact been directed to her. Perhaps more importantly, given the capacity for speakers/animators to move between different authors/principals in producing reported speech, they also are able to animate conflicting points of view and conflicting ideologies. We find in this stretch of interview talk with Lan that she performs particular but competing language ideologies. Lan's irate customer is constructed as orienting to the normative expectation that English is rightly the default language for public spaces in the United States. Such usage is treated as needing no defense or explanation. Blommaert (2005, 2010) notes that for relative newcomers to immigrant receiving countries the use of their non-dominant languages for normal communication in public contexts is typically treated as 'commonsensically' problematic.

Lan displays herself as broadminded in recognizing both 'sides' of the issue: the discomfort Americans feel when they cannot understand the non-English languages spoken in their presence, but also the pragmatic need for her Vietnamese worker to communicate in his own language in order to do his work. In re-performing the words and actions of concrete individuals interacting in a particular business space, Lan can interrogate the ideologically normative understanding that English should 'of course' be the default language for communication in her shop. When a particular individual, such as her employee, just needs to communicate, he or she will commonsensically do so in the language(s) he or she knows. Attributions of rudeness are shown to be non-sensical in this reconstructed interactional event, populated by 'real' individuals and animated by their 'real' words. At the same time, it is important to note that the customer's anger in reaction to Lan's and her employee's use of Vietnamese in his presence is not merely an individualistic sensation arising only from him, but a socially constructed value system by which some languages (and their speakers) are deemed appropriate and others are devalued in particular contexts or spaces. The customer's alleged utterance 'you [should] speak English' (15) ought thus be understood as dialogically produced. It is more than just an interactional reconstruction of words produced by an author/principal at a particular time and place, it also bears the 'traces' of others' words and values (Bakhtin, 1981). As such, the constructed 'speaking personality' here reconstitutes the 'social vicissitudes of … verbal-ideological communication' (Vološinov, 1973: 157).

Conclusion

Language ideologies are never uniformly adopted and/or reconstituted, and though powerful, they are not absolute. Lan's narrative in Excerpt (10) serves to interrogate, in part, the ideology that governs the 'sense' driving the questions and answers in all of the interviews – that, of course, it is the interviewees who should have taken action to learn a new language. For the most part, however, as interviewees constructed reported speech utterances in their accounts directed to me, someone who is recognizably 'local' as an English-speaking American, who also happens to be Caucasian, and who incited interviewees' accounts regarding their use and learning of English, these individuals supplied evidence to their implicit claims to be regarded as active, responsible language-learning and language-using individuals, in part, through accommodating, linguistically, to native speakers of the language. This performatively constituted identity was mobilized in Kay's account as she performed utterances that acknowledged her English language limitations and which requested correction from her native-English-speaking clients (Excerpt (5)). We saw this identity emerge in Hee's account in which she positioned herself as agentively seeking to compensate for her English-language limitations when speaking with lawyers and doctors (Excerpt (3)). In co-constructing Hee's narrative, I never made relevant any expectation that these English-speaking lawyers and doctors should exert themselves to be understood in their immigrant clients' languages. Such efforts would undoubtedly have been treated as exceptional overtures by both Hee and me.

Though the ideological assignment of responsibility for being understood may be unfair in who benefits most from it (i.e. native speakers, see Grin, 2005), it simultaneously creates some small entitlements for immigrant language learners. That is, the normatively recognized accommodation by non-English speaking immigrants to their native-English-speaking interlocutors also positions them as legitimate objects for positive assessment. If an immigrant's English language capacity is not taken as a given, and if gaining such capacity requires agentive effort, then it can serve as a touchstone for positive evaluations as we saw in Kay's account of her nail salon clients complimenting her progress in learning English (Excerpt (7)). Further, demonstrating that one is able to communicate successfully in order to accomplish 'normal' but consequential interactions for running one's business, points to the ideological valuing of such learning achievements (Hannah, Excerpt (5)). Individuals who have responsibly taken action to learn English can 'sensibly' be complimented for the 'same' language capacities that native speakers will not be complimented for, and they sometimes can gain social capital in the dominant culture just for making the effort.

The efficacy of evidential demonstrations in the form of reported speech utterances extends beyond the local interactional context. They performatively re-sediment previously spoken utterances and their ideological 'sense', even as they can serve as mediating material for constituting Self as agentive in the local interaction. When one displays awareness and conformity to ideologies of 'legitimated' language dominance (Miller, 2009), one can enter into a 'domain of speakability' (Butler, 1997: 33), a desirable and necessary space for constituting Self in desirable ways. But of course, the terms of speakability simultaneously construct constraints on how one can speak and act and still be 'recognized'. Even as Lan's and other interviewees' complaint accounts challenged the 'common sense' valuation assigned to English usage in the United States, they also re-sedimented such values. That is, the act of critiquing or resisting a social norm still constitutes it as a 'real' social phenomenon, and gives evidence of its efficacy in local, micro-level discursive practices. In this way, our socially and ideologically mediated Selves are performatively constituted through (re)sedimenting as well as sometimes resisting normative ways of being in the world. And such 'ways of being' take form and become meaningful, in part, through our acts of (re)narrating them.

7 Local Production of Ideology and Discursive Agency

Constituting Reality

When the interviewees who participated in this study talked about their experiences learning and using English and other languages, they constructed accounts that drew on their memories of past and ongoing personal encounters, thoughts and actions. That they should do so may seem almost too trivial to mention given that they were participating in interview conversations. Atkinson and Coffey (2001), however, speak to the sociality of memory and remind us that when someone remembers and speaks about his or her *individual* experiences, these *personal* memories are socially, historically, interactionally and semiotically mediated occasions. They note that 'memory is a cultural phenomenon, and is therefore a collective one. What is "memorable" is a function of the cultural categories that shape what is thinkable and what is not, what is counted as appropriate, what is valued, what is noteworthy, and so on' (Atkinson & Coffey, 2001: 810).

Furthermore, our sense of ourselves as individuals in the world, though varying depending on culture, context and social situation, needs to be understood as socially constituted as well. In advocating a performativity perspective, Judith Butler contends that our sense of our own idiosyncratic and internal subjectivity, which we typically believe serves as the basis for our actions, is an effect of our participation in renewing social conventions. Likewise, from a performativity perspective, interviewees' 'individual' utterances are treated as discursive performances that generate or create social reality through reiterating, reformulating and transforming social conventions and values. In this way, in the most mundane moments of human sociality, we enact and reconstitute social ideologies. Our diffuse utterances, rather than 'being caused or explained by external social forces or internal motives', need to be taken as 'the working mechanism of social life itself' (Holstein & Gubrium, 2005: 490). Ideologies only survive and remain real when reissued and recycled in such myriad social locations.

Gubrium and Holstein (2012) provide an expansive description of how to conceptualize reality construction as mediated through discursive practices:

> Discursive activity, on the one hand, and discursive resources and conditions, on the other, are mutually constitutive. Each inevitably involves the other. We have variously described discursive activity as employing vocabularies, schemes of interpretation, background expectations, collective representations, stocks of knowledge, local cultures, language games, institutional environments, and discourses—along with other related concepts—that have, from time to time, become working parts of our analytic vocabulary. These are all aspects of the context of interpretation that must be actively, situationally articulated to render experience sensible, orderly, meaningful. Without these resources, discursive activity conveys nothing; it is empty and, as such, unrecognizable. (Gubrium & Holstein, 2012: 350)

In their list of discursive resources or conditions, Gubrium and Holstein do not explicitly mention ideology though I believe it is implicated, perhaps as one of the 'related concepts'. In what follows, I will describe how I define ideology and discuss how I regard it as a central principal for understanding agency as socially derived, maintained and performatively constituted.

What is Ideology?

Referring to ideology when discussing discourses on learning English or other languages seems inevitable. It is also dangerous. Blommaert (2005: 158) noted, somewhat cynically, that nearly every scholar who explores discourse has described it as a 'site of ideology', and he adds that 'few terms are as badly served by scholarship as the term ideology'. So why the hubris to attempt it nonetheless? It seems there is no better conceptual apparatus for arriving at a 'big picture' understanding for why the individuals in these interviews positioned themselves and others as they did when discussing their experiences related to learning and using English. I cannot explain comprehensively why these individuals produced accounts as they did, and I certainly cannot identify in any comprehensive fashion the explicit factors – historical, cultural, economic, or social – which caused them to construct themselves as particular kinds of (in)agentive participants in these accounts. However, it is possible to explore why their personal accounts of past experiences and their 'theories of agency' (Ahearn, 2010) can be received as 'sensible' and 'natural' ways to speak about themselves as learners and users of English. Exploring these accounts from the perspective of ideology allows the varying types of discourse analysis used in the preceding chapters to move beyond linguistic analysis and/or interactional analysis to social analysis (Verschueren, 2012).

Numerous scholars of ideology have commented on the range of definitions of ideology, the frequent incompatibility between such definitions, as well as the inevitability of such incommensurability (e.g. Eagleton, 1991; Woolard, 1998). Given that others have discussed many of these diverse perspectives taken in research on language and ideology (Blommaert, 1999; Kroskrity, 2000; McGroarty, 2010; Schieffelin *et al.*, 1998; Thompson, 1987), I will focus on identifying my own perspective and address the connection between ideologies of language learning (in relation to immigrants in the United States) and ideologies of agency in this chapter. I have found Verschueren's (2012) approach to ideology most compatible with my developing understanding of the constraints and enablements mediating the production of discursive practices and our understanding of agency. Verschueren's view of discourse and ideology 'centers around meaning' (Verschueren, 2012: 2) that involves 'relations between groups of people' (Verschueren, 2012: 2). He sees ideology as constituted in and constitutive of 'mundane and everyday processes' (Verschueren, 2012: 3), and as something that can be understood as common sense thinking and explanation – all of which is discursively produced by individuals but is not the invention of individuals. Verschueren adds that an ideology is 'common sense with a history', the kind of common sense that 'members of a wider community appeal to in order to be persuasive' (Verschueren, 2012: 8) and, as such, as that which is taken for granted and not questioned.

Similarly, in addressing the constitutive effects of language and ideology, Thompson (1987: 517) comments that:

> 'ideas' or 'meanings' do not drift aimlessly through the social world, like so many shapeless clouds in a summer sky. Rather, ideas circulate in the social world as utterances, as expressions, as words which are spoken or inscribed. Hence, to study ideology is, in some part and in some way, to study language in the social world.

So the abstractly ideological becomes empirical in this way. Ideologies are not typically conspiratorially hidden from view (though they can be); rather, they are most frequently performed and constituted as implicit, common sense knowledge. Furthermore, ideologies do not reside merely in the realm of ideas, values and beliefs. Rather, ideologies are enacted as common sense rationality that is actively practiced and ongoingly reconstituted in social interactions – not typically as an explicit topic of conversation, but as practical discursive methods for sense-making, rationalizing, perspective-taking, evaluating, configuring actors in narratives, providing evidence, among many others. My emphasis in this book is on the reconstitution of ideologies through mundane discursive practice, but I recognize that values and orientations to social relations do not necessarily develop organically. They often develop out of deliberate institutional policies and economic practices. However, in many cases the 'sense' of these policies and practices come to be treated as the natural order and likewise come to be indexed in discursive practice as normal and inevitable rather than as exceptional.

Ideologies and Discursive Practice

In taking the approach that ideologies are materialized in discursive practice through mundane interactional displays of accountability and recognizability, we can explore interlocutors' methods of mobilizing accounts and of positioning Self as actor or benefactor with an eye to what they treat as common sense configurations. Occasions for ideological exploration emerge as interviewees supply normative assessments of social actions and/or individual capacities, or produce evidential displays – the discursive constructs and practices explored in this book. Such analysis does not entail a straightforward 'reading from the surface'. Researchers must always be cautious in treating utterances as explicit descriptions of individuals' beliefs or in taking interview responses as clear indicators of what interviewees actually value. As discussed in Chapter 3, treating interview talk as discourse rather than as transparent content allows us to avoid the epistemological fallacy of research in which 'you ask, they answer, and then you know' (Hollway, 2005: 312, cited in Talmy, 2011: 27). Verschueren (2012: 18) argues for the need to treat interviews as 'discourse, subject to all the processes of interaction that shape any other type of discourse rather than as straightforward and factual reflections of ideological content'. Treating interviews as social practices (Talmy, 2011) requires that we give close attention to how people say what they say (Holstein & Gubrium, 1995). This emphasis on the *how* in addition to the *what* becomes particularly important when a researcher's analytic as well as theoretical concerns include exploration of the performative constitution of social reality, individual identity and ideology in language in use. Furthermore, exploring ideologies in discursive practices requires attention to the implicit ways we orient to normalcy, naturalness and mundane reality. Lee and Beattie (2000: 73), for example, note that 'what counts as normal is indexical' just as 'abnormality has to be constructed in discourse'.

The varying approaches to analyzing talk that have been adopted in this book focus on synchronic language performances in the sense that they explore what was produced and performed at particular moments in time. Even so, I view these moment-in-time interactions as showing 'traces' of previous practices for as Bakhtin (1981: 341) has proposed, 'the ideological becoming of a human being ... is the process of selectively assimilating the words of others'. What is uttered in a given interaction is never a mirror image of what happened before, but it can only be produced because of what happened before – even when it transforms what was said or done on previous occasions. Blommaert describes this as the 'synchronicity of discourse' (Blommaert, 2005: 131) in which history is 'crystalised in particular ... ways of speaking' (Blommaert, 2005: 134). For this reason, he urges researchers to move beyond the 'one time event' and to consider it as indexical of 'slower layers, longer spans of time' (Blommaert, 2005: 174).

Working from a performativity perspective, Pennycook (2007b) argues that the sedimentation of previous utterances that are mobilized in current practices requires a reversal in our perspectives on language and human subjectivity. He promotes a view in which difference, renewal and flow are treated as primary in linguistic and social life, and where stability and essential interiority are understood to be the products of repeated social acts. He adds that taking the view that language and human subjectivity derive from a common core 'is an illusion brought about by a misrecognition of sedimented performance in terms of underlying rules' (Pennycook, 2005: 592). Pennycook (2007b: 592) thus argues for the need to treat human activity, linguistic and otherwise, not as 'divergence from a core but rather as repeated acts of quotidian language use [which thus] shifts the focus from stability to flow'. Linguistic constructs, when (re)issued in social practice, are never 'merely' language structures, they are always integrated into meaning-making, which 'bring realities and who we are into being' (Miller, 2008: 261).

In viewing discursive practice as creative iteration and sedimentation, and language structure as emergent from such processes, one can then examine the production of utterances in discursive practice as cases of 'reification within language', an analytic approach that can 'facilitate the analysis of ideology' (Thompson, 1987: 527). Thompson addresses the need for (cautious) interpretation of linguistic structure, including features such as 'grammar, syntax and style' along with 'patterns of exchange' with the goal of understanding how ideological 'meaning is mobilized in the social world'

(Thompson, 1987: 520). Likewise, critical discourse analyst Van Dijk (1995: 24) discusses the 'ideological implications of syntactic sentence structures'. Thompson (1987: 526) is very clear that the 'structural relations' between, say, subjects and predicates are not 'ideological as such'. However, their implementation in constructing relationships between people and places and events mobilizes normative meanings and thereby helps to constitute commonsensical (i.e. ideological) social reality.

Thompson (1987: 527) also advocates examining narrative structure and focusing particularly on:

> ways in which relations of domination are sustained by being represented as legitimate, for the legitimation of social relations is a process that commonly assumes a narrative form. Stories are told which seek to justify the exercise of power by those who possess it and which serve to reconcile others to the fact that they do not.

Thus, Thompson views the often implicit legitimation of domination in social relations as key to ideology. Verschueren (2012: 9), however, cautions against treating domination as always part of ideology, noting that 'powerless and dominated groups may—and usually do—have their ideologies too'. That said, if we conceptualize ideologies as always involving social relations, our exploration of how ideologies are (re)instantiated will almost inevitably need to account for differential relations and power struggles. It seems then that ideologies can be understood as the discursive effects of how we demonstrate what is commonsensical, and in so doing, orient to who is 'legitimately' expert or 'commonsensically' dominant or 'naturally' more powerful in any social sphere. Our commonsensical meaning-making actions often contradict each other, and for this reason 'social reality' is never monolithic or static.

When it comes to the 'contents' of language ideologies one is indeed treading on dangerous terrain. To identify 'an ideology' is an exercise in extreme simplification. Kroskrity (1998: 195) noted that language ideologies are never simply singular beliefs, but should be understood as 'cluster concepts' in which a number of values and social relationships coalesce. Likewise, our normative procedures for making sense of the world are rarely coherent or uniform world views. We often align with and enact conflicting and multiple values and beliefs in the same conversations (Schildkraut, 2005). Furthermore, if we orient to ideologies as common sense beliefs regarding how people are positioned in relation to each other in all social spaces, then it is less about 'beliefs' and more about who is allowed to 'call the shots', when and where and with whom. Despite the dangerous simplification of discussing particular ideologies, the endeavor can still be useful for analytic purposes. As one explores the relationships among people, events and expectations that are presupposed in interlocutors' sense-making discursive actions, one can work to identify ways in which the creation of often-implicit values, differentiated social relationships and differentiated social responsibilities are performatively materialized as normal and inevitable.

Ideologies of Language Learning for Immigrants to the United States

Though it is factually true that English is still the dominant language in the United States, the conviction that it should remain so is an ideological perspective, based on stratified relationships between speakers of different languages. A historical and contemporary outline of attitudes towards English and other languages among people in the United States shows that these attitudes have changed over time depending on world events, immigration cycles, domestic and international economic conditions, among other events (see Potowski, 2010). Historical studies also indicate that early 20th century efforts to link American national identity and national loyalty to English language usage were deliberate efforts to promote nationalistic loyalties. In the late 1800s and early 1900s, the 'Great Migration' to the United States of nearly 24 million immigrants, who brought with them diverse languages, religions, cultures and skin colors, resulted in widespread fears of a loss of national unity among the 'native' Americans (see Ricento, 2005; Wiley & Lukes, 1996). It was during this period that Congress in 1906 added English language proficiency as a requirement for individuals seeking American citizenship. With the advent of World War I came an even greater increase in xenophobic attitudes, particularly anti-German fears. Ricento (2005) documents that by 1923, 22 states had outlawed all foreign language teaching in primary grades. Pavlenko (2002: 185) argues that the cultural, linguistic and ethnic diversity in the United States during these early decades in the 20th century came to be seen as a 'national crisis' and immigrant bilingualism and language maintenance came to be seen as '"un-American" in spirit'. Pavlenko adds that:

> the linking of English monolingualism as Americanness ... entered the public discourse during the World War I era and has remained there ever since co-existing with more inclusive versions of what it means to be an American. Eventually, the fact that abandonment of native languages was a socially enforced process was edited out of the national identity narrative and immigrant families came to see their linguistic choices [and

that of their parents and grandparents] as individual and voluntary. (Pavlenko, 2002: 191)

Ricento (2005: 353) also notes that the sharp decrease in the use of non-English languages in churches, in business, in the print media, as well as in schools during this time period negates the 'folk belief' that immigrants from this earlier era 'voluntarily assimilated'.

Ricento, however, attributes the development of an ideology of a mono-lingual English-speaking country to an even earlier period in American history, one dependent on discursive rather than policy effects. He quotes from *The Federalist Papers* of 1788 in which John Jay characterized the new nation as 'one united people—a people descended from the same ancestors, speaking the same language, professing the same religion ... very similar in their manners and customs' (cited in Ricento, 2005: 350). As Ricento argues:

> By discursively subtracting non-Protestants, non-whites, non-Europeans, and non-English speakers from the 'nation,' the Founding Fathers helped create a template for 'authentic' American identity that has privileged certain groups (white/European), religions (Protestantism), and languages (English, and to a lesser degree European languages) over all others. (Ricento, 2005: 350)

With an ideology of English as legitimately dominant defended in the nation's founding documents and in later language policies, it has come to seem only natural and right that 'the existence and protection [of English] is unquestioned, while other non-national languages [are believed to] have no natural right, or warrant, to exist' (Ricento, 2005: 357) in the United States. Of course, our beliefs about which language is 'naturally' warranted to remain dominant are really beliefs about *whose* language(s) are maintained and *whose* language(s) may be merely tolerated as appropriate for use in private spheres.

Schmid (2001) notes that the dramatic increase in migration to the United States, starting in the late 1970s and continuing through the present, has been met by many 'native' Americans as a threat to the 'natural' order of language and culture. In response to these on-the-ground fears and naturalized ideologies of language, nation and identity, governmental bodies have intermittently promoted English Only or Official English laws. As of 2012, 31 states have passed (largely symbolic) Official English laws (proenglish.org). Conservative organizations such as ProEnglish (proenglish.org) or the Federation for American Immigration Reform (fairus.org), which promote Official English policies, also promote liberal sounding arguments to justify such policies. For example, on the ProEnglish website, one of the guiding principles for the organization includes this proclamation: 'Our nation's public schools have the clear responsibility to help students who don't know English to learn that language as quickly as possible. To do otherwise is to sentence the child to a lifetime of political and economic isolation' (proenglish.com, n.p.). As Crawford (1992) has argued, the ideological common sense incorporated into such stances is that people will learn to speak English only if forced to do so.

Of course, as Schmidt (2000) argues, states and other elite institutions must use *someone's* language in order to function. But we need to recognize that these choices, however pragmatic, regarding which language(s) to use, will inevitably enfranchise some individuals and disenfranchise others. Even without promoting particular legislative policies, decisions regarding which language(s) to use in public and institutional contexts are never neutral, even when it seems 'logical' to adopt the language of the majority or of the more powerful. Furthermore, most immigrants to countries such as the United States recognize and accept their need to learn English (or whatever the dominant languages of public institutions in a given context) in order to live and advance their lives when living in that country. As May (2008: 155) argues, 'those whose habitus are assigned a lesser value by the market come to accept this diminution as legitimate'. This 'symbolic violence' (Bourdieu, 1991) occurs 'when a particular (linguistic) habitus, along with the hierarchical relations of power in which it is embedded, is "misrecognized" (méconnaissance) as legitimate and tacitly accepted—even by those who do not have access to it—as "natural" rather than a socially and politically constructed phenomenon' (May, 2008: 155).

However, in describing how people typically align with multiple and conflicting viewpoints, Schildkraut (2005) cautions against a too simplistic generalization in treating Americans as racist and anti-immigrant for insisting that immigrants should learn English when living in the United States. As she contends:

> a wide range of American ideals, including individualism, economic opportunity, participatory democracy, openness to immigration and tolerance, are all implicated in debates about language use. People seek to protect the images of American identity that they cherish; for some this leads to support for official-English laws, whereas for others it leads to opposition to them. (Schildkraut, 2005: 4)

Ricento (2003) too notes that alternative ideological stances have long been part of the American cultural history, including a 'progressive discourse' that emerged during the early 20th century Americanization campaigns when learning English was made mandatory for gaining citizenship.

Schildkraut (2005: 194) refers to 'images of America' and 'symbolic predispositions', but she could well use the term 'ideologies' to index the conflicting beliefs held by contemporary Americans regarding responsibility for learning English by immigrants to the United States. For example, she points to survey and focus group data, which reveal that many Americans advocate hybrid ideological perspectives, such as promoting the validity of individual rights as well as promoting the need for citizens to take up their responsibility for civic participation. Similarly, beliefs about tolerance and individual liberty are often blended with celebrations of diversity, which often leads to an uneasy relationship between the right to maintain one's own language and culture, and the desire for assimilationist and participatory civic engagement. There is often a simultaneous fear of 'balkanization' and loss of community cohesion promoted along with the celebration of diversity and individual rights. Thus we can be pulled in opposite directions simultaneously, but as Schildkraut (2005: 198) notes, most Americans seem 'to genuinely want both diversity and unity … On a deep level, they sense that diversity and unity need not be mutually exclusive and they subscribe to an image of American identity that allows for both'. Though policies that enable that image to become reality remain 'elusive', Schildkraut (2005: 197) argues that it is important to recognize the everyday reality of 'consensual and conflictual civic myths'.

There are, thus, multiple rationales for the normative 'logic' that immigrants who come to the United States have a responsibility to learn English. Furthermore, when language is viewed as merely a neutral tool or resource that can be learned at will – if perhaps with some difficulty – then there is typically an erasure of the complexities of power relationships, of dominance, of distinctions regarding whose language counts and whose does not. Taking a view of language as a neutral, autonomous system can further reinforce the belief that responsibility for learning a language lies with an individual, and that failure by individuals to learn a dominant language can straightforwardly explain their lack of upward mobility, or that their failure to assimilate to a dominant culture explains their lack of inclusion in socially valued cultural practices (though of course whole populations are dismissively characterized as willfully choosing not to learn English as well). The other 'side' of this logic is that individuals who are already English speakers in the United States have no 'moral' responsibility to learn other languages. They may have other motivations for learning an additional language related to educational or career goals or to maintain a heritage language identity, but the same kind of moral imperative is often missing for many of these English-speaking Americans when engaged in learning non-English languages while living in the United States.

In arguing that perspectives which assign responsibility to *individual* immigrants for learning the dominant language are ideological, I do not mean to suggest that we should therefore discourage them from learning English. I too have taught English as a Second Language classes to immigrants and see the provision of such classes as an important resource for newcomers to the United States. It is clearly true that many immigrants who come to the United States find that their day-to-day lives are easier and that they have more choices and better opportunities when they learn English. However, such factual phenomena do not erase the ideological sense driving these actions, and their ideological basis becomes more apparent when we consider who is affected or unaffected by such 'common sense'.

In approaching the issue of minority language rights from an economic perspective, Grin (2005) outlines several benefits for native speakers of a dominant language in a given society. For example, he identifies the 'communication savings effect' for native speakers by which he means 'native speakers of the dominant language are spared the effort required to translate messages directed to them by speakers of other languages' (Grin, 2005: 456). Another benefit is the 'language learning savings effect' in which native speakers of the dominant language do not need to invest time and effort in learning other languages, and this 'amounts to a considerable savings' (Grin, 2005: 456). Yet another benefit is the 'alternative human capital investment effect', which identifies how 'the money not invested in foreign language acquisition can be diverted to other forms of human capital investment and give native speakers of the dominant language an edge in other areas' (Grin, 2005: 456). As such, the status quo in which native speakers are naturally, rightfully and commonsensically allowed to continue using their language for public or institutional purposes, as well as in their private interactions, grants them considerable advantage. Even if we agree that such disparity remains the most viable (i.e. practical) situation for immigrant-receiving countries, we must recognize that the situation is not ideologically neutral in terms of how people are positioned in relation to each other. Deetz (1994: 194) comments that 'the quiet, repetitive micro-practices . . . which function to maintain normalized, conflict-free experiences and social relations', such as, from my perspective, the mundane discursive practices through which we legitimize who needs to learn what language, in fact need to be conceptualized as 'arbitrary, power-laden manners of world-, self- and other-constitution'. Thus, when immigrants to the United States develop a desire to learn English, which then motivates them to attend language classes and/or to buy pedagogical books or tapes, we need to treat their agentive individual actions as emerging, in part, in relation to the affordances available (classes or materials) in their social contexts, but more powerfully in relation to how they are interpellated as subjects who must do so. This 'natural' assignment of responsibility for language learning to the newcomers can be understood as one of the commonsensical 'practices and routines which constitute identities and experiences', which in turn produce 'unproblematic asymmetries' so that 'privileged knowledge and expertise [are] located in some and not others' (Deetz, 1994: 194).

Ideologies of Agency and Responsibilization

The previous discussion on the ideological common sense regarding immigrants' responsibility to learn a dominant language covers familiar territory for many second language scholars. However, the existing research has paid much less attention to the ideological common sense in treating and constructing individuals as *essentially* agentic. Some scholars use the term 'ideology of agency' (Gaonkar, 1997; Geisler, 2005; Gunn & Cloud, 2010) to critique this normative orientation to people as autonomous entities in the world who automatically 'have' agency. Interestingly, Keltner *et al.* (2008: 41) argue that individuals who have greater power within a particular social group will typically align with an 'ideology of agency' because they perceive their own co-constructed and socially mediated powerful positions to have emerged from their own actions. These individuals regard their more powerful positioning as a natural reward for their 'individually' derived and implemented efforts.

One critique of agency research conducted by Western scholars is that it does not account for culturally varied perspectives of agency (Donzelli, 2010). While this is undoubtedly true, it is also important to understand that *within* a culture and language group, if such an entity is definable, there is variation in how we understand individuals to be agentive. Cassaniti (2012) presents an interesting case of how varied religious affiliations among Thais living in two neighboring communities in rural northern Thailand influenced how they constructed their (in)agentive religious Selves. For example, in commenting on the role of prayer in their religious life, those adhering to Buddhist traditions positioned agency within themselves; that is, their acts of praying created positive karma within and for themselves. By contrast, those adhering to Christian traditions believed prayer to be efficacious because of interacting with 'an external, powerful agent' or God (Cassaniti, 2012: 308). As Cassaniti summarizes, 'the agency of the individual is mediated through the agency of God in Christian Mae Min, while the agency of the individual remains unmediated in Buddhist Mae Jaeng' (Cassaniti, 2012: 309). This variation in how culturally similar groups of people construct themselves as differently agentive in their religious lives, helps us better understand the problem that comes with constituting Selves in terms of an essential agency.

In deconstructing an 'ideology of agency', Jennifer Miller (2008) investigates how the 'responsibilized actor' is performatively constituted and ideologically generated. Our common sense understanding of an individual is of someone who 'actively participates in his or her own life management' rather than functioning as 'docilely' subject to determinant powers. She writes, the 'responsibilized actor, though cloaked in the "appearance of freedom" is nevertheless an effect' (Miller, 2008: 262–263). Notions of self-responsibility, for some actions but not for others, are mobilized in the construction and implementation of an ethical, moral Self. This construction, according to Miller, is not a 'natural state', but a socially and ideologically positioned Self in the world. Miller links contemporary notions of the responsiblized actor to neoliberal ideologies in Western states that have erased or pathologized many of our notions of communal responsibility or of social welfare and have reconstructed responsibility for the welfare of people to the 'enterprising' individuals themselves (Miller, 2008: 262; see also Purvis & Hunt, 1999).

Numerous other studies exploring ideologies of the 'responsiblized Self' point to neoliberal beliefs and policies that place responsibility for actions *in* individuals. For example, Turnbull and Hannah-Moffat (2009), who have studied how parole boards in Canada help prepare women prisoners for life outside of prison, note that these boards do so by mobilizing particular techniques of self-governance and responsibility, which are often contradictory. As they put it, the paroled subject is framed as 'unprepared to self-govern' and yet responsibilized for her reintegration (Turnbull & Hannah-Moffat, 2009: 533). They add:

Notions about what is (or should be) 'meaningful' and 'prosocial' for paroled women are based on 'idealized lifestyles' that reflect whiteness, heterosexuality, ablebodiedness and middle-class norms. Under the conditions of their release, paroled women are expected to pursue such lifestyles as a way to change themselves and avoid being returned to prison. In particular, such prosocial pursuits appear to be 'healthy' homes, places of (legitimate) employment or education and 'meaningful' relationships with intimate partners, kids, family and friends. Arguably, these pursuits are considered respectable because they conform to the gendered characteristics of *normative citizenship*; that is, they relate to notions of domesticity, motherhood, property, self-reliance (through paid employment) and self-improvement. Presumably, these idealized lifestyles will help women break the cycle of crime, establish prosocial associations, avoid problematic consumption of substances and distance themselves from criminogenic spaces. These lifestyles, however, do not resonate with many paroled women's experiences and, for some, are not feasible possibilities. (Turnbull & Hannah-Moffat, 2009: 548)

Though Turnbull and Hannah-Moffat are primarily seeking to understand why so many parolees are unable to maintain such 'responsible' behaviour, even though these women desperately want to stay out of prison, their exploration of this situated social production of responsibility points very clearly to the production of responsibilized individuals according to particular sociocultural definitions regarding the kinds of behavior that can be accepted as evidence of taking responsibility. These authors do not criticize the promotion of such 'prosocial' behaviors, and, in fact, see them as desirable. What their study seeks to expose is the socially constructed nature of such 'naturally' responsibilized individuals.

Similarly, Pitts-Taylor (2010: 646) argues that a broad neoliberal understanding of the responsibilized Self emerges in discourses that attribute 'maintaining the body and avoiding illness and even aging ... [to be individual or personal] responsibilities'. Grady (2010: 164) does the same for retirement funding, indicating that an individual's inadequate retirements savings are often discursively attributed to 'individual reluctance to prepare for retirement' according to neoliberal discourses. These quite different case studies again help to illustrate how discursive practices performatively constitute individuals as responsible for particular acts and outcomes. Though few would dispute that individuals can and should, in most cases, work to save money toward retirement and engage in healthy lifestyles, such actions alone are often insufficient in themselves. We can readily imagine scenarios when all the responsible efforts in the world are inadequate for inoculating an individual from disease or for allowing one to accumulate sufficient savings to self-fund one's retirement years.

These disparate examples of 'ideologies of agency' and the 'responsibilized Self', I hope, can help us understand how the same ideologies are manifest in constituting language learners as particular kinds of individuals. When responsibility for gaining communicative proficiency in English is assigned to individuals who migrate to the United States, their (lack of) efforts to learn the language becomes 'legitimately' sanctionable. Individuals' acceptance of this responsibility can motivate them to learn English, and for many immigrants, such agentive action leads to desirable outcomes for them. Park (2010: 23) explores contemporary discourses in South Korea that promote and celebrate individual achievement in learning English well and that treat success as 'deeply grounded in subjective, human qualities of the learner', but which ignore the 'learner's social provenance or institutional privileges'. He argues for the pervasiveness of neoliberal views that constitute these individual learners of English as a neoliberal subject type, that is, as free to act toward their own goals but 'also held accountable for the consequences of [their] choices and actions' (Park, 2010: 25). He adds, 'any success or failure that is experienced in the neoliberal system' is no longer attributed to social or economic inequalities but becomes 'a matter of the individual's aspirations and capabilities—that is, a reflection of one's naturalized inner qualities' (Park, 2010: 25). Ullman (2012) similarly explores neoliberal discourses of responsibilization emerging in the narratives of Mexican migrants living in the Southwestern United States. The ideologies to which they oriented include 'personal responsibility to educate [themselves] in English' (Ullman, 2012: 461), the view that 'speaking English everywhere' is normal and desirable (Ullman, 2012: 462), and an acceptance that one 'must learn English in order to succeed' (Ullman, 2012: 464). This is performativity par excellence. Such 'neoliberal personhood' (Park, 2010: 25) is a discursive construction, but it is performatively materialized in an active recognition by Self and Others as objectively real.

Taking a feminist poststructuralist perspective to discourse and subjectivity, Davies (1991: 51) sees agency as, in part, 'the discursive constitution of that person as author of their own multiple meanings and desires (though only to the extent that they have taken on as their own the discursive practices and the attendant *moral commitments of the collective(s) of which they are members)*' (italics added). What Davies (1991) foregrounds and what Ullman (2012) and Park (2010) implicitly point to is the performative constitution of agency and responsibility. That is, when we perform our investment in socially constituted 'moral commitments' (Davies, 1991: 51), we (co)construct ourselves as agentive, responsible individuals. One becomes *recognizable* as an actor or agent when one acts as one, actions made possible 'precisely to the extent that [one] is constituted as an actor' (Butler, 1997: 16).

Conclusion

The immigrant interviewees in this study performatively constituted themselves as, and were positioned as, responsible and thus moral individuals. They effected this, in part, through claiming and demonstrating that they have pursued the learning of English, often at great sacrifice, while living in the United States. They were constituted as individuals who 'naturally' chose to do this by me, the interviewer, as I asked them questions related to *when* and *how* they learned English. Such interview practices were used even though I align with theories of language learning that frame such learning as mediated and as distributed. There are many 'ideologies of language learning' in circulation that have been discussed by scholars, such as the acquisition versus the participation metaphors for conceptualizing language learning (Pavlenko & Lantolf, 2000) or the belief that the younger one is, the easier the language learning process is and the more successful the outcomes (Razfar, 2012).

Though they did not use the phrase 'ideologies of language learning', Firth and Wagner (1997, 2007) argued strongly against prevailing views that treat language learners as individuals who experience in-the-brain learning rather than socially situated individuals who experience language learning in interaction. And numerous second language scholars have advocated an orientation to the social, distributed and mediated activity of language learning over the past two decades (see Zuengler & Miller, 2006, for a review). Given this approach to second/additional language learning, it seems, in retrospect, inappropriate for me to have constructed interview questions that presuppose that interviewees have managed to learn languages on their *individual* powers. Perhaps what researchers, including myself, need to figure out are ways to position and address individuals as always mediated, and to frame agency and action as always emergent from discursive practice, rather than to reissue language constructs that perpetuate 'common sense' ideologies of language learning as individual endeavor, of agency as essentially individual and of individual responsibility for learning languages as inevitable.

8   Conclusion

A Researcher's Account

This book presents an account of how I have made sense of slippery and broad-scale theoretical concepts such as *agency, ideology* and *discursive practice* by exploring concrete moments of language production and performance in interviews with a small group of adult immigrants to the United States. In creating an integrated explanatory discussion, I engage in what Briggs (2007) would deem an ideological act in the practice of knowledge-making. The practice of scholarly research and publication is comprised of multiple 'knowledge practices' (Briggs, 2007: 574); the ideological aspect of research, according to Briggs, emerges as scholars create a text that construes these multiple research actions as inevitably and naturally coherent and that positions research 'findings' as the inevitable and natural outcome of these various actions. Briggs contends that researchers, in fact, engage in discursive *transformation* as they collect interviewees' 'individual expressions', fit them into 'collective portraits', and then, transport them into 'professional texts and contexts', thereby taking 'a complex array of practices stretching over multiple times and places [to form] a single coherent, integrated package' (Briggs, 2007: 558). This is productive and constitutive work rather than a discovery mission. Briggs does not suggest that this is somehow devious or unprofessional labor. There do not appear to be desirable alternatives at present for how to engage in such knowledge-making practices. What he does advocate is for researchers to acknowledge their research practices as ideological and to show, as clearly as possible, how the 'integrated package' was constructed.

Overview of Linguistic Constructs Produced by Interviewees

The analysis chapters in this book focused on three types of linguistic constructs that interviewees produced as they talked about how they learned

English, their use and ongoing learning of English at their workplaces, and their use and learning of non-English languages in these business spaces. Chapter 4 examined how interviewees positioned themselves as agents or non-agents in the subject-predicate configurations produced when addressing these topics. Chapter 5 analyzed how interviewees produced evaluative stances in relation to their capacity to learn and use English and other languages. Chapter 6 focused on their use of reported speech utterances by which they were able to supply discursive evidence for the legitimacy of their claims to have acted responsibly and agentively to learn English, and to use English and/or other languages competently. In this overview section, I would like to consider how these separate analytic foci, when compared, point to overlapping discursive effects as well as nuanced distinctions that contribute to a more complex understanding of how the *hows* intersected with the *whats* of interview talk.

In my analysis of subject-predicate constructs in Chapter 4, I found that all interviewees exhibited a greater tendency to construct themselves as agentive when addressing each of the focal interview topics. When speaking about their efforts to learn English soon after arriving in the United States, a greater percentage of their subject-predicate utterances positioned them as obligated to act, compared with their utterances addressing their use and continued learning of English at work, and their use and learning of non-English languages at work. By constructing their story-world Selves as agentive relatively more frequently, and also as responsive to the perceived obligation and/or need to learn English after arriving in the United States, interviewees were able to co-construct themselves as responsible individuals. Both they, and I as the interviewer, treated their account-giving regarding their effortful actions to learn English as normal and appropriate discursive actions for the interview context. When Hannah reported that she 'picked' an American friend who also knew Chinese to be her English teacher, or when Kay indicated that she attended a community college after she realized that she needed to 'practice more and more' English, they created mundane performances of their story-world Selves acting deliberately and effortfully and exercising agency.

Of course, the interviewees also displayed variability in how they positioned themselves in their narrative accounts. That is, they also positioned themselves as benefactors of Others' actions and thus as non-agentive. Their greater likelihood to perform agentive positioning is thus also more telling, suggesting an orientation to the normativity of this positioning, perhaps 'seeded' through the way my questions positioned them as agents of learning. It also points to our jointly produced orientation to ideologies of responsibility for learning English (as self-evidently assigned to immigrants to the

United States who do not know English) and ideologies of agency (as self-evidently located *in* individuals). In these mundane encounters in which I address interviewees as 'you' and they speak of themselves as an 'I' who acts in particular ways, we reify ourselves as separate individuals. These linguistic choices are not optional. We must work within the constraints of English linguistic constructs, including the ordering of personal pronouns, to speak intelligibly. However, as Butler (2005: 132) would argue, such commonsensical and necessary ways of 'recognizing' ourselves and others make opaque the ways the 'acting, telling and showing' Self, performed as an 'I' emerges from 'a crucible of social relations'.

The seeming preference for an agentive characterization of interviewees' language-learner Selves, performed through their subject-predicate constructs, is supported in their use of reported speech utterances. Reported speech utterances are multi-functional, but one of their discursive effects is that they appear to provide evidence of 'actual' interactive events that occurred at another time and place (Tannen, 1995). For example, when Hannah performed the reported speech utterances *'You got the choice of that and that'*, which she allegedly directed to customers at her catering business, she provided an example utterance that is appropriate to the context being described, thus lending evidential credibility of what actually transpired, of what she actually said. Interviewees produced comparatively more reported speech utterances in which they were constructed as the author and principal, and by far the greatest percentage of these utterances, such as Hannah's utterance above, positioned them as agentive. Even when they produced reported speech utterances that highlighted their limitations in English, some interviewees still constructed them as demonstrations of agentive actions to learn English, such as Kay's performance of what she directs her nail salon clients to do: *'something I say, if you think it not right, you please correct me'*. As such, the performance of many of their reported speech utterances and the greater likelihood for interviewees to position their story-world Selves as agentive in their subject-predicate constructs have overlapping and reinforcing language effects.

Even so, in my analysis of their production of evaluative stance toward their capacity to learn English, I showed that the majority of the interviewees consistently produced negative evaluations. Many of them disparaged their language proficiency as still limited and problematic. These negative stance acts were typically embedded in accounts that also highlighted constraints to their capacity to learn English well. In this way, their discursive acts of evaluation worked in tandem with accounts that supplied rationales for their imperfect learning of the language. In describing constraints to learning as owing to external factors, such as the inherent difficulties in the language, work responsibilities or family needs, they construct the terrain in which agentive action is curtailed. Interestingly, descriptions of constraints simultaneously provided a context for interviewees to demonstrate their agentive efforts. As noted in Chapter 2, one's socially constituted agency is ongoingly enabled or constrained in relation to the 'cultural, discursive, and political forces' that 'pattern[] the grounds for what [is] possible' in one's life (Desjarlais, 1997: 246). By supplying evidence of trying hard and of desiring to learn English until they encountered socially legitimated constraints to action, interviewees produced 'theories of agency' of themselves acting as responsible, agentive individuals. While their negative stance acts positioned them in the local interview interaction as 'appropriately' modest in making claims about their English learning achievements, they also constructed the interviewees as aware of the social valuation placed on learning 'good' English. I believe that producing such negative evaluations in relation to their English learning achievements helps to re-sediment an 'ideology of competence' (Park, 2010: 22) in which something akin to native-speaker-like competence serves as the comparative standard for determinations of good versus poor English proficiency. By implicitly orienting to this ambiguous standard, interviewees displayed their sensitivity to the need for *them* to act to meet this goal, and their recognition that when their individual actions have not been sufficient for meeting this standard, however ill-defined, the outcomes can be legitimately critiqued.

Interviewees' acute sensitivity to the normative place of English in the United States, to their own responsibility to learn the language well and to use it in their workplace transactions, was further demonstrated when several of them performed reported speech utterances to dramatize what English-speaking Americans have allegedly said to them in reaction to their use of non-English languages in their work spaces or to evaluate interviewees' English competence. For example, Lan performed a dramatic re-enactment of the alleged words of one of her hair salon clients, *'you need to speak English'*, in reaction to her use of Vietnamese with one of her Vietnamese-speaking employees. Donna enacted how employees at the Department of Motor Vehicles told her *'you need to go learn some more English'* after she failed her written exam for her driver's license. Kay, on the other hand, performed compliments she received from her nail salon clients: *'Your English really well. You speak English good'*, which, in their positive orientation, still construct a differential responsibility for who must make the effort to achieve sufficient communicative competence for the settings in which 'native speakers' and 'immigrant non-native speakers' operate.

While the general propensity among interviewees toward agentive positioning emerged as I analyzed linguistic constructs across the interview corpus, I could also see how a different kind of agentive Self was performed in interviewees' accounts when I undertook a micro-analytic approach. This different type of agency was construed as less effortful, as more contingent, distributed and responsive. It was performed in their production of subject-predicate utterances in which they described unplanned occasions in which they agentively managed their limitations in English 'on the fly' as they interacted with clients or employees. A subset of the interviewees also performed such an 'easy agency' when they described how they learned and used bits of the non-English languages spoken by their clients and/or employees. For example, Lan constructed such agentive actions as emerging unplanned and effortlessly when she simply asks her Spanish- and/or Arabic-speaking hair salon customers who 'sit [in her] chair' how to 'speak hello' or 'say come here' in their languages. She described such learning as 'they told me, so I remember', construing it as relatively effortless.

This easy agency was constructed simultaneously with more positive evaluative stances toward interviewees' capacity to learn and use English and other languages at work – this in contrast to their much greater tendency to produce negative evaluations of their capacity to learn English well outside of their workplace interactions. Even though they described occasions of miscommunication and interactional difficulty, nearly all of the interviewees performed positive evaluations of their ability to conduct their work-place interactions in English well enough. They further demonstrated the credibility of such positive evaluations through performing reported speech utterances that enacted their sufficiently competent workplace interactions. That is, by performing what they say to customers or to employees in carrying out their work, they produced examples, appropriate to the contexts, which supplied evidence that these positive evaluations are not empty *claims*. Interviewees constructed these interactional successes as matter-of-course occurrences, as desirable but not extraordinary.

Thus, in contrast to interviewees' characterizations of their effortful but also less successful actions to learn English, they characterized their use and ongoing learning of English in the situated contexts of their small businesses as less effortful but also as more successful. Here too, their agentive Selves pattern with the social and material terrain. In this context they seem to encounter fewer constraints to their capacity to use and learn English and more mediating affordances. Given the interactional affordances of their work spaces, which, in some cases, include multilingual interlocutors as well as interviewees' authority to control, to some degree, how such workplace interactions develop, it seems their performed 'theories of agency' orient to a different kind of language regime. Rather than orienting to an ambiguous native-speaker-like standard in evaluating their English, they seemed to orient to local valuations of good-enough English. In orienting to a locally constituted language regime, their language expertise is evaluated more positively. But also it is treated as more trivial. The production of mitigative qualifiers, such as 'just' as in Lan's description of 'just some small bit' to characterize her learning of Arabic and Spanish from her customers, positions her actions as relatively inconsequential.

But why should these interviewees tend to downgrade the significance of their interactional successes in their workplaces? Perhaps it develops in response to the ideological valuation that is assigned to particular kinds of agentive acts when it comes to language learning and use. Blommaert and his colleagues' notions of 'regimes of language' helps us to conceptualize why 'truncated competence' is often evaluated differently, depending on which language one knows well, on who speaks to whom and on where the interaction occurs (Blommaert, 2010; Blommaert *et al.*, 2005a, 2005b). Likewise, Desjarlais (1997) views differential orientations to agentive actions as rooted in 'political exigencies' (Desjarlais, 1997: 246) and adds that our acts of 'reasoning, narrating and feeling are political through and through' (Desjarlais, 1997: 248). It seems that our evaluations of differential competence and the desirability of different language competences emerge out of ideological valuations, rather than objective measures of good or poor language usage (Park, 2010).

I believe that rather than pointing to a triumph of individual will, control and power as interviewees positioned their story-world Selves as agentive, relatively more frequently than as inagentive, they are in fact re-sedimenting normative perceptions of responsibilized individuals who are agentive in essence. This does not mean that these interviewees are determined by ideology. We see a vivid demonstration of this when Lan voices an alternative orientation to a taken-for-granted expectation that one can rightfully expect to use and hear (only) English in business spaces in the United States. However, her capacity to challenge this dominant ideology does not arise only from within herself or in an ideological vacuum. She can do so *in relation to* existing sense-making norms. Her actions to defend the use of Vietnamese in her hair salon with her employee performatively constitute those actions as a challenge to the dominant social norm because that social norm is part of their meaning, or part of their semiotic 'apparatus' as Otsuji and Pennycook might say (2010: 244). While resistant stances such as that demonstrated by Lan are more easily understood to enact discursive agency, the far more mundane and compliant stances performed by all the interviewees also need to be understood as instances of performativity. Lu and Horner (2013: 31) contend that if we view discursive patterns and regularities as an 'achievement of recontextualization or re-forming' of language, then we can recognize that even the most 'clichéd' and 'conventional' language usages are products of agentive discursive work.

In the language analysis chapters just reviewed, I selected particular language constructs for close scrutiny and then compared their meaning-making 'effects' across the interview corpus. This effort was an attempt to take up Butler's challenge to 'call into question ordinary language and the ways in which we structure the world on its basis' (in Olson & Worsham, 2000: 732). She suggests that if one is ever to understand the effects of ordinary language on how we make sense of ourselves and others, then we need to 'see the ways in which grammar is both *producing* and *constraining* our sense of what the world is' (in Olson & Worsham, 2000: 732–733, italics added). Clearly we cannot and do not order words in any fashion we like if we want to be understood and recognized as a legitimate interlocutor, but such limits are also the springboard for discursive action, for making meaning and for creating new meanings.

When one produces an account of oneself, then one must generally use the indexical 'I' in some way, one must position that 'I' somewhere within a subject-predicate construct, and given the limited options for how that 'I' can be positioned, one effects a particular kind of performance in relation to that constructed story-world Self. Such 'obligatory' positioning is rarely contemplated carefully and is typically 'inaccessible to the average speaker's consciousness', but the reiteration of such under-the-radar language forms can 'play a key role in structuring cognitive categories and social fields by constraining the onotology that is taken for granted by speakers' (Hill & Mannheim, 1992: 387). It is true that individuals, such as adult language learners who still struggle to produce 'grammatical' constructs, often need to think about and 'plan' what they say, to some extent, in order to produce utterances that make 'sense' in relation to patterned forms of discourse. Working with and within the obligatory constraints of English allowed them to create a degree of mutual understanding with me as interviewer. However, even though they were likely somewhat conscious of desiring to create a positive impression within the interview context, they – like most interlocutors – undoubtedly produced particular subject-predicate configurations, enacted evaluative stances and performed reported speech utterances without extensive forethought as to how they were constructing their story-world Selves.

Awareness of how we 'structure the world' through 'ordinary language' (Butler in Olson & Worsham, 2000: 728) depends on retrospective analysis of how meanings are mobilized in discursive practices. Interviewees' accounts ought not be treated as objective reports of what really happened, though the reported events often do have a basis in actual events. These accounts provide a means by which I could explore how interviewees constructed 'theories of agency' that they deemed appropriate to the context of speaking. I treat the agency configurations in these accounts as performatively re-sedimenting and sometimes challenging common-sense ways of knowing and acting in the world.

Implications of Treating Agency as Socially Mediated

This book evolved out of an attempt to arrive at a better understanding of agency and second language learning. Drawing on the research and insightful proposals elaborated by many scholars, representing diverse disciplinary traditions, I have come to understand that agency – when reified as a namable social entity – is a socially mediated construction. It is not something that one can locate; one does not necessarily even 'know it when you see it'. It is a concept that has been generated to identify an ambiguous, socially generated and maintained capacity by which individuals perceive themselves to be able to act in meaningful ways. This sensibility that one has the capacity to act toward desired ends emerges in relationship with Others and in relation to (i.e. patterned with) the world around us, both in the present and through the accumulation of such relationships over time. The perception that one has of one's agentive capacity to learn a second or additional language clearly differs across individuals, and some individuals, such as a number of the interviewees cited in this book, need to contend with difficult material constraints that prevent them from engaging in language learning practices, even when they value such practices and perceive themselves as responsible to and capable of learning English. Though social and material constraints often prevent individuals from pursuing particular actions, the agency of individuals as potential language learners depends most profoundly on their being 'recognized' and 'recognizing' (Butler, 1997) themselves as particular kinds of social entities.

But where does this performatively constituted recognition come from? How do we know ourselves to be agentive in relation to taking actions such as learning a language? I would argue that such recognition or social sensibility develops out of one's participation in discursive practices. It is in such jointly constituted meaning-making activity that we come to see ourselves *as individuals* who bear particular kinds of responsibilities. It is in such participation, over time and in multiple discursive practices, whether by choice or through imposed participation or through everyday socialization, that we develop differential understandings regarding the kinds of agentive acts we are able to and responsible to engage in. Indeed, for some immigrants living in 'ethnic enclaves' in the United States, who interact almost entirely with others who share their native non-English languages in their work, family and cultural life, it is likely that they will develop little or perhaps no sense of a responsibility to learn English. In fact, many of these individuals find it more desirable and more economically advantageous to maintain their cultural and linguistic identities and to police intrusions from outsiders into their enclaves (Zhou, 2005).

However, immigrants living in more heterogeneous communities, such as the interviewees in this study, typically find it essential to learn at least some English. In order to be 'recognized' as agentive, one must be both inter-pellated as or assigned a socially recognized identity, and one must also respond in some way to that designation. As such, an immigrant language learner's capacity to act arises out of a nexus of social, cultural, political and ideological affordances, expectations and responsibilities. Such 'discursive agency', i.e. agency that is performatively constituted in discursive practice, does not exist as a latent entity and then get dusted off and brought into the light of day at the moments when individuals exercise it. Agency is a compo-nent of discursive practice and exists *in* practice rather than *in* bounded indi-viduals (Reckwitz, 2002). We know and see and do things in the world because they have been made recognizable and enactable through discursive, semiotically mediated practices. Agentive action can also be curtailed in the nexus of mediating factors that comprise the social terrain.

To trace the lineage of language learners' discursively constituted agen-tive capacities that develop out of incredibly complex affordances and con-straints, with clarity and certainty, is impossible. However, we can explore how such individuals construct their 'theories of agency' in concrete moments in time, recognizing that such moments, in themselves, do not performatively mobilize agentive Selves. Rather, they are points of re-enact-ment or sedimentation of myriad and intersecting discursive practices that are ongoingly reaffirmed, legitimated and sometimes transformed through such local performances. Gunn and Cloud (2010: 75) contend that agency is probably only 'definitively sensible in retrospect'. I make no claims to provid-ing a definitive discussion of how the interviewees in this study performed their 'theories of agency', but I do believe we can gain some understanding of how they were rendered 'sensible' in the mundane interview interactions by analyzing them retrospectively to see *how* they said *what* they did, in order to begin to understand how (non)responsible, (in)agentic language learning and language using story-world Selves are mobilized in such talk.

Just as sociocultural theories of language and learning have helped us come to understand that processes of language learning develop in relation-ship with others, rather than enclosed in an individual brain, so too learners' agentive capacity should be understood to develop in relationship with others and with the world. For this reason, I caution researchers and language teachers to avoid the too-simple equation of *agent* with *human individual*. We

as researchers and language teachers also need to take care in how we construe causation. Though events and experiences in our histories and in our
immediate surroundings clearly do bear on how we see ourselves as agentive
or not, most of our complex social histories remain beyond our conscious
awareness. Creating causal links between our experiences and our ensuing
actions will undoubtedly always be partial explanations. That does not
mean we should not try to understand such links or avoid seeking to create
experiences and opportunities within discursive practices that we think
could enable agentive actions to emerge. However, I would argue that viewing agency for language learning as socially mediated does lead us to a greater
understanding of our limitations. Language teachers, though often strongly
consequential to the language learning process, are but one factor in these
relational constructs. Mercer (2012: 56) suggests that when language teachers understand 'that not one single intervention may affect learner agency',
they can then 'work at creating momentum by attending to a range of
dimensions and components in the agentic system such as creating a range
of conditions and learning environments (in and out of class) designed to
enhance and facilitate learner agency'. This is a tall order for any teacher.
Importantly, however, it positions teachers (and researchers) within the constraints and enablements of 'learning environments' along with language
learners. Teachers enter into complex, dialogically achieved social relationships in interacting with students and such relationships are constituted,
made possible as it were, on the basis of foreclosures as well.

Feminist poststructuralist scholars in the 1990s warned against bestow-
ing too much authority and responsibility onto teachers for empowering students (Ellsworth, 1992; Gore, 1992), worrying that doing so would lead to
individual hubris, or, more likely, to despair when the individual teacher is
unable to effect empowerment among his or her students. So too, we need to
be cautious in how we assign responsibility to teachers for enabling agency
among language learners in a classroom. At the same time, because of the
inevitable dialogic engagement with others that transpires in language classrooms, teachers do help shape the semiotic terrain on which language learners
can build their own capacities to mean, to understand and to act in a second/
additional language. Given the profound influence of our implicit, common
sense perceptions regarding how we learn, how we know and how we can
act, teachers may find it useful to have students make their beliefs and perceptions explicit through journaling or other reflective activities. Teachers can,
perhaps, ask students to consider their 'theories of agency' regarding language
learning and to discuss what they see as constraints and enablements to their
actions. Bringing implicit perceptions to the forefront may help to transform
some aspects of how students engage in learning practices. Butler contends

that 'though we are constituted socially ... through certain kinds of limitations, exclusions and foreclosures ... those limitations are not there as struc-
turally static features of myself. They are subject to renewal, and I perform
(mainly unconsciously or implicitly) that renewal in the repeated acts of my
person' (in Olson & Worsham, 2000: 739).

Even if defining agency is not something that can be decided once and for
all, such a relativist view does not mean that anything goes. Our perspectives
have consequences. It is difficult to wrest ourselves away from the 'weighty
inevitability of common knowledges' (Davies, 2000: 165), but seeing how
common sense is routinely performed might allow us to begin entertaining
other possibilities. Davies addresses this perspective eloquently:

> In abandoning the automatic connection between ways of speaking and
> essential self, and in heightening the awareness of the different discourses
> and relations of power at play and their effects, I find a different mor(t)
> ality. I am no longer tied down by questions as to whether my actions
> constitute one coherent package called the 'real me.' The emphasis shifts
> away from 'Is this how I would speak or act?' to 'If I speak or act this
> way, what emerges in that speaking or acting?' And as I watch/listen/
> smell/feel the emergent speaking or acting, I can see what is emerging
> not just as the effect of my acting or speaking in particular ways, but also
> as a new moment in which the context, the lived history of the partici-
> pants and their understanding of the present moment, will all be consti-
> tutive of my speech, my action. (Davies, 2000: 168)

Such a view does not construe agency as the mere waving of a magic
wand or view the performance of language as creating something out of
nothing. Rather, it treats discourse as the epistemological mechanism by
which we come to see and know (i.e. to recognize) what is treated as valued
and real. Discourse is not static language, but language in use in concert with
other semiotic and bodily activities. Performativity is not mere action, but a
way of understanding and constituting the world. Drawing on performativity theory can thus allow us to begin to understand how social realities, such
as learner agency, are made recognizable in discursive practice in the myriad
performances by which we re-sediment and reconstitute those realities.

Appendix

Transcription Conventions

Contiguous utterances

=	A single uninterrupted turn continues at the next ' = ' on the next line. If ' = ' is inserted at the end of one speaker's turn and at the beginning of the next speaker's turn, it indicates that there is no audible gap between the two turns.

Intervals within and between utterances

(1.3)	A number in parentheses indicates the duration in seconds of a pause in speech.
(...)	A brief pause, usually less than 0.2 seconds. More dots signal slightly longer pauses and fewer dots signal slightly shorter pauses.

Characteristics of speech delivery

transcript.	A period indicates falling pitch.
transcript?	A question mark indicates rising pitch, not necessarily a question.
transcript,	A comma indicates continuing intonation.
trans-	A hyphen indicates an abrupt cut-off of utterance.
transcri:::pt	One or more colons indicate lengthening of the preceding sound; each additional colon represents a lengthening by one beat.
transcript	Underlined type indicates marked stress.
°transcript°	The degree sign indicates the beginning and end points of a whisper or reduced volume speech.

| >transcript< | Arrow markers enclose faster speech. |
| ha ha | Laughter tokens |

Commentary in the transcript

(xx)	Indicates a stretch of talk that is unintelligible.
(transcript)	Single parentheses indicate speech that is unclear or in doubt in the transcript.
((laugher))	Double parentheses contain descriptions of non-verbal actions.
transcript	Italic type marks reported speech utterances.

References

Ahearn, L.M. (2001) Language and agency. *Annual Review of Anthropology* 30, 109–137.

Ahearn, L.M. (2010) Agency and language. In J. Jasper, J. Vershueren and J. Östman (eds) *Society and Language Use* (pp. 28–48). Amsterdam: John Benjamins Publishing.

Altheide, D.L. (2008) The evidentiary narrative: Notes toward a symbolic interactionist perspective about evidence. In N.K. Denzin and M.D. Giardina (eds) *Qualitative Inquiry and the Politics of Evidence* (pp. 137–162). Walnut Creek, CA: Left Coast Press.

Arundale, R.B. (2010) Constituting face in conversation: Face, facework, and interactional achievement. *Journal of Pragmatics* 42 (8), 2078–2105.

Atkinson, P. and Coffey, A. (2001) Revisiting the relationship between participant observation and interviewing. In J.F. Gubrium and J.A. Holstein (eds) *Handbook of Interview Research* (pp. 801–814). Thousand Oaks, CA: SAGE Publications.

Bakhtin, M.M. (1981) *The Dialogic Imagination: Four Essays by M.M. Bakhtin.* (M. Holquist, ed.; C. Emerson and M. Holquist, trans.). Austin, TX: University of Texas Press.

Bakhtin, M.M. (1984) *Problems of Dostoyevsky's Poetics.* (Caryl Emerson, ed. and trans.). Minneapolis: University of Minnesota Press.

Bakhtin, M.M. (1986) *Speech Genres and Other Essays.* (M. Holquist and C. Emerson, eds; V. McGee, trans.). Austin TX: University of Texas Press.

Banfield, A. (1993) Where epistemology, style, and grammar meet literary history: The development of represented speech and thought. In J.A. Lucy (ed.) *Reflexive Language: Reported Speech and Metapragmatics* (pp. 339–363). Cambridge: Cambridge University Press.

Barad, K. (2003) Posthumanist performativity: Toward an understanding of how matter comes to matter. *Signs* 8 (3), 801–831.

Barker, C. and Galasinski, D. (2001) *Cultural Studies and Discourse Analysis: A Dialogue on Language and Identity.* Thousand Oaks, CA: SAGE Publications.

Baszanger, I. and Dodier, N. (2004) Ethnography: Relating the part to the whole. In D. Silverman (ed.) *Qualitative Research: Theory, Method and Practice* (pp. 9–34). Thousand Oaks, CA: SAGE Publications.

Baynham, M. (2006) Agency and contingency in the language learning of refugees and asylum seekers. *Linguistics and Education* 17 (1), 24–39.

Baynham, M. (2011) Stance, positioning and alignment in narratives of professional experience. *Language in Society* 40 (1), 63–74.

Bell, J.S. (2002) Narrative inquiry: More than just telling stories. *TESOL Quarterly* 36 (2), 207–213.

Biber, D. and Finegan, E. (1989) Styles of stance in English: Lexical and grammatical marking of evidentiality and affect. *Text-Interdisciplinary Journal for the Study of Discourse* 9 (1), 93–124.

Billig, M. (1995) *Banal Nationalism*. Thousand Oaks, CA: SAGE Publications.

Block, D. (2009) Identity in applied linguistics: The need for conceptual exploration. In V. Cook (ed.) *Contemporary Applied Linguistics: Volume 1 Language Teaching and Learning* (pp. 215–232). London: Continuum.

Block, D. (2010) Unpicking agency in sociolinguistic research with migrants. In M. Martin-Jones and S. Gardner (eds) *Multilingualism, Discourse and Ethnography*. New York: Routledge.

Block, D. (2013) The structure and agency dilemma in identity and intercultural communication research. *Language and Intercultural Communication* 13 (2), 126–147.

Blommaert, J. (ed.) (1999) *Language-Ideological Debates*. Berlin: Walter de Gruyter.

Blommaert, J. (2005) *Discourse: A Critical Introduction*. Cambridge: Cambridge University Press.

Blommaert, J. (2010) *The Sociolinguistics of Globalization*. Cambridge: Cambridge University Press.

Blommaert, J., Collins, J. and Slembrouck, S. (2005a) Spaces of multilingualism. *Language and Communication* 25 (3), 197–216.

Blommaert, J., Collins, J. and Slembrouck, S. (2005b) Polycentricity and interactional regimes in 'global neighborhoods'. *Ethnography* 6 (2), 205–235.

Blommaert, J., Creve, L. and Willaert. E. (2006) On being declared illiterate: Language-ideological disqualification in Dutch classes for immigrants in Belgium. *Language and Communication* 26 (1), 34–54.

Bourdieu, P. (1977a) *Outline of a Theory of Practice* (R. Nice, trans.). Cambridge: Cambridge University Press.

Bourdieu, P. (1977b) The economics of linguistic exchange. *Social Science Information* 16 (6), 645–668.

Bourdieu, P. (1990) *The Logic of Practice*. Stanford, CA: Stanford University Press.

Bourdieu, P. (1991) *Language and Symbolic Power: The Economy of Linguistic Exchanges*. Cambridge, MA: Harvard University Press.

Bourdieu, P. (2000) *Pascalian Meditations*. Stanford, CA: Stanford University Press.

Bourne, J. (2001) Doing 'What comes naturally': How the discourses and routines of teachers' practice constrain opportunities for bilingual support in UK primary schools. *Language and Education* 15 (4), 250–268.

Briggs, C.L. (1986) *Learning How to Ask: A Sociolinguistic Appraisal of the Role of the Interview in Social Science Research*. Cambridge: Cambridge University Press.

Briggs, C.L. (2007) Anthropology, interviewing, and communicability in contemporary society. *Current Anthropology* 48 (4), 551–580.

Bucholtz, M. and Hall, K. (2005) Identity and interaction: A sociocultural linguistic approach. *Discourse Studies* 7 (4–5), 585–614.

Busch, B. (2012) The linguistic repertoire revisited. *Applied Linguistics* 33 (5), 503–523.

Butler, J. (1990) *Gender Trouble: Feminism and the Subversion of Identity*. New York: Routledge.

Butler, J. (1993) *Bodies that Matter: On the Discursive Limits of 'Sex'*. New York: Routledge.

Butler, J. (1997) *Excitable Speech: A Politics of the Performative*. New York: Routledge.

Butler, J. (2005) *Giving an Account of Oneself*. New York: Fordham University Press.

Butler, J. (2009) Performativity, precarity and sexual politics. *AIBR Revista de Antropologia Iberoamericana* 4 (3), i–xiii.

Butler, J. (2010) Performative agency. *Journal of Cultural Economy* 3 (2), 147–161.

Bybee, J.L. and Hopper, P.J. (eds) (2001) *Frequency and the Emergence of Linguistic Structure*. Amsterdam: John Benjamins Publishing.

Bybee, J., Perkins, R. and Pagliuca, W. (1994) *The Evolution of Grammar: Tense, Aspect, and Modality in the Languages of the World*. Chicago: University of Chicago Press.

Canagarajah, A.S. (1996) From critical research practice to critical research reporting. *TESOL Quarterly* 30 (2), 321–330.

Canagarajah, A.S. (2007) Lingua Franca English, Multilingual Communities, and Language Acquisition. *The Modern Language Journal* 91 (s1), 923–939.

Canagarajah, A.S. (2013) *Translingual Practice: Global Englishes and Cosmopolitan Relations*. New York: Routledge.

Capps, L. and Ochs, E. (1995) *Constructing Panic: The Discourse of Agoraphobia*. Cambridge, MA: Harvard University Press.

Cassaniti, J. (2012) Agency and the other: The role of agency for the importance of belief in Buddhist and Christian traditions. *Ethos* 40 (3), 297–316.

Chafe, W. and Nichols, J. (1986) *Evidentiality: The Linguistic Coding of Epistemology in Language*. Norwood, NJ: Ablex.

Cicourel, A.V. (1964) *Method and Measurement in Sociology*. New York: Free Press of Glencoe.

Cicourel, A.V. (1974) *Language Use and School Performance*. New York: Academic Press.

Clark, H.H. and Gerrig, R.J. (1990) Quotations as demonstrations. *Language* 66 (4), 764–805.

Clark, K. and Holquist, M. (1984) *Mikhail Bakhtin*. Cambridge, MA: The Belknap Press of Harvard University Press.

Clifford, J. (1986) Introduction: Partial truths. In J. Clifford and G.E. Marcus (eds) *Writing Culture: The Poetics and Politics of Ethnography* (pp. 1–26). Berkeley and Los Angeles: University of California Press.

Clift, R. (2007) Getting there first: Non-narrative reported speech in interaction. In E. Holt and R. Clift (eds) *Reporting Talk: Reported Speech in Interaction* (pp. 120–149). Cambridge: Cambridge University Press.

Clift, R. and Holt, E. (2007) Introduction. In E. Holt and R. Clift (eds) *Reporting Talk: Reported Speech in Interaction* (pp. 1–15). Cambridge: Cambridge University Press

Cook, H.M. (2011) Language socialization and stance-taking practices. In A. Duranti, E. Ochs and B.B. Schieffelin (eds) *The Handbook of Language Socialization* (pp. 315–339). Malden, MA: Blackwell Publishing.

Cornwall, A. (2007) Taking chances, making choices: The tactical dimensions of 'reproductive strategies' in southwestern Nigeria. *Medical Anthropology* 26 (3), 229–254.

Cortazzi, M. and Jin, L. (2000) Evaluating evaluation in narrative. In S. Hunston and G. Thompson (eds) *Evaluation in Text: Authorial Stance and the Construction of Discourse* (pp. 102–120). Oxford: Oxford University Press.

Couper-Kuhlen, E. (2007) Assessing and accounting. In E. Holt and R. Clift (eds) *Reporting Talk: Reported Speech in Interaction* (pp. 81–119). Cambridge: Cambridge University Press.

Crawford, J. (1992) What's behind Official English? In J. Crawford (ed.) *Language Loyalties: A Source Book on the Official English Controversy* (pp. 171–177). Chicago, IL: University of Chicago Press.

Cudworth, E. and Hobden, S. (2013) Of parts and wholes: International relations beyond the human. *Millennium: Journal of International Studies* 41 (3), 430–450.

Damari, R.R. (2010) Intertextual stancetaking and the local negotiation of cultural identities by a binational couple. *Journal of Sociolinguistics* 14 (5), 609–629.

DaSilva Iddings, A.C. and Katz, L. (2007) Integrating home and school identities of recent-immigrant Hispanic English language learners through classroom practices. *Journal of Language, Identity, and Education* 6 (4), 299–314.

Davies, B. (1990) Agency as a form of discursive practice: A classroom scene observed. *British Journal of Sociology of Education* 11 (3), 341–361.

Davies, B. (1991) The concept of agency: A feminist poststructuralist analysis. *Social Analysis* 30, 42–53.

Davies, B. (2000) *A Body of Writing, 1990–1999*. Walnut Creek, CA: AltaMira Press.

Deetz, S. (1994) The new politics of the workplace: Ideology and other unobtrusive controls. In M. Billig and H.W. Simons (eds) *After Postmodernism: Reconstructing Ideology Critique* (pp. 172–199). Thousand Oaks, CA: SAGE Publishing.

De Fina, A. (2003) *Identity in Narrative: A Study of Immigrant Discourse*. Philadelphia: John Benjamins Publishing.

De Fina, A. (2009) Narratives in interview—the case of accounts: For an interactional approach to narrative genre. *Narrative Inquiry* 19 (2), 233–258.

De Fina, A. and Georgakopoulou, A. (2008) Analysing narratives as practices. *Qualitative Research* 8 (3), 379–387.

De Fina, A. and Georgakopoulou, A. (2012) *Analyzing Narrative: Discourse and Sociolinguistic Perspectives*. Cambridge: Cambridge University Press.

De Silveira, C. and Habermas, T. (2011) Narrative means to manage responsibility in life narratives across adolescence. *The Journal of Genetic Psychology* 172 (1), 1–20.

Desjarlais, R. (1997) *Shelter Blues: Sanity and Selfhood among the Homeless*. Philadelphia, PA: University of Pennsylvania Press.

Deters, P. (2011) *Identity, Agency and the Acquisition of Professional Language and Culture*. London: Continuum.

Dixon, J. and Durrheim, K. (2000) Displacing place-identity: A discursive approach to locating self and other. *British Journal of Social Psychology* 39 (1), 27–44.

Doerr, N.M. (ed.) (2009) *The Native Speaker Concept: Ethnographic Investigations of Native Speaker Effects*. Berlin: De Gruyter Mouton.

Donzelli, A. (2010) Is ergativity always a marker of agency? Toraja and Samoan grammar of action and the contribution of emancipatory pragmatics to social theory. *Applied Linguistics Review* 1, 193–220.

Du Bois, J.W. (1980) Beyond definiteness: The trace of identity in discourse. In W. Chafe (ed.) *The Pear Stories: Cognitive, Cultural, and Linguistic Aspects of Narrative Production* (pp. 203–274). Norwood, NJ: Ablex.

Du Bois, J.W. (1987) The discourse basis of ergativity. *Language* 63 (4), 805–855.

Du Bois, J.W. (2003) Discourse and grammar. In M. Tomasello (ed.) *The New Psychology of Language: Cognitive and Functional Approaches To Language Structure*, Volume 2 (pp. 47–88). Mahwah, NJ: Lawrence Erlbaum.

Du Bois, J.W. (2007) The stance triangle. In R. Englebretson (ed.) *Stancetaking in Discourse: Subjectivity, Evaluation, Interaction* (pp. 139–182). Amsterdam: John Benjamins Publishing.

Du Bois, J.W. (2011) Co-opting intersubjectivity: Dialogic rhetoric of the self. In C. Meyer and F. Girke (eds) *The Rhetorical Emergence of Culture* (pp. 52–84). New York: Berghahn Books.

Duff, P. (2012) Issues of identity. In A. Mackay and S. Gass (eds) *The Routledge Handbook of Second Language Acquisition* (pp. 410–426). New York: Routledge.

Duranti, A. (2001) Performance and encoding of agency in historical-natural languages. *Proceedings from the Ninth Annual Symposium about Language and Society—Austin* 44, 266–287.

Duranti, A. (2006) Agency in language. In A. Duranti (ed.) *A Companion to Linguistic Anthropology*, 2nd edn (pp. 451–473). Oxford, UK: Blackwell Publishing Ltd.

Eagleton, T. (1991) *Ideology: An Introduction*. London: Verso.

Eggins, S. and Slade, D. (2004) *Analysing Casual Conversation*. Sheffield, UK: Equinox Publishing Ltd.

Ellsworth, E. (1992) Why doesn't this feel empowering? Working through the repressive myths of critical pedagogy. In C. Luke and J. Gore (eds) *Feminisms and Critical Pedagogy* (pp. 90–119). New York: Routledge.

Emirbayer, M. and Mische, A. (1998) What Is agency? *American Journal of Sociology* 103 (4), 962–1023.

Enfield, N.J. (2011) Sources of asymmetry in human interaction: Enchrony, status, knowledge and agency. In T. Stivers, L. Mondada and J. Steensig (eds) *The Morality of Knowledge in Conversation* (pp. 285–312). Cambridge: Cambridge University Press.

Englebretson, R. (2007) Stancetaking in discourse: An introduction. In R. Englebretson (ed.) *Stancetaking in Discourse: Subjectivity, Evaluation, Interaction* (pp. 1–25). Amsterdam: John Benjamins Publishing.

Feldman, G. (2005) Essential crises: A performative approach to migrants, minorities, and the European nation-state. *Anthropological Quarterly* 78 (1), 213–246.

Fillmore, C.J. (1968) The case for case. In E. Bach and E.T. Harms (eds) *Universals of Linguistic Theory* (pp. 1–88). New York: Holt.

Firth, A. and Wagner, J. (1997) On discourse, communication, and (some) fundamental concepts in SLA research. *The Modern Language Journal* 81 (3), 285–300.

Firth, A. and Wagner, J. (2007) Second/foreign language learning as a social accomplishment: Elaborations on a reconceptualized SLA. *The Modern Language Journal* 91 (Supplement 1), 800–819.

Foley, W. and Van Valin, R. (1984) *Functional Syntax and Universal Grammar*. Cambridge: Cambridge University Press.

Ford, C.E., Fox, B.A. and Thompson, S.A. (2003) Social interaction and grammar. In M. Tomasello (ed.) *The New Psychology of Language: Cognitive and Functional Approaches to Language Structure*, Volume 2 (pp. 119–43). Mahwah, NJ: Lawrence Erlbaum.

Foster, P. and Ohta, A. (2005) Negotiation for meaning and peer assistance in second language classrooms. *Applied Linguistics* 26 (3), 402–430.

Fox, B.A. and Thompson, S.A. (1990) A discourse explanation of the grammar of relative clauses in English conversation. *Language* 66 (2), 297–316.

Gao, X. (2010) *Strategic Language Learning: The Roles of Agency and Context*. Bristol: Multilingual Matters.

Gaonkar, D.P. (1997) The idea of rhetoric in the rhetoric of science. In A.G. Gross and W.M. Keith (eds) *Rhetorical Hermeneutics: Invention and Interpretation in the Age of Science* (pp. 25–85). Albany, NY: State University of New York Press.

Geisler, C. (2005) Teaching the post-modern rhetor continuing the conversation on rhetorical agency. *Rhetoric Society Quarterly* 35 (4), 107–113.

Gergen, K.L. (2009) *Relational Being: Beyond Self and Community*. Oxford: Oxford University Press.

Giddens, A. (1979) *Central Problems in Social Theory: Action, Structure and Contradiction in Social Analysis*. Berkeley, CA: University of California Press.

Givón, T. (1979) *On Understanding Grammar*. New York: Academic Press.

Givón, T. (ed.) (1983) *Topic Continuity in Discourse: A Quantitative Cross-language Study*. Amsterdam: John Benjamins Publishing.

Goffman, E. (1971) *Relations in Public: Microstudies of the Public Order*. New York: Harper and Row.

Goffman, E. (1974) *Frame Analysis: An Essay on the Organization of Experience*. York, PA: Northeastern University Press.

Goffman, E. (1981) *Forms of Talk*. Oxford: Blackwell Publishing.

Goodwin, C. (2011) Contextures of action. In J. Streeck, C. Goodwin and C. LeBaron (eds) *Embodied Interaction: Language and Body in the Material World* (pp. 182–193). Cambridge: Cambridge University Press.

Gore, J. (1992) What we can do for you! What *can* 'we' do for 'you'? In C. Luke and J. Gore (eds) *Feminisms and Critical Pedagogy* (pp. 54–73). New York: Routledge.

Grady, J. (2010) From Beveridge to Turner: Laissez-faire to neoliberalism. *Capital & Class* 34 (2), 163–180.

Grin, F. (2005) Linguistic human rights as a source of policy guidelines: A critical assessment. *Journal of Sociolinguistics* 9 (3), 448–460.

Gubrium, J.F. and Holstein, J.A. (2012) Theoretical validity and empirical utility of a constructionist analytics. *The Sociological Quarterly* 53 (3), 341–359.

Gumperz, J. (1982) *Discourse Strategies*. Cambridge: Cambridge University Press.

Gunn, J. and Cloud, D.L. (2010) Agentic orientation as magical voluntarism. *Communication Theory* 20 (1), 50–78.

Günthner, S. (1999) Polyphony and the 'layering of voices' in reported dialogues: An analysis of the use of prosodic devices in everyday reported speech. *Journal of Pragmatics* 31 (5), 685–708.

Günthner, S. (2000) Constructing scenic moments: Grammatical and rhetoric-stylistic devices for staging past events in everyday narratives. *Interaction and Linguistic Structures* InLiSt No. 22, 1–22.

Haakana, M. (2007) Reported thought in complaint stories. In E. Holt and R. Clift (eds) *Reporting Talk: Reported Speech in Interaction* (pp. 150–178). Cambridge: Cambridge University Press

Hak, T. (2003) Interviewer laughter as an unspecified request for clarification. In H. van den Berg, M. Wetherell and H. Houtkoop-Steenstra (eds) *Analyzing Race Talk: Multidisciplinary Perspectives on the Research Interview* (pp. 200–214). Cambridge: Cambridge University Press.

Hantzis, D.M. (1995) Reflections on 'A dialogue with friends': 'Performing' the 'Other/ Self'. In S.J. Dailey (ed.) *The Future of Performance Studies: Visions and Revisions* (pp. 203–206). Annandale, VA: National Communication Association.

Harissi, M., Otsuji, E. and Pennycook, A. (2012) The performative fixing and unfixing of subjectivities. *Applied Linguistics* 33 (5), 524–543.

Heritage, J. (1984) *Garfinkel and Ethnomethodology*. Cambridge: Polity Press.

Heritage, J. and Raymond, G. (2005) The terms of agreement: Indexing epistemic authority and subordination in talk-in-interaction. *Social Psychology Quarterly* 68 (1), 15–38.

Herndl, C.G. and Licona, A.C. (2007) Shifting agency: Agency, kairos, and the possibilities of social action. In M. Zachry and C. Thralls (eds) *Communicative Practices in Workplaces and the Professions: Cultural Perspectives on the Regulation of Discourse and Organizations* (pp. 133–154). Amityville, NY: Baywood Publishing.

Hill, J.H. and Mannheim, B. (1992) Language and world view. *Annual Review of Anthropology* 21 (1), 381–406.

Hill, J.H. and Zepeda, O. (1993) Mrs. Patricio's trouble: The distribution of responsibility in an account of personal experience. In J.H. Hill and J.T. Irvine (eds) *Responsibility and Evidence in Oral Discourse* (pp. 197–225). Cambridge: Cambridge University Press.

Hitlin, S. and Elder, G.H. (2007) Time, self, and the curiously abstract concept of agency. *Sociological Theory* 25 (2), 170–191.

Holland, D., Lachicotte Jr, W., Skinner, D. and Cain. C. (1998) *Identity and Agency in Cultural Worlds*. Cambridge, MA: Harvard University Press.

Holliday, A. (1996) Developing a sociological imagination: Expanding ethnography in international English language education. *Applied Linguistics* 17 (2), 234–255.

Holquist, M. (1993) Foreword. In M. Bakhtin *Toward a Philosophy of the Act*. (V. Liapunov and M. Holquist, eds; V. Liapunov, trans.). Austin, TX: University of Texas Press.

Holsanova, J. (2006) Quotations and social positioning. In H. Hausendorf and A. Bora (eds) *Analysing Citizenship Talk: Social Positioning in Political and Legal Decision-making Processes* (pp. 251–275). Philadelphia: John Benjamins Publishing.

Holstein, J.A. and Gubrium, J.F. (1995) *The Active Interview*. Thousand Oaks, CA: SAGE Publishing.

Holstein, J.A. and Gubrium, J.F. (2003) Inside interviewing: New lenses, new concerns. In J.A. Holstein and J.F. Gubrium (eds) *Inside Interviewing: New Lenses, New Concerns* (pp. 1–32). Thousand Oaks, CA: SAGE Publishing.

Holstein, J.A. and Gubrium, J.F. (2005) Interpretive practice and social action. In N.K. Denzin and Y.S. Lincoln (eds) *The SAGE Handbook of Qualitative Research*, 3rd edn (pp. 483–506). Thousand Oaks, CA: SAGE Publishing.

Holt, E. (1996) Reporting on talk: The use of direct reported speech in conversation. *Research on Language and Social Interaction* 29 (3), 425–454.

Holt, E. (2000) Reporting and reacting: Concurrent responses to reported speech. *Research on Language and Social Interaction* 33 (4), 219–245.

Holt, E. (2007) 'I'm eyeing your chop up mind': Reporting and enacting. In E. Holt and R. Clift (eds) *Reporting Talk: Reported Speech in Interaction* (pp. 47–80). Cambridge: Cambridge University Press.

Hopper, P.J. (1998) Emergent grammar. In M. Tomasello (ed.) *The New Psychology of Language: Cognitive and Functional Approaches to Language Structure*, Volume 1 (pp. 155–176). Mahwah, NJ: Lawrence Erlbaum.

Hopper, P.J. and Thompson, S.A. (1984) The discourse basis for lexical categories in universal grammar. *Language* 60 (4), 703–752.

Hunston, S. (2007) Using a corpus to investigate stance quantitatively and qualitatively. In R. Englebretson (ed.) *Stancetaking in Discourse: Subjectivity, Evaluation, Interaction* (pp. 27–48). Amsterdam: John Benjamins Publishing.

Hunston, S. and Thompson, G. (eds) (2000) *Evaluation in Text: Authorial Stance and the Construction of Discourse*. Oxford: Oxford University Press.

Jackendoff, R. (1990) *Semantic Structures*. Cambridge, MA: MIT Press.

Jaffe, A. (2009) *Stance: Sociolinguistic Perspectives*. Oxford: Oxford University Press.

Jefferson, G. (1984) Transcript notation. In J. Heritage and J.M. Atkinson (eds) *Structures of Social Action: Studies in Conversation Analysis* (pp. ix–xvi). Cambridge: Cambridge University Press.

Jespersen, O. (1965/1924) *The Philosophy of Grammar*. New York: W.W. Norton.

Johansen, M. (2011) Agency and responsibility in reported speech. *Journal of Pragmatics* 43 (11), 2845–2860.

Joseph, J.E. (2006) Applied linguistics and the choices people make (or do they?). *International Journal of Applied Linguistics* 16 (2), 237–241.

Kärkkäinen, E. (2006) Stance taking in conversation: From subjectivity to intersubjectivity. *Text and Talk: An Interdisciplinary Journal of Language, Discourse Communication Studies* 26 (6), 699–731.

Keltner, D., Van Kleef, G.A., Chen, S. and Kraus, M.W. (2008) A reciprocal influence model of social power: Emerging principles and lines of inquiry. *Advances in Experimental Social Psychology* 40, 151–192.

Kerbrat-Orecchioni, C. (2010) The case for an eclectic approach to discourse-in-interaction. In J. Streeck (ed.) *New Adventures in Language and Interaction* (pp. 71–98). Amsterdam: John Benjamins Publishing.

Kishner, J.M. and Gibbs, R.W. (1996) How 'just' gets its meanings: Polysemy and context in psychological semantics. *Language and Speech* 39 (1), 19–36.

Klewitz, G. and Couper-Kuhlen, E. (1999) Quote-unquote: The role of prosody in the contextualization of reported speech sequences. *Pragmatics* 9 (4), 459–485.

Kockelman, P. (2007) Agency. *Current Anthropology* 48 (3), 375–401.

Kramsch, C. (2008) Ecological perspectives on foreign language education. *Language Teaching* 41 (3), 389–408.

Kroskrity, P.V. (1998) Arizona Tewa Kiva speech as a manifestation of a dominant language ideology. In B.B. Scheiffelin, K.A. Woolard and P.V. Kroskrity (eds) *Language Ideologies: Practice and Theory* (pp. 103–122). Oxford: Oxford University Press.

Kroskrity, P.V. (2000) Regimenting languages: Language ideological perspectives. In S. Gal, J.H. Hill, R. Bauman and C. Briggs (eds) *Regimes of Language: Ideologies, Polities, and Identities* (pp. 1–34). Santa Fe, NM: School of American Research Press.

Kulick, D. (2003) No. *Language and Communication* 23 (2), 139–151.

Kvale, S. and Brinkmann, S. (2008) *Interviews: Learning the Craft of Qualitative Research Interviewing* (2nd edn). Thousand Oaks, CA: SAGE Publishing.

Labov, W. (1972) *Language in the Inner City*. Philadelphia, PA: University of Pennsylvania Press.

Laihonen, P. (2008) Language ideologies in interviews: A conversation analysis approach. *Journal of Sociolinguistics* 12 (5), 668–693.

Langellier, K.M. (1999). Personal narrative, performance, performativity: Two or three things I know for sure. *Text and Performance Quarterly* 19 (2), 125–144.

Lantolf, J.P. and Genung, P.B. (2002) 'I'd rather switch than fight': An activity-theoretic study of power, success, and failure in a foreign language. In C. Kramsch (ed.) *Language Acquisition and Language Socialization: Ecological Perspectives* (pp. 175–196). London: Continuum.

Lantolf, J.P. and Pavlenko, A. (2001) (S)econd (L)anguage (A)ctivity theory: Understanding second language learners as people. In M. Breen (ed.) *Learner Contributions to Language Learning. New Directions in Research* (pp. 141–158). London: Longman.

Lantolf, J. and Thorne, S.L. (2006) *Sociocultural Theory and the Genesis of Second Language Development*. Oxford: Oxford University Press.

Lave, J. and Wenger, E. (1991) *Situated Learning: Legitimate Peripheral Participation*. Cambridge: Cambridge University Press.

Lee, V. and Beattie, G. (2000) Why talking about negative emotional experiences is good for your health: A microanalytic perspective. *Semiotica* 130 (1/2), 1–81.

Lu, M. and Horner, B. (2013) Translingual literacy and matters of agency. In A.S. Canagarajah (ed.) *Literacy as Translingual Practice: Between Communities and Classrooms* (pp. 26–38). New York: Routledge.

Lucy, J. (ed.) (1993) *Reflexive language: Reported Speech and Metapragmatics*. Cambridge: Cambridge University Press.

Macaulay, R. (2001) You're like 'why not': The quotative expressions of Glasgow adolescents. *Journal of Sociolinguistics* 5 (1), 3–21.

Madison, D.S. (2008) Narrative poetics and performative interventions. In N.K. Denzin and M.D. Giardina (eds) *Qualitative Inquiry and the Politics of Evidence* (pp. 221–249). Walnut Creek, CA: Left Coast Press.

Mathis, T. and Yule, G. (1994) Zero quotatives. *Discourse Processes* 18 (1), 63–76.

May, S. (2008) *Language and Minority Rights: Ethnicity, Nationalism and the Politics of Language*. New York: Routledge.

Mayes, P. (1990) Quotation in spoken English. *Studies in Language* 14 (2), 325–363.

McCollum, C. (2002) Relatedness and self-definition: Two dominant themes in middle-class Americans' life stories. *Ethos* 30 (1–2), 113–139.

McGroarty, M. (2010) Language and ideologies. In N.H. Hornberger and S.L. McKay (eds) *Sociolinguistics and Language Education* (pp. 3–39). Bristol: Multilingual Matters.

McKay, S.L. and Wong, S.C. (1996) Multiple discourses, multiple identities: Investment and agency in second-language learning among Chinese adolescent immigrant students. *Harvard Educational Review* 66 (3), 577–608.

McNamara, T. (2006) Validity in language testing: The challenge of Sam Messick's legacy. *Language Assessment Quarterly* 3 (1), 31–51.

Menard-Warwick, J. (2009) *Gendered Identities and Immigrant Language Learning*. Bristol: Multilingual Matters.

Mercer, S. (2011) Understanding learner agency as a complex dynamic system. *System* 39 (4) 427–436.

Mercer, S. (2012) The complexity of learner agency. *Apples—Journal of Applied Language Studies* 6 (2), 41–59.

Miller, E.R. (2009) Orienting to 'being ordinary': The (re)construction of hegemonic ideologies in interactions among adult immigrant learners of English. *Critical Inquiry in Language Studies* 6 (4), 315–344.

Miller, E.R. (2010) Agency in the making: Adult immigrants' accounts of language learning and work. *TESOL Quarterly* 44 (3), 465–487.

Miller, E.R. (2011a) Indeterminacy and interview research: Co-constructing ambiguity and clarity in interviews with an adult immigrant learner of English. *Applied Linguistics* 32 (1), 43–59.

Miller, E.R. (2011b) Performativity theory and language learning: Sedimenting, appropriating, and constituting language and subjectivity. *Linguistics and Education* 23 (1), 88–99.

Miller, E.R. (2013) Positioning selves, doing relational work and constructing identities in interview talk. *Journal of Politeness Research* 9 (1), 75–95.

Miller, J. (2008) Foucauldian constructionism. In J.A. Holstein and J.F. Gubrium (eds) *The Handbook of Constructionist Research* (pp. 251–274). New York: The Guilford Press.

Mishler, E.G. (1986) *Research Interviewing: Context and Narrative*. Cambridge, MA: Harvard University Press.

Morgan, B. (2004) Teacher identity as pedagogy: Towards a field-internal conceptualization in bilingual and second language education. *Bilingual Education and Bilingualism* 7 (2–3), 172–185.

Morita, N. (2004) Negotiating participation and identity in second language academic communities. *TESOL Quarterly* 39 (4), 573–603.

Muntigl, P. and Ventola, E. (2010) Grammar: A neglected resource in interaction analysis? In Jürgen Streeck (ed.) *New Adventures in Language and Interaction* (pp. 99–124). Amsterdam: John Benjamins Publishing.

Nelson, L. (2010) Bodies (and spaces) do matter: The limits of performativity. *Gender, Place & Culture: A Journal of Feminist Geography* 6 (4), 331–353.

Norton, B. (2000) *Identity and Language Learning*. London: Longman.
Norton, B. and Toohey, K. (2001) Changing perspectives on good language learners. *TESOL Quarterly* 35 (2), 307–322.
O'Loughlin, K. (2001) (En)gendering the TESOL classroom. *Prospect* 16 (2), 33–44.
Ochs, E. (1993) Constructing social identity: A language socialization perspective. *Research on Language and Social Interaction* 26 (3), 287–306.
Ochs, E. and Schieffelin, B. (1989) Language has a heart. *Text* 9 (1), 7–25.
Olson, G.A. and Worsham, L. (2000) Changing the subject: Judith Butler's politics of radical resignification. *JAC* 20 (4), 727–765.
Ortner, S.B. (2006) *Anthropology and Social Theory: Culture, Power, and the Acting Subject*. Durham, NC: Duke University Press.
Otsuji, E. and Pennycook, A. (2010) Metrolingualism: Fixity, fluidity and language in flux. *International Journal of Multilingualism* 7 (3), 240–254.
Overstreet, M. (1999) *Whales, Candlelight, and Stuff Like That: General Extenders in English Discourse*. Oxford: Oxford University Press.
Packer, M. (2011) *The Science of Qualitative Research*. Cambridge: Cambridge University Press.
Park, J.S.Y. (2010) Naturalization of competence and the neoliberal subject: Success stories of English language learning in the Korean conservative press. *Journal of Linguistic Anthropology* 20 (1), 22–38.
Park, J.S.Y. and Wee, L. (2008) Appropriating the language of the other: Performativity in autonomous and unified markets. *Language & Communication* 28 (3), 242–257.
Pavlenko, A. (2001) 'How am I to become a woman in an American vein?': Transformations of gender performance in second language learning. In A. Pavlenko, A. Blackledge, I. Piller and M. Teutsch-Dwyer (eds) *Multilingualism, Second Language Acquisition, and Gender* (pp. 134–174). Berlin: Mouton de Gruyter.
Pavlenko, A. (2002) 'We have room for but one language here': Language and national identity in the US at the turn of the 20th century. *Multilingua* 21 (2/3), 163–196.
Pavlenko, A. (2007) Autobiographic narratives as data in applied linguistics. *Applied Linguistics* 28 (2), 163–188.
Pavlenko, A. and Lantolf, J.P. (2000) Second language learning as participation and the (re)construction of selves. In J.P. Lantolf (ed.) *Sociocultural Theory and Second Language Learning* (pp. 155–177). Oxford: Oxford University Press.
Peirce, B.N. (1995) Social identity, investment, and language learning. *TESOL Quarterly* 29 (1), 9–31.
Pennycook, A. (2004) Performativity and language studies. *Critical Inquiry in Language Studies: An International Journal* 1 (1), 1–19.
Pennycook, A. (2005) Performing the personal. *Journal of Language, Identity, and Education* 4 (4), 297–304.
Pennycook, A. (2007a) *Global Englishes and Transcultural Flows*. New York: Routledge.
Pennycook, A. (2007b) 'The rotation gets thick. The constraints get thin': Creativity, recontextualization, and difference. *Applied Linguistics* 28 (4), 579–596.
Pennycook, A. (2010) *Language as a Local Practice*. New York: Routledge.
Pitts-Taylor, V. (2010) The plastic brain: Neoliberalism and the neuronal self. *Health* 14 (6), 635–652.
Pomerantz, A. (1984) Agreeing and disagreeing with assessments: Some features of preferred/dispreferred turn shapes. In M. Atkinson and J. Heritage (eds) *Structures of Social Action: Studies in Conversation Analysis* (pp. 57–101). Cambridge: Cambridge University Press.

Potowski, K. (ed.) (2010) *Language Diversity in the USA*. Cambridge: Cambridge University Press.

Potter, J. and Hepburn, A. (2010) Putting aspiration into words: 'Laugh particles,' managing descriptive trouble and modulating action. *Journal of Pragmatics* 42 (6), 1543–1555.

Poynton, C. (1993) Grammar, language and the social: Poststructuralism and systemic-functional linguistics. *Social Semiotics* 3 (1), 1–21.

Price, S. (1996) Comments on Bonny Norton Peirce's 'Social identity, investment, and language learning': A reader reacts. *TESOL Quarterly* 30 (2), 331–337.

Purvis, T. and Hunt, A. (1999) Identity versus citizenship: Transformations in the discourses and practices of citizenship. *Social Legal Studies* 8 (4), 457–482.

Quigley, J. (2000) The child's autobiographical self: A developmental linguistic investigation. *The Irish Journal of Psychology* 21 (3–4), 171–180.

Quigley, J. (2001) Psychology and grammar: The construction of the autobiographical self. *Theory and Psychology* 11 (2), 147–170.

Rampton, B. (1990) Displacing the 'native speaker': Expertise, affiliation and inheritance. *ELT Journal* 44 (2), 97–101.

Rampton, B. (2001) Critique in interaction. *Critique of Anthropology* 21 (1), 83–107.

Razfar, A. (2012) Narrating beliefs: A language ideologies approach to teacher beliefs. *Anthropology and Education Quarterly* 43 (1), 61–81.

Reckwitz, A. (2002) Toward a theory of social practices: A development in culturalist theorizing. *European Journal of Social Theory* 5 (2), 243–263.

Relaño Pastor, A.M. (2004) Living in a second language: Self-representation in reported dialogues of Latinas' narratives of personal language experiences. *Issues in Applied Linguistics* 14 (2), 91–114.

Ricento, T. (2003) The discursive construction of Americanism. *Discourse and Society* 14 (5), 611–637.

Ricento, T. (2005) Problems with the 'language-as-resource' discourse in the promotion of heritage languages in the U.S.A. *Journal of Sociolinguistics* 9 (3), 348–368.

Romaine, S. and Lange, D. (1991) The use of like as a marker of reported speech and thought: A case of grammaticalization in progress. *American Speech* 66 (3), 227–279.

Ros i Solé, C. (2007) Language learners' sociocultural positions in the L2: A narrative approach. *Language and Intercultural Communication* 7 (3), 203–216.

Rosenblatt, P.C. (2002) Interviewing at the border of fact and fiction. In J.F. Gubrium and J.A. Holstein (eds) *Handbook of Interview Research: Context and Method* (pp. 893–910). Thousand Oaks, CA: SAGE Publications.

Sacks, H. (1984) On doing 'being ordinary'. In J.M. Atkinson and J. Heritage (eds) *Structures of Social Action: Studies in Conversation Analysis* (pp. 513–529). Cambridge: Cambridge University Press.

Sacks, H., Schegloff, E.A. and Jefferson, G. (1974) A simplest systematics for the organization of turn-taking for conversation. *Language* 50 (4), 696–735.

Scheibman, J. (2002) *Point of View and Grammar: Structural Patterns of Subjectivity in American English Conversation*. Amsterdam: John Benjamins Publishing.

Scheibman, J. (2007) Subjective and intersubjective uses of generalizations in English conversations. In R. Englebretson (ed.) *Stancetaking in Discourse: Subjectivity, Evaluation, Interaction* (pp. 111–138). Amsterdam: John Benjamins Publishing.

Schieffelin, B.B., Woolard, K.A. and Kroskrity, P.V. (eds) (1998) *Language Ideologies: Practice and Theory*. Oxford: Oxford University Press.

Schildkraut, D. (2005) *Press One For English: Language Policy, Public Opinion, And American Identity*. Princeton, NJ: Princeton University Press.

Schmid, C.L. (2001) *The Politics of Language: Conflict, Identity, and Cultural Pluralism in Comparative Perspective*. Oxford: Oxford University Press.

Schmidt, R. (2000) *Language Policy and Identity Politics in the United States*. Philadelphia, PA: Temple University Press.

Scollon, R. (2001) *Mediated Discourse: The Nexus of Practice*. New York: Routledge.

Smolka, A.L.B., de Goes, M.C.R. and Pino, A. (1995) The constitution of the subject: A persistent question. In. J.V. Wertsch, P. del Rio and A. Alvarez (eds) *Sociocultural Studies of Mind* (pp. 165–184). Cambridge: Cambridge University Press.

Speer, S.A. (2012) The interactional organization of self-praise: Epistemics, preference organization, and implications for identity research. *Social Psychology Quarterly* 75 (1), 52–79.

Stivers, T., Mondada, L. and Steensig, J. (2011) Knowledge, morality and affiliation in social interaction. In T. Stivers, L. Mondada and J. Steensig (eds) *The Morality of Knowledge in Conversation* (pp. 3–25). Cambridge: Cambridge University Press.

Swain, M. (2000) The output hypothesis and beyond: Mediating acquisition through collaborative dialogue. In J.P. Lantolf (ed.) *Sociocultural Theory and Second Language Learning* (pp. 97–114). Oxford: Oxford University Press.

Swain, M. (2006) Languaging, agency and collaboration in advanced second language proficiency. In H. Byrnes (ed.) *Advanced Language Learning: The Contribution of Halliday and Vygotsky* (pp. 95–108). London: Continuum.

Tagliamonte, S. and Hudson, R. (1999) Be like et al. Beyond American: The quotative system in British and Canadian youth. *Journal of Sociolinguistics* 3 (2), 147–172.

Talmy, S. (2011) The interview as collaborative achievement: Interaction, identity, and ideology in a speech event. *Applied Linguistics* 32 (1), 25–42.

Tannen, D. (1989) *Talking Voices: Repetition, Dialogue, and Imagery in Conversational Discourse*. Cambridge: Cambridge University Press.

Tannen, D. (1990) Gender differences in topical coherence: Creating involvement in best friends' talk. *Discourse Processes* 13 (1), 73–90.

Tannen, D. (1995) Waiting for the mouse: Constructed dialogue in conversation. In D. Tedlock and B. Mannheim (eds) *The Dialogic Emergence of Culture* (pp. 198–218). Urbana, IL: University of Illinois Press.

Ten Have, P. (2004) *Understanding Qualitative Research and Ethnomethodology*. Thousand Oaks, CA: SAGE Publishing.

Thompson, G. and Hunston, S. (2000) Evaluation: An introduction. In S. Hunston and G. Thompson (eds) *Evaluation in Text: Authorial Stance and the Construction of Discourse* (pp. 1–27). Oxford: Oxford University Press.

Thompson, J.B. (1987) Language and ideology: A framework for analysis. *The Sociological Review* 35 (3), 516–536.

Thompson, S.A. and Hopper, P.J. (2001) Transitivity, clause structure, and argument structure: Evidence from conversation. In J. Bybee and P. Hopper (eds) *Frequency and the Emergence of Linguistic Structure* (pp. 27–60). Amsterdam: John Benjamins Publishing.

Thorne, S.L. (2008) Mediating technologies and second language learning. In J. Coiro, C. Lankshear, M. Knobel and D. Leu (eds) *Handbook of Research on New Literacies* (pp. 417–449). Mahwah, NJ: Lawrence Erlbaum.

Todorov, T. (1984) *Mikhail Bakhtin: The Dialogical Principle*. Minneapolis: University of Minnesota Press.

Tomasello, M. (2009) *Constructing a Language: A Usage-based Theory of Language Acquisition.* Cambridge, MA: Harvard University Press.

Toohey, K. and Norton, B. (2003) Learner autonomy as agency in sociocultural settings. In D. Palfreyman and R.C. Smith (eds) *Learner Autonomy across Cultures: Language Education Perspectives* (pp. 58–74). Hampshire, UK: Palgrave MacMillan

Trester, A.M. (2009) Discourse marker 'oh' as a means for realizing the identity potential of constructed dialogue in interaction. *Journal of Sociolinguistics* 13 (2), 147–168.

Turnbull, S. and Hannah-Moffat, K. (2009) Under these conditions: Gender, parole and the governance of reintegration. *British Journal of Criminology* 49 (4), 532–551.

Ullman, C. (2012) 'My grain of sand for society': Neoliberal freedom, language learning, and the circulation of ideologies of national belonging. *International Journal of Qualitative Studies in Education* 25 (4), 453–470.

Van De Mieroop, D. (2005) An integrated approach of quantitative and qualitative analysis in the study of identity in speeches. *Discourse and Society* 16 (1), 107–130.

Van Dijk, T.A. (1995) Discourse semantics and ideology. *Discourse and Society* 6 (2), 243–289.

van Lier, L. (2007) Action-based teaching, autonomy and identity. *Innovation in Language Learning and Teaching* 1 (1), 46–65.

van Lier, L. (2008) Agency in the classroom. In J.P. Lantolf and M.E. Poehner (eds) *Sociocultural Theory and the Teaching of Second Languages* (pp. 163–186). London: Equinox.

Vasterling, V. (1999) Butler's sophisticated constructivism: A critical assessment. *Hyptia* 14 (3), 17–38.

Verhagen, A. (2005) *Constructions of Intersubjectivity. Discourse, Syntax, and Cognition.* Oxford: Oxford University Press.

Verschueren, J. (2012) *Ideology in Language Use: Pragmatic Guidelines for Empirical Research.* Cambridge: Cambridge University Press.

Vitanova, G. (2005) Authoring the self in a non-native language: A dialogic approach to agency and subjectivity. In J.K. Hall, G. Vitanova and L. Marchenkova (eds) *Dialogue with Bakhtin on Second Language Learning: New Perspectives* (pp. 149–169). Mahwah, NJ: Lawrence Erlbaum.

Vitanova, G. (2010) *Authoring the Dialogic Self.* Amsterdam: John Benjamins Publishing.

Vološinov, V.N. (1973) *Marxism and the Philosophy of Language* (L. Matejka and I.R. Titunik, trans.). New York: Seminar Press.

Vygotsky, L.S. (1978) *Mind in Society: The Development of Higher Psychological Processes* (M. Cole, V. John-Steiner, S. Scribner and E. Souberman eds). Cambridge, MA: Harvard University Press.

Vygotsky, L.S. (1987a) *The Collected Works of L.S. Vygotsky, Volume 1, Problems of General Psychology Including the Volume Thinking and Speech.* (R.W. Rieber and A.S. Carton, eds; N. Minick, trans.). New York: Plenum Press.

Vygotsky, L.S. (1987b) *The Collected Works of L.S. Vygotsky, Volume 4, The History of the Development of Higher Mental Functions.* (R.W. Rieber, ed.; M.J. Hall trans.). New York: Plenum Press.

Wacquant, L.J.D. (1992) The social logic of boxing in black Chicago: Toward a sociology of pugilism. *Sociology of Sport Journal* 9 (3), 221–254.

Wertsch, J.V. (1998) *Mind as Action.* Oxford: Oxford University Press.

Wertsch, J.V., Tulviste, P. and Hagstrom, F. (1993) A sociocultural approach to agency. In E.A. Forman, N. Minick and C.A. Stone (eds) *Contexts for Learning: Sociocultural Dynamics in Children's Development* (pp. 336–356). Oxford: Oxford University Press.

Wertsch, J.V., del Rio, P. and Alvarez, A. (1995) Sociocultural studies: History, action, and mediation. In J.V. Wertsch, P. del Rio and A. Alvarez (eds) *Sociocultural Studies of Mind* (pp. 1–34). Cambridge: Cambridge University Press.

Wetherell, M. (1998) Positioning and interpretative repertoires: Conversation analysis and post-structuralism in dialogue. *Discourse and Society* 9 (3), 387–412.

Wiley, T.G. and Lukes, M. (1996) English-only and standard English ideologies in the U.S. *TESOL Quarterly* 30 (3), 511–535.

Willett, J., Solsken, J. and Wilson-Keenan, J.A. (1998) The (im)possibilities of constructing multicultural language practices in research and pedagogy. *Linguistics and Education* 10 (2), 165–218.

Woolard, K.A. (1998) Introduction: Language ideology as a field of inquiry. In Schieffelin, B.B., Woolard, K.A. and Kroskrity, P.V. (eds) *Language Ideologies: Practice and Theory: Practice and Theory* (pp. 3–47). Oxford: Oxford University Press.

Young, R. (2009) *Discursive Practice in Language Learning and Teaching*. Malden, MA: Wiley-Blackwell.

Zhou, M. (2005) Ethnicity as social capital: Community-based institutions and embedded networks of social relations. In G.C. Loury, T. Modood and S.M. Teles (eds) *Ethnicity, Social Mobility, and Public Policy: Comparing the US and UK* (pp. 131–159). Cambridge: Cambridge University Press.

Zuengler, J. and Miller, E.R. (2006) Cognitive and Sociocultural Perspectives: Two Parallel SLA Worlds? *TESOL Quarterly* 40 (1), 35–58.

Author Index

Ahearn, L. M. 2, 3, 9, 13, 20, 28, 32, 38, 43, 52, 95, 121
Altheide, D. L. 99, 106
Arundale, R. B. 58, 83
Atkinson, P. 35, 36, 119

Bakhtin, M. M. 7, 8, 9, 13, 18, 19, 21, 28, 36, 37, 42, 96, 97, 117, 123
Banfield, A. 98
Barad, K. 26
Barker, C. 23
Baszanger, I. 31
Baynham, M. 7
Beattie, G. 123
Bell, J. S. 33
Biber, D. 74
Billig, M. 59
Block, D. 4, 8, 22
Blommaert, J. 9, 20, 21, 28, 59, 88, 91, 92, 116, 120, 121, 123, 140
Bourdieu, P. 2, 12, 22, 23, 127
Bourne, J. 7
Briggs, C. L. 34, 40, 41, 135
Brinkmann, S. 35
Bucholtz, M. 43, 80, 81
Busch, B. 52, 60
Butler, J. 2, 9, 13, 23, 24, 25, 26, 27, 28, 29, 30, 52, 60, 118, 119, 133, 137, 141, 142, 144
Bybee, J. L. 37, 42, 45

Canagarajah, A. S. 33, 69, 85, 89
Capps, L. 43
Cassaniti, J. 130
Chafe, W. 74

Cicourel, A. V. 34
Clark, H. H. 18, 98
Clifford, J. 35
Clift, R. 94, 95
Cloud, D. L. 12, 22, 130, 143
Coffey, A. 35, 36, 119
Cook, H. M. 74
Cornwall, A. 71
Cortazzi, M. 75
Couper-Kuhlen, E. 94, 95, 96, 99, 102, 103, 104
Crawford, J. 127
Cudworth, E. 13, 20

Damari, R. R. 75
DaSilva Iddings, A. C. 6
Davies, B. 11, 59, 133, 145
De Fina, A. 35, 36, 39, 48, 94, 97
De Silveira, C. 47
Deetz, S. 27, 129, 130
Desjarlais, R. 12, 13, 27, 138, 140
Deters, P. 7
Dixon, J. 59
Dodier, N. 31
Doerr, N. M. 85
Donzelli, A. 44, 45, 46, 130
Du Bois, J. W. 37, 47, 73, 74, 75, 77, 78, 81, 82, 84, 92, 93
Duff, P. 7
Duranti, A. 2, 43, 44, 45, 46, 47, 65, 73
Durrheim, K. 59

Eagleton, T. 121
Eggins, S. 38
Elder, G. H. 71

Ellsworth, E. 144
Emirbayer, M. 17, 18, 71
Enfield, N. J. 99, 100, 108
Englebretson, R. 73

Feldman, G. 1, 2
Fillmore, C. J. 47
Finegan, E. 74
Firth, A. 3, 30, 134
Foley, W. 44
Ford, C. E. 37
Foster, P. 14
Fox, B. A. 47

Galasinski, D. 23
Gao, X. 7
Gaonkar, D. P. 130
Geisler, C. 130
Genung, P. B. 7
Georgakopoulou, A. 39, 94
Gergen, K. L. 3
Gerrig, R. J. 98
Gibbs, R. W. 61, 80, 90
Giddens, A. 2, 4, 17
Givón, T. 37, 47
Goffman, E. 96, 98
Goodwin, C. 42
Gore, J. 144
Grady, J. 132
Grin, F. 118, 129
Gubrium, J. F. 29, 33, 34, 120, 122
Gumperz, J. 39
Gunn, J. 12, 22, 130, 143
Günthner, S. 96, 97

Haakana, M. 98
Habermas, T. 47
Hak, T. 58
Hall, K. 43, 80, 81
Hannah-Moffat, K. 131, 132
Hantzis, D. M. 2
Harissi, M. 44, 93
Hepburn, A. 111
Heritage, J. 40, 99
Herndl, C. G. 25
Hill, J. H. 94, 141
Hitlin, S. 71
Hobden, S. 13, 20

Holland, D. 16, 17, 18
Holliday, A. 33
Holquist, M. 18, 36
Holsanova, J. 95, 96
Holstein, J. A. 29, 33, 34, 120, 122
Holt, E. 94, 95, 96, 97, 98, 99, 100, 102
Hopper, P. J. 37, 42, 44, 45, 47
Horner, B. 140
Hudson, R. 95
Hunston, S. 73, 75, 76
Hunt, A. 131

Jackendoff, R. 47
Jaffe, A. 73, 75
Jefferson, G. 39
Jespersen, O. 74
Jin, L. 75
Johansen, M. 94
Joseph, J. E. 8

Kärkkäinen, E. 75
Katz, L. 6
Keltner, D. 130
Kerbrat-Orecchioni, C. 37, 38
Kishner, J. M. 61, 80, 90
Klewitz, G. 95, 96, 103, 104
Kockelman, P. 70, 74
Kramsch, C. 88
Kroskrity, P. V. 121, 124
Kulick, D. 25
Kvale, S. 35

Labov, W. 94, 98
Laihonen, P. 54
Lange, D. 95
Langellier, K. M. 108
Lantolf, J. P. 7, 8, 14, 46, 134
Lave, J. 46
Lee, V. 123
Licona, A. C. 25
Lu, M. 140
Lucy, J. 94, 98
Lukes, M. 109, 125

Macaulay, R. 95
Madison, D.S. 36
Mannheim, B. 141
Mathis, T. 95

May, S. 127
Mayes, P. 97
McCollum, C. 51, 52
McGroarty, M. 121
McKay, S. L. 5, 6, 7
McNamara, T. 28
Menard-Warwick, J. 7
Mercer, S. 7, 144
Miller, E. R. 3, 28, 29, 35, 37, 42, 52, 54, 59, 61, 71, 75, 84, 118, 134
Miller, J. 123, 131
Mische, A. 17, 18, 71
Mishler, E. G. 34, 53
Morgan, B. 28
Morita, N. 6, 7
Muntigl, P. 43

Nelson, L. 27
Nichols, J. 74
Norton, B. 6, 7, 22, 23

O'Loughlin, K. 28
Ochs, E. 43, 74
Ohta, A. 14
Olson, G. A. 141, 145
Ortner, S. B. 12, 18
Otsuji, E. 91, 140
Overstreet, M. 113

Packer, M. 24, 33, 36
Park, J. S. Y. 85, 132, 133, 138, 140
Pavlenko, A. 8, 28, 33, 46, 59, 125, 126, 134
Pennycook, A. 21, 25, 28, 29, 42, 91, 123, 140
Pitts-Taylor, V. 132
Pomerantz, A. 110
Potowski, K. 59, 125
Potter, J. 111
Poynton, C. 43
Price, S. 7
Purvis, T. 131

Quigley, J. 37, 38, 46, 73

Rampton, B. 20, 39, 40
Raymond, G. 99
Razfar, A. 134

Reckwitz, A. 143
Relaño Pastor, A. M. 96
Ricento, T. 59, 125, 126, 127
Romaine, S. 95
Ros i Solé, C. 7
Rosenblatt, P. C. 29, 30

Sacks, H. 39, 54
Scheibman, J. 45, 47, 51, 75
Schieffelin, B. B. 74, 121
Schildkraut, D. 124, 127, 128
Schmid, C. L. 126
Schmidt, R. 127
Scollon, R. 28
Slade, D. 38
Smolka, A. L. B. 16
Speer, S. A. 112
Stivers, T. 99
Swain, M. 14, 15

Tagliamonte, S. 95
Talmy, S. 34, 122
Tannen, D. 58, 95, 97, 98, 137
Ten Have, P. 53
Thompson, G. 73, 75, 76
Thompson, J. B. 121, 123, 124
Thompson, S. A. 37, 44, 45, 47
Thorne, S. L. 8, 14, 46
Todorov, T. 7
Tomasello, M. 15, 16
Toohey, K. 6, 7
Trester, A. M. 75
Turnbull, S. 131, 132

Ullman, C. 133

Van De Mieroop, D. 39
Van Dijk, T. A. 124
van Lier, L. 4
Van Valin, R. 44
Vasterling, V. 24
Ventola, E. 43
Verhagen, A. 75
Verschueren, J. 121, 122, 124
Vitanova, G. 7, 8
Vološinov, V. N. 19, 37, 96, 97, 117
Vygotsky, L. S. 9, 13, 14, 15, 16, 18, 19, 21

Wacquant, L. J. D. 17
Wagner, J. 3, 30, 134
Wee, L. 85
Wenger, E. 46
Wertsch, J. V. 13, 19, 37, 47,
Wetherell, M. 38
Wiley, T. G. 109, 125
Willett, J. 33
Wong, S. C. 5, 6, 7

Woolard, K. A. 121
Worsham, L. 141, 145

Young, R. 24
Yule, G. 95

Zepeda, O. 94
Zhou, M. 143
Zuengler, J. 134

Subject Index

Account(s)
Interview 3, 13, 35–36, 43–44, 51
Narrative 66, 73, 94, 136
Accountable 36, 84, 99, 133
Accounting 5, 36, 47, 49, 71, 83
Accountability 70, 75, 122
Active interview 34
Addressed (or recognized) 2, 60
Addressivity 8
Affordances 14, 17, 22–23, 27, 38, 71, 72, 98, 129, 139, 143
Agency
Agency constructs 44–48
Agency-enhancement 5, 7
Agency of spaces 9, 13, 20–21
Definition 8, 13, 46
Discursive agency 47, 140, 143
Distributed agency 70, 139
Easy agency 62–63, 89, 139
Grammar and agency 42–46
Human agency 2, 7, 11, 20, 28
Ideologies of agency 10, 22, 121, 130–134, 137
Individual agency 3, 9, 12, 142
Lacking or reduced agency 9, 65, 71
Learner agency 2–9, 12–14, 18, 21, 23, 28, 30, 65, 142–145
Linguistic encoding 44–47
Performativity and agency 24–28, 133, 143
Responsibility and 10, 12, 14, 28, 32, 60, 94, 133, 138
Socially mediated agency 3–4, 8–9, 11, 13, 18–19, 22–23, 26–27, 120, 138, 142–144

Theories of agency 9, 11, 22, 28, 32, 38, 43, 45, 52, 95, 121, 138, 139, 141, 143, 144
Agentive
Actions/Acts 3, 6, 13, 17, 23–24, 32, 46, 48, 52–56, 58, 60–61, 65, 71, 84, 93, 95, 102–103, 109, 112, 114, 132, 137–140, 142–144
Actors 30, 71
Efforts 65, 88, 93, 109, 118, 138
Figures 51, 55, 66
Participants 121
Relationships 44–45
Self/Selves 9, 60, 63, 69, 72, 85, 103, 138–139, 143
Agonistic 11, 19, 21, 26
Animator 96, 98, 111, 116
Appropriate (verb) 8, 16, 38, 88, 97
Appropriation 11, 17, 85
Author (role) 96, 101, 104, 110–111, 116–117, 137
Authorship 96, 112
Autonomous (Language system) 19, 37, 128
Autonomous agents 27, 130

Biological individual 7, 8
Body 16, 22, 132
Socialized 12, 17
Boxing gym 17

Capacity
Agentive 13, 18–19, 21, 27, 69, 73, 76, 93, 142–143
English 84–85, 87, 109, 111–112
Language learning 76, 83, 93

Language/Linguistic 80, 85, 88, 92, 95, 111, 118
    Speaking 87–88
Choices 7, 12–13, 26, 38, 43, 46, 51, 55, 60, 75, 107–108, 125, 127, 129, 133, 137, 142
Citation 26
Commonsensical 10–11, 21, 59–60, 81, 109, 116–117, 124, 129–130, 137
Competence
    Communicative 138
    Identities of 6
    Ideology of 85, 138
    Language/linguistic 13, 20, 71, 85, 140
    Learning 77, 81
    Multilingual 80, 92
    Performative 69
    Symbolic 88
    Truncated 91–92, 140
Complaint
    Accounts 113, 116, 118,
Compliments 111–112, 138
Configuration
    Agency 141
    Common sense 122
    Interactional 9, 28
    Relational 23
    Subject-Predicate 136, 141
Configuring 42, 122
Consciousness 15–16, 18, 96, 141
Constitutive 9–10, 40, 120, 135, 145
    Effects 2, 23, 121
    Power 27
    Process 41, 121
Constraints 13, 26, 57, 60, 64, 69–70, 87, 118, 137–139, 141
    Affordances and 22–23, 27, 38, 72 143
    Economic 22
    Enablements and 38, 121, 144,
    Enabling 24
    Language 38, 137
    Material 26, 87, 142
    Political 12
    Social 4, 27
Constructed dialogue 97
Constructivist 3, 9, 36
Control 43, 46, 49, 55, 65, 71, 87, 98, 113–114, 139–140

Self-Controlled 16
    Spaces 20
Conversation analysis 39
Counterdiscourses 5

Depreciatory qualifier 61, 65, 80, 89, 90
Deterministic 2
Determined 12
    Ideologically 81, 140
Dialectic 7–8, 19, 26, 92
Dialogic (al/ly) 9, 18–19, 25–26, 28, 36–37, 42, 74–75, 81–82, 84, 92–93, 97, 117, 144
Dialogism 9, 13, 19, 36, 96–97
Discourse analysis 9–10, 38–40, 121
Discourses 2, 11, 120, 132, 145
    Neoliberal 132–133
    Policy-level 2
    Political 1–2
    School 6
    Social 5, 35
Discrimination 9
Discursive constructs (-ion) 33, 38, 40–41, 43, 49, 73, 94, 122, 133
Discursive practice(s) 2, 4, 9, 11–12, 18–19, 22–27, 37–38, 42, 52, 73, 75, 82, 103, 118, 120–123, 129, 132–135, 141–145
Discursive regularity 38, 43, 44–45
Discursively constituted 9, 33, 47, 143
Disempowered 8–9, 22
Distributed 8, 15, 37, 42, 46, 70, 134, 139
Domain of speakability 26, 118
Dominant language 13, 20–22, 26, 88, 116, 125, 127–130
Dynamic 7, 12–13, 22, 31, 37, 42, 84, 96

Efficacy 23, 33, 36, 47, 118
Emergent 10, 13, 37, 39, 91, 103, 123, 134, 145
Enabled 7, 18, 21, 26, 40, 52, 70, 138
Enablements 38, 46, 121, 144
Epistemic rights 98
Epistemic stance 74, 80
Epistemology
    Constructivist 9, 36
Ethnic 30, 125, 142
Ethnographic 5, 17, 33, 35,

Evaluative stance 10, 38, 73–77, 79, 100, 136–137, 139, 141
Evidence
  Discursive 10, 136
  For agentive actions 95, 103, 105, 109, 112
  In reported speech 98–103, 105–109, 112, 117–118, 137, 139
  Of taking responsibility 132, 138
Evidential 94, 99, 116, 118, 122, 137
Expertise in English 6, 23, 38, 69
  Language/Linguistic 20–21, 23, 69, 72, 91, 140

Feminist 43, 133, 144
Flow 17, 71, 123
Footing 96
Foreclosure 29, 60, 144–145
Free-willed 25, 46

Habitual 16–17, 43
Habitus 22, 127
Hegemony 19
Higher mental functioning 15, 18
History-in-person 17, 25
Homeless 9, 27

I-experience 19
Identity(ies) 8, 15, 20, 23, 26–29, 35, 39, 46, 59, 69, 71, 80, 93, 106, 122, 128, 130
  Agency and 3–4, 6–7, 22
  American 59, 125–128
  Enactment 44, 71
  Gendered 25, 28
  Immigrant 76, 100, 143
  In interaction 22, 74, 84
  Learner 3, 5–6, 28, 69
  Nation/national 1–2, 125–126
  Performatively constituted 2, 29, 93, 117
  Responsible 45, 69
  Recognizable 11, 24, 81, 143
  Socially mediated 5, 8
Ideology(ies) 7, 13, 19, 23, 25, 27–28, 33, 35–36, 38, 40, 43, 45, 52, 54, 58–60, 72, 74–76, 80–81, 95, 100, 105, 108, 118–138, 140, 143
  Of competence 85
  Of agency 10, 22, 121, 130–133, 137

Of language 9, 20–22, 85, 92–93, 102, 109, 116–117, 121, 124, 126, 134
Of language learning 20, 76, 112, 121, 125–130, 134
Imagined subject 29–31
Immigrant(s) 1–6, 8–10, 13, 20–23, 26–27, 29–30, 44, 56, 60, 62, 67, 70, 76, 81, 88, 91–92, 95, 100, 116–118, 121, 125–130, 132–133, 135–136, 138, 142–143
Immigration 1, 2, 125–127
Inagentive 10, 22, 48–49, 51–52, 87, 140
Index 47, 69, 75, 80–82, 85, 107–108, 114, 122, 128
Indexical 80–81, 92, 123, 141
Inner speech 16
Intention 8, 15, 17, 21, 56, 63, 65, 70, 95, 97, 102
Interactional performance 25, 43
Interactional sociolinguistics 39
Internalization 11, 16–17
Interpellate 23, 27, 130, 143
Intersubjectivity 37, 75, 91, 93
Intersubjective 74, 81, 84, 92
Intransitive 47
Investment 5, 23, 129, 133

Joint attention 15

Language learner 6, 17, 20, 28, 30, 46, 60, 81, 88, 91, 100, 113, 118, 132, 134, 141–144
  Agency (see Agency)
  Identity (see Identity)
  Selves 63, 70, 73, 137
Language learning 2, 10, 15, 17–18, 22, 26, 28–30, 32, 41–42, 46, 56–57, 59, 65, 74, 76, 81, 83–84, 87, 91, 93, 95, 100–102, 117, 129–130, 134, 140, 142–143
  Ideologies of (see Ideology)
  In work place 65, 67–69, 71, 106
  Processes 5, 13, 55, 134, 144
  Research 3–8
Languaging 14
Language structure 10, 14, 37–38, 75, 123, 124
Language systematicity 37
Legitimate(d)(ing) 6, 56, 84, 93, 99, 131–132, 138, 143

Actions 23, 29, 129
Language expertise 20
Languages 21
Language dominance 109, 118, 124, 127
    (Non)-legitimate speaker 23, 141
    Participant 23
Legitimation 124
Limitation(s) 36, 103, 105, 109–110, 117,
    137, 139, 144–145
Linguistic agent 43–44, 47
Local(ly) 10, 13, 20–21, 24–26, 59, 69, 74,
    76, 91–93, 117, 120, 139
    Interaction 34, 52, 75–76, 81, 85, 89,
        111, 118, 138
    Language regime 139–140
    Performances 25, 93, 143
    Practices 2, 24
    Positioning 10, 52
Localization 7

Materialized 37, 42–43, 122, 125, 133
Meaning-making 15–17, 123–124,
    141–142
Mediated 17–19, 24–25, 28, 31, 60, 120
    Ideologically 13, 20, 23, 25, 27, 81, 118
    Interactionally 8, 19, 23, 26, 119
    Semiotically 13–16, 26, 119, 143
    Socially 3, 9, 11, 13–16, 21–23, 26–27,
        130, 134, 142, 144
    Unmediated 16, 130
Memory 63, 83, 92, 119
Micro-analysis 10, 39–40, 52, 82, 100,
    103, 139
Microgenetic 14, 18
Migration 20, 125–126
Modal verb 47–48
    Agent-oriented modality 44–45,
        48, 56
Monolingual(ism) 91, 125–126
Moral(ly) 2, 35, 45, 54, 74–75, 94 109,
    114, 128, 131, 133
Multilingual 21, 67, 80, 88–93, 139

Narrative(s) 114, 117, 122, 125, 133
    Account (see Account)
    In interviews 35–36
    Narrative agency 47
    Reported speech and 75, 95, 98, 103,
        105, 113–114

Research 33, 39
    Stance and 75, 84
    Structures 36, 124
Nation 1, 126
National 2, 59, 125–126
    Banal nationalism 59
Nationalistic 125
Native speaker(s) 14, 22–23, 78, 83–85,
    88, 91–93, 117–118, 129, 138–139
Non-native speaker(s) 3, 30, 78, 85,
    98, 138
Naturalize(d) 27, 108, 126, 133
Negative assessment 87, 109–110, 113
Negative evaluation 76, 82–84, 86–87,
    137–139
Neoliberal 22, 131–133
Neutral stance 54, 73, 76–77
Non-legitimate 20, 23
Non-positivist 33, 35
Normalcy 123
Normative 20–21, 23, 25, 28, 31, 42–43,
    52–55, 58–59, 72, 75, 81, 84, 91–92,
    95, 99–100, 116, 118, 122, 124, 128,
    130–131, 138, 140
Norms 26, 37, 46, 52, 73, 80–81, 85–86,
    88–89, 92, 100, 118, 131, 140

Obligation 11, 45, 48–49, 56–58, 63–64,
    67–68, 71–72, 99, 114, 136
Obligatory 50–51, 141
Official English 126–127

Participant(s)
    In interaction/practice 21, 24, 30, 39,
        97, 121, 145
    Interview 32, 34, 43, 51, 60,
        65–67, 100
    Legitimate 23
    Research 3–4, 6, 29–31, 33, 80
Participate in
    Civic 128
    Communities of practice 46
    Constitutive process 41, 119
    Discursive practices 8, 11–12, 16, 18,
        19, 22, 24, 26, 27, 142
    Invention 35
    Learning contexts 6, 7
    Research study 119
Patterned grounds 27

Performance 25, 35, 43–44, 46, 55, 73–74, 93, 95, 99, 100, 106, 108, 113, 119, 123, 135–137, 141, 143, 145
Performative effects 39–40, 42, 44–46, 52, 59, 69, 74, 92, 98
Performatively
    Constitute 1, 24–26, 28, 76, 100, 117–118, 120, 131–133, 140, 142–143
    Materialize 95, 125, 133
    Produced 27
    Realized 43–44, 81
    Reconstruct 92–93, 109
Performativity 1–3, 9, 13, 23–25, 27–29, 85, 119, 123, 133, 140, 145
Position(ed)(ing) 4–10, 22–23, 29–30, 32, 34, 44–55, 58–61, 65–66, 69, 71, 73–74, 78, 86–87, 100, 102–103, 107, 111–114, 116–118, 120, 122, 124, 129–131, 133–138, 140–141, 144
Positive assessment 66, 111–112, 118
Positive evaluation 76, 81, 83, 87–89, 90, 118, 139
Postfoundational 3
Poststructural(ist) 3–4, 11–13, 43, 133, 144
Power 12, 22–27, 33, 37, 49, 52, 92, 108, 117, 124, 127–131, 134, 140, 145
    Disempowered 8–9, 22
    Empower(ment) 23, 144
    Relation(ships) 2, 5, 22, 25, 128
    Unequal power 13, 22
Principal (role) 96, 98, 101, 104, 110–112, 116–117, 120, 137
Proficiency(-ies)
    English 21, 93, 109, 111, 112, 138
    Language 6, 83–85, 89, 91, 93, 109–110, 125, 137
    Communicative 132
Prosody 95–96, 101, 107

Qualitative research 2–3, 33
Quotative 95–96, 101

Reconstitute(ing) 4, 10, 17, 21, 25, 28, 42, 45–46, 59, 73–74, 81, 91, 117, 119, 122, 145
Receipt tokens 53–57, 62, 67, 87, 90, 114
Recognition 5, 7, 23, 26, 46, 57, 75, 133, 138, 142

Recognizable 2, 7, 11, 20, 24–25, 29, 38, 43–44, 49, 81, 120, 133, 143, 145
Recognized as 11, 23–24, 26, 43, 60, 81, 92, 141, 143
    Misrecognized 123, 127
Reflexivity 33
Regimes of languages 21, 59, 91–92, 140
Reification 123
Reify 27, 137, 142
Relational 3, 13, 18, 23, 36, 71, 93, 144
Relationship(s) 2, 8, 10, 27, 31, 36, 43–46, 63, 67, 71, 77–78, 82, 84, 97, 107, 124–125, 128, 131, 142–144
    Agentive 44–45
Religion 125–126
Reported speech utterances 38, 76, 94–95, 98–105, 107–114, 116–118, 136–139, 141
Resistance 5, 7, 140
Responsibilized 131–132, 140
Responsible(ity) 26, 28, 32, 58, 70, 87, 144
    Ideology and 20, 105, 125, 127–128, 131–134, 136
    Individual 14, 20, 84–85, 109, 133, 136,
    Language learn(er)(ing) 10, 48, 56, 64, 69, 84, 103, 112–113, 117–118, 128–130, 132–134, 136, 138, 142–143
    Morally 2, 45, 133
    Reported speech and 94, 96, 98, 111
    Self 11–12, 38, 52, 60, 71, 85, 93, 96, 98, 136, 142
    Stance and 75, 81, 84
    To act/actions 19, 27, 33, 46, 56, 65, 99–100, 105, 112, 131–132

Second language research 3–11, 13–14, 28, 33–34
    Learning 5, 8, 13, 17, 29, 142
Sediment(ing) 17, 37, 45, 59, 81, 123
    Re-sediment(ing) 25, 43, 93, 118, 138, 140, 142, 145
Sedimentation 93, 123, 143
    Re-sedimentation 26–28
Self regulation 14, 17
Semi-structured interview 40
Semiotic 17, 37, 42, 144–145
    Semiotic apparatus 91, 140
    Mediation (*see* Mediated)

Sense-making 33, 35, 40, 52, 76, 109, 122, 125, 140
Situated 2, 8, 12–13, 18, 21, 25, 40, 46, 65, 86, 89, 91, 132, 134, 139
  Situated agency 26, 88
Small business 21, 29, 30, 69, 88, 92, 139
Social 'birth' 8
Social action 2, 16, 74, 81, 122
Social actor 32, 43, 74, 84
Social practice 7, 11, 21, 29, 34, 36, 65, 73, 122–123
Social structure 2, 3, 8, 92
Socialized 5, 12, 17, 38, 93
Socially constituted 8, 18, 46, 119, 133, 138
Sociocultural 8–9, 13, 16, 18–19, 23, 37, 74, 81, 93, 132
Sociocultural theory/approach 3–4, 14, 46, 143
Sovereign agent 12
Sovereignty 24
Space(s) 1, 8–9, 20–21, 23, 25, 28, 31, 37, 42, 52, 59–60, 69, 84, 91–93, 116–118, 124, 132
  Workplace 21, 30, 60, 65, 71, 88, 91, 113, 116, 136, 138–140
  Agency (See Agency of spaces)
Speakability 26, 118
Stance 10, 38, 43, 54, 58, 85, 93, 96, 99, 127, 140
  Acts 78–81, 83–84, 87–89, 92, 137–138
  Dialogic 74–75, 82, 84
  Evaluative 10, 38, 73–81, 87–90, 92, 100, 136–139, 141
  In Reported speech 95–96, 100, 113, 141
Stance diagram 77–80, 82
Story-world figure 10, 43, 45, 47, 49–51, 54, 58, 65

Story-world self 39, 43, 46–48, 52–53, 55, 59–60, 72, 74, 82, 86–87, 89, 95, 98, 100, 103, 136–137, 140–141, 143
Stratified spaces 20
Stratified relationships 125
Structure 12–13, 19, 22, 26–27, 80–81, 91, 141
  Social 2, 3, 8, 92
Structuring 4
Struggle 9, 18–19, 26, 39, 124, 141
Subject-Predicate 10, 42–44, 47, 50, 52, 55, 73, 76, 136–137, 141
Subjectivity 1, 8, 10, 23–25, 34, 37, 82, 119, 123, 133
Symbolic violence 127

Target language 14
Theories of agency (see Agency)
Traces 12, 17, 19, 117, 123
Transglobal 20
Transitivity 44–45
Triangulated 35
Truncated competence (see Competence)
  Language forms 88
  Multilingualism 90–91

Value system 45, 75, 86, 117
Values 7–8, 12, 19, 21, 23–24, 27, 32, 58, 75–76, 84–85, 90, 92–93, 95, 113, 117–119, 122, 124–125, 127, 142
Verbal-ideological 97, 117
Volitional 16, 43

Willful 70, 128
Workplace(s) 63, 65, 69–72, 78–80, 88–90, 108, 136, 138–140